What it Takes
from $20 *to*
$200 Million

"*What It Takes, From $20 to $200 Million* is a true story about the fact that a great business idea, coupled with passion and compassion in the heart of an entrepreneur, resulted in Jerry Azarkman accomplishing the ultimate American Dream."

— **Maelia Macin**, Univision.

"Jerry Azarkman's memoir is about a pioneer in marketing to the Hispanic market and how he has experienced great success due to his respect for and innate understanding of these consumers. Jerry is a visionary with a golden touch that has succeeded where countless others failed. From Tel Aviv to East Los Angeles, Jerry not only crossed oceans but cultural barriers. His success is a testament to his hard work and business acumen."

— **Leonard Lieberman**, Lieberman Broadcast

"Jerry Azarkman's memoir is a true American story about an immigrant entrepreneur who overcame countless obstacles to build a retail powerhouse. He created opportunity by giving opportunity to a Hispanic community looking to improve their lives and begin living the American dream. This is a story of passion, creativity and vision in connecting with the immigrant experience and capitalizing on the changing demographics of the American consumer."

— **Andy Barnet**, Telemundo

What it Takes
from $20 *to*
$200 Million
A Memoir

Jerry Azarkman *and*
Ruth Garcia-Corrales

NEW YORK

NASHVILLE • MELBOURNE • VANCOUVER

What it Takes *from* $20 *to* $200 Million
A Memoir

Published in New York, New York, by Morgan James Publishing. Morgan James is a trademark of Morgan James, LLC. www.MorganJamesPublishing.com

The Morgan James Speakers Group can bring authors to your live event. For more information or to book an event visit The Morgan James Speakers Group at www.TheMorganJamesSpeakersGroup.com.

ISBN 978-1-68350-454-2 paperback
ISBN 978-1-68350-455-9 eBook
Library of Congress Control Number: 2017902073

Cover Design by:
Rachel Lopez
www.r2cdesign.com

Interior Design by:
Bonnie Bushman
The Whole Caboodle Graphic Design

In an effort to support local communities, raise awareness and funds, Morgan James Publishing donates a percentage of all book sales for the life of each book to Habitat for Humanity Peninsula and Greater Williamsburg.

Get involved today! Visit
www.MorganJamesBuilds.com

To All Entrepreneurs

Table of Contents

Foreword

It is a book of a man who started his business with nothing, and accomplishes great success. It's truly explained that he has engaged powerfully to change many rules of the business world with his innovative ideas. However, the reason for his success has not been due to these changes, rather to the one thing he has never changed, 'Contributing to Society.' I consider this as the real American dream.

— **Shiro Kitajima**, Panasonic North America, COO,
Panasonic Consumer Electronics Company, President.

Preface

In my post as Consul General of Costa Rica in Los Angeles I've had the opportunity to attend a zillion activities. Cultural, sporting and civic events, beauty pageants, fundraisers, you name it. Our consulate reached the point of having over 100 volunteers, a big accomplishment for a small Central American country and very small immigrant population in Los Angeles.

On many occasions we approached business organizations for support; Jerry Azarkman and his company were always willing to help by providing product to raffle off. The push he showed our volunteers was precious, this was a matter of doing or not doing an event, and when Jerry's help came through it motivated all of us to keep going.

A fellow citizen once showed me a magazine listing the richest Hispanics living in the United States, and one was from Costa Rica. I made an appointment to see my wealthy countryman because Costa Rica's National Symphonic Orchestra was traveling to Asia and in route were stopping in Los Angeles. This offered an opportunity for the orchestra to play in L.A., and they needed me to create that event.

In the middle of our luncheon the millionaire asked me if I had any challenges, and I shared with him that 110 musicians were coming to L.A. on their way to Asia and they wanted to perform here. The gentleman asked what was stopping me, and I said "money." "How much?" he asked, and I told him $20,000. "That's nothing," he replied, "I have a friend who will give you guys this money, and if he won't, I have a nonprofit organization that will give it to make this concert happen."

I remember going back to the office and calling Maria M., President of the Cultural Committee, and telling her we had gotten the money, so carry on with the arrangements for the concert. We had begun the promotion with no money and in the end we were able to bring them to L.A. The Cultural Committee covered all of the expenses: Hotel, airfare from Costa Rica to Los Angeles, pocket money and local transportation. The Coast Rican millionaire bought six seats, although they remained empty during the concert, that's it. He gave us the confidence to do the event; it was inside us, but our fear had been holding us back.

It was a different case for Jerry when he started to walk the streets of Los Angeles; he had a strong will and knew everything was in his hands. He was the only one selling, buying, collecting the payments; he had to make it happen. He knew he was the only alternative to this niche market of otherwise overlooked people.

During this period I served this society as Consul General and it was clear that to make any change for this community we could not act alone. We created a Central American Federation with the participation of all the Consuls General of Central America, we went to events together, and we prepared activities together. It made us stronger in the eyes of the community.

When my service finished with the change of governments I went to say goodbye to Jerry. He asked me to work for the company he had created and developed and which now had two stores. I started in the Purchasing and Merchandising Department and after several promotions became the Advertising and Marketing Manager. Many years have passed since Jerry hired me and today the chain has eleven mega-stores, offering services such as local and long distance phone calling and lots of other good stuff.

Year after year I've observed Jerry's way of treating people, how he'd approach any associate with respect, a warm smile and handshake. How he'd make his points in a soft voice but with strong words and examples. Within the company Jerry is recognized as its heart and during the entire economic crisis he was instrumental in developing campaigns and special sales to bring traffic to the stores.

Throughout the years Jerry has learned Spanish, especially so he could communicate better with associates and they'd understand him fully. When a radio or TV commercial is sent to him for approval Jerry needs to understand what it says, in order to ensure that everyone else will understand it, too.

I remember one time that he was unhappy about a table set we were selling in the furniture department. I called the vendor and told him he'd sold me a set that was being sold for less at other stores. The vendor came to our outlet, investigated and showed us pictures. Yes, he was right, there were similar models for sale elsewhere with lower prices, but our table set was thicker and bigger. But for Jerry the customer's perception was what mattered, and if you don't have one set next to the other the buyer could say, "I saw it for less at one of your competitor's stores." Jerry very cleverly has the ability to put himself in the consumer's shoes, and as a strategist, he's simply fabulous.

You will find in this book many stories as the one of Rocio Morales' born in Mexico with six siblings, her family was so poor that she decided to run up North for a better life with no money in her pockets. Her neighborhood friends paid for her bus up to Mexicali and train to Guadalajara. The police will stop them and make her sing the national anthem to verifying her nationality.

Rocio started working at the age of nine cleaning a house, she never had a Christmas gift, and she remembered how she washed floors in her knees. Once in the US she started working at McDonalds cleaning floors where she would fall in love and her boyfriend introduced her to Curacao. At Curacao she thrived and her American Dream started.

Jerry is an inspirational leader who always has a simple way of seeing everything, and the ability to explain it to you. I remember he told me once that when he was in the military, it was very complicated to get tribes to provide information, even though the army had offered a $10,000 reward to whoever gave them tips. Jerry had insisted that instead of posting signs with the amount of money informants would be awarded, the signs should, instead, state that tipsters would receive 1,000 sheep, 500 hens, 200 rabbits, etc., and then people would understand and deliver the information.

There are many stories about Jerry we need to share in order to let everyone know what this incredible man has done to create a multi-million dollar operation with his family and with over 2,000 associates. In reading about Jerry's exploits, the reader will learn how he/she can also find success in the marketplace and life.

Overview

Perseverance when you have nothing. Determination when you have no resources, when you do not even know how to speak the language of the place you live in. Firmness? Keep on going? Even when your circumstances don't look good? Hope that the day will come, when all you can do, for now, is to give it all you've got because nothing will change if you don't put on a better face and go out and keep trying.

That is the face of this book, the face of Jerry Azarkman, who, at 24 years old, with only $20 in his pocket and his heart full of hope, went looking for an opportunity. As he walked the streets of Los Angeles trying to find a way to survive, he and his wife both homeless, Jerry exchanged those $20 dollars for merchandise he bought wholesale in downtown L.A. Looking to sell it he went door-to-door knocking on doors in a community where no one wanted to be found, where a knock at the door could mean coming face to face with the authorities asking for the correct residency papers. That day in 1978, Jerry Azarkman made his first sale, and from there on he would turn it into a multimillion dollar operation.

His customers were immigrants, people, like him, who were forced to live in the shadows because of their legal status, people with under-the-radar jobs, whose everyday existence was determined by whom no one could actually say existed; the false identities they were forced to acquire in order to get a job, names used that were not their birth names. Some used names of relatives, family or friends, most of them with jobs that paid them in cash, people with years of toiling in their adoptive country, working but with hardly anything to show for it, not even something as basic as a credit history.

Although most of his customers were immigrants from Latin America Jerry found himself in the faces of these people who purchased his products, faces full of the familiar pain and desperation that he saw in his own face. But he also saw their hope, their dreams, their fierce desire to succeed—that mirrored his own. Even though they couldn't talk, hold a conversation or share their stories through words with each other, both understood they needed each other and that together they could make a difference.

That group of people who opened their doors and their hearts to Jerry became the first customers of what 30 years later would turn out to be a powerhouse in retail, services and community issues—Curacao. Today, with over 2 million credit applications and over $200 million in sales, this company, Curacao, represents the vast majority of the growing Hispanic community. A community of many skin and eye colors, different dialects and numerous variations of cultures, but in the end they're the same as any other individual with a family and children, with the same needs and aspirations as members of any other group.

Starting a business in any society requires a thick skin, a strong will to resist rejection after rejection and still persist in pursuing the dream of success. According to the Small Business Administration, for every ten businesses that open, only three will survive the first two years, while only half of these will still exist five years later. Building a successful business is not an easy task for anyone. Finding a niche market, giving your customers a unique service, making your business grow and keeping it going through the years requires a strong fiber.

The story that you will find in this book is a story of success, a story of real people who, with perseverance and the leadership of Jerry Azarkman, were able to change and conquer an American Dream. In this story you will identify with Jerry who—despite having Attention Deficit Disorder and being the last in his class—with the help of a motivating teacher overcame all of his obstacles and reached to the top of his class.

I am also an immigrant, one who came to this country for a short time but stayed a long while, as the government in my country changed hands. After 25 years I'm still here, I've worked tailoring advertising and marketing campaigns to more than 2 million Hispanics, most of whom have received credit lines of Curacao to obtain their basic home needs.

Every time I meet immigrants in elevators, parking lots or malls, I can feel their struggles due to leaving loved ones back in their countries, leaving their homes, towns, churches, playgrounds. I sense the lives they've constructed together with their parents, the lives they once had with their families back home and that exist today only in their memories. Many immigrants won't ever go back to their homelands, not even for funerals, not even to see their parents for the last time. Not because they don't want to, but because they are unable to.

Writing this book tells the story not only of Jerry Azarkman. This is the real life story of an immigrant from Israel who started walking the streets of Los Angeles with $20 in his pocket, and today, with his brother, has created a multi-million dollar company by giving credit and products to the "great unwashed huddled masses" of immigrants who were ignored by all of the established credit houses. This is a success story and tale of very hard work, but it is also a story of immigrants who, working together, have grown and created a company of 2,500 hundred associates, 11 mega-stores, e-commerce and multiple services.

Readers of this book will learn the path through Jerry's life and about his business philosophy. They will benefit by discovering the four D's for success and how to apply them in their own lives. In addition, Jerry shares the seven steps that made him who he is today—a millionaire.

Part I

The Origins

The beginning of a family will be marked by their circumstances.

Chapter One

What It Takes

W hat does it take for an individual to become successful? Is it simply a matter of character, or the sum total of their experiences? Destiny, perhaps? What about their family of origin, their birthplace, the political and socio-economic situation in which they were raised? Could a harsh climate be a factor in shaping an individual? What of their parents' background, education, and their own life-altering decisions?

Walking in hot, desert, sands gives you strong legs as you fight to gain a foothold in the shifting sands. Sometimes it makes you feel that you are not going anywhere, like walking on a treadmill; the sand moves beneath your feet and yet you are left in the same spot. Your lungs feel as if they're on fire every time you inhale the hot, dry, air, and you yearn for relief. Your mind focuses on reaching a cool and safe place to rest and recover. The same is true about walking in the snow or mountains. Weather can be a factor in determining your character development as it trains you to survive in hostile conditions.

The better prepared you are for life's challenges, the greater your chances of becoming successful.

This is the story of a family, their struggles, and successes.

Oscar Azarkman was born in 1891 in Kermanshah, a city in western Persia. Kermanshah is close to the border of Iraq, in a land where Kurds live today. This region has the Middle East's oldest known prehistoric village, dating back to 9800 BP. "BP" stands for "Before Present," present being 1950, when radiocarbon dating methods began. The name of the city changed to Bakhtaran in 1979. Name changes are frequent in this region.

With its beautiful mountains and balmy climate, Kermanshah was considered to be a summer resort for kings. When the Russians invaded and many Jews were killed, the Azarkman family decided to move to Qasr-e Shirin—a safer place to live. Oscar was six years old.

Located closer to the border of what is today Iraq, Qasr-e Shirin is where members of Persia's royal family, the Sassanids, spent their vacations. It was also known as the city of love due to a legend reminiscent of the story of Romeo and Juliet. It took place here centuries ago, during the days of the Qajar Dynasty. Princess Shirin ("sweet" in Persian), was the daughter of the Queen of Armenia, and was known for her great beauty and her gentle disposition. Shirin fell in love with Khosrow II, the 22nd King of Sassanid. He ordered Farhad, the Kingdom's best master stone carver, to build her a palace in Qasr-e Shirin, with rock quarried from Mount Bistun. During this period, the King was at war with the Arabs, and had to fight many battles before declaring complete victory. Khosrow II suffered the pain of separation from his beloved princess and yearned to see her again. It took him many days and nights to come home and make her his bride.

However, His Majesty was not the only man who fell in love with the princess—the craftsman who built the palace found himself enamored of her, too. Skillfully carving the stones, Farhad built a beautiful castle for Shirin, and she, too, found herself falling for him. The king found out about the secret love while still at war and banished Farhad before returning and marrying the Princess himself. However, the king was eventually killed by his son, and Shirin committed suicide over the dead body of her husband.

This palace was the pride and glory of the city under the rule of the Qajar Dynasty. In 1988, during the Iraq and Iran War, Iraqi forces occupied the palace;

the Iraqis lost the battle but before Saddam's army left the city, they made sure not even a single wall of the palace was left standing. Oscar played while a small child in the gardens and surroundings of the palace.

Oscar's father was a merchant, trading in precious metals and minerals. He sold his wares at the local market, knowing fully that they could command higher prices if he traveled. However, taking his treasures on the road would expose him to the dangers of thieves, so Oscar's father came up with an ingenious plan: he melted his gold and silver trinkets and converted them into ordinary pans and skillets, painting them black to disguise them. This way, they were thought to be inexpensive cooking items. When he reached his destination, the jeweler would reverse the process and melt everything back to raw material. The merchant was very prosperous, but, eventually, he came under suspicion. On his next trip, Oscar's father was followed and he was murdered.

His death changed the course of Oscar's destiny, the oldest of ten kids, who from one day to the next went from being a child to playing the role of father and head of the family. He had to put food on the table, and take care of his family and their business.

Every time you're confronted with dire circumstances—whether they are the death of family members, drastic changes in the direction of your business, losses hard to recuperate from, or a major, unexpected turn of events, you must persist in order to survive and succeed. During those moments you'll always have doubts, but you have no choice except to plow ahead.

Working under a hot, blazing sun can impede your progress and make you want to give up, but you can choose not to. Those freezing nights when the cold seeps into your bones, or the exhaustion of many sleepless nights in a row—these are all things that can drag you down, wear you out, and keep you from doing your best. But whatever is preventing you from accomplishing your goal; you can overcome and triumph if you have the will. Even the darkest night will become a fresh new day. You will see the light and gain a new perspective. Every setback can be an opportunity for growth, if you have vision and determination.

Now that his father was no longer there for him and the entire family, Oscar was determined to protect their assets and the fortune his father had created for them. The changes started with their last name: Javahery meant "jeweler", so Oscar decided to change it to Azarkman, which translates to "bow and arrow of fire."

Oscar had always wanted to become a physician. He now resolved to accomplish his goal and moved to Tehran to study in a French school of medicine. Leaving behind his mother and nine siblings was a difficult decision for Oscar, but he knew he had no choice; he needed to lay the groundwork for providing for his family, and he was not going to let anything stop him. He started by learning French. He studied day and night. It was challenging but he knew this was what he wanted to do. He studied hard and developed his skills in order to become a recognized doctor of medicine.

When life puts extraordinary obstacles in your path and you reach that crossroads, will you despair and give up, or double your efforts and move on? Will you recognize the opportunity that it brings? What does it take to change your course to where you want it to go? Are you ready to take over and make it happen? How many times have you asked yourself these questions? When you have nothing, even the smallest accomplishment means the world to you, and when your circumstances drive your reality, there's no other choice but to put on a brave face, confront your challenges and make things better.

Oscar had to succeed in his studies because his family needed him to be successful. He had to make it happen, and he couldn't let the difficulty of the subject matter, the language, finances, or anything else hold him back. His goal was set and he summoned his willpower to work hard and accomplish his dreams.

Iran's school of medicine staff consisted of doctors that had graduated from French, English, and other European universities. To be on this prestigious staff or to even be considered for a position as a professor, one had to have earned degrees abroad. Students were trained to determine diagnoses by observing symptoms of diseases, mostly through external observations of symptoms, such as fever.

Doctors studied the science of pain and the medicines required for controlling the symptoms. Physicians were taught how to prepare their own medicines by mixing varying amounts of chemicals and plants in order to develop the right treatment for each patient. At the time, the region was besieged by the biggest cholera epidemic of the time, wiping out entire families, and challenging the medical community to come up with better treatments. Oscar was proud to be on the forefront of these emerging cures.

Oscar was living in a time of great change, when Russia and Britain had strong interests in Persia. Both great powers aggressively pursued policies that brought development to the area along with big business interests. Concessions were made by the shah to develop roads, railroads, mines, telegraphs, banks, and tobacco, and many of these new endeavors conflicted with the nation's businesses, causing internal revolts and ultimately giving more power and ammunition to the anti-modernism movements and Islamic groups.

Persia was part of the changes occurring in the region. The shah separated mosque and state and the royal family was removed from power. The Jews received political rights from the shah, which was a huge step forward for the Jewish community. This news caused Jews to travel long distances in order to reach this more progressive society.

Oscar didn't know then if he'd ever marry and have kids. All he wanted was to accomplish his goal, serve his community, serve people in pain, and help families with sick relatives. Iran's population growth was on a fast track: its demographics were doubling in number, urbanization was taking over, and doctors were in big demand. In this land, Oscar was to find his fulfillment as a well-known doctor.

Life is easier when the weather is pleasant. Similarly, if there is a climate of tolerance in the region's religious practices, and if the political climate around you is on your side, it affords you many liberties and allows you to thrive and to take the necessary actions for your cause. This is what was happening for Jews in Iran. However, their lives could change in an instant if any of these factors were altered.

The Azarkmans stayed in Qasr-e Shirin, and when Oscar finished his studies in Tehran, he took his practice to Iraq for five years. He worked briefly with an established doctor who had an office and a pharmacy in the same location, and his

1898 the vanished Jewish Kurdish Trip. Oscar Azarkman is the boy standing in the front. This is the oldest picture of the family.

eyes were opened to the possibilities of his combined professions: medicine and pharmacy. When Oscar returned to Qasr-e Shirin, he opened a successful practice and made a handsome living.

Many Persian Jews made their home in Iranian towns, including Tehran, and Oscar now had established an office and pharmacy on the border between Iran and Iraq. Big jars of chemicals and weighing scales covered the shelves of his walls and he'd create his own mixtures and medicines to treat his patients. In the backyard of his home, he kept rabbits to test his mixtures and for experimentation. These were the early days of medicine, when the world was discovering vaccinations for dreaded diseases, as well as supplements for enhancing health.

Oscar was always mixing leaves, seeds, and flowers, and trying to develop new combinations for cures to many kinds of conditions, from a simple cold to a more serious heart condition. In the Jewish community, traditional remedies were handed down from one generation to the next, with cures for many illnesses. Oscar's family was no exception, so he had the family concoctions to draw from in addition to his own compounds.

The family lived in Qasr-e Shirin until Oscar made up his mind to move them to Tehran. Oscar was suffering acute asthma attacks and came close to choking to death several times. It was recommended that he live closer to better sources of medicine and a dryer climate, so the family made the decision to leave their birthplace. The trip from Qasr-e Shirin took them many days and nights and required moving all their belongings in cars, carts, and horses. It was a complex and challenging move.

When his patients became too ill to go to his office, Oscar made frequent visits to their homes, and it was in one such house call that he met a beautiful girl. Muluk had found food at the entrance of the apartment building where she and her family lived during a time when food was scarce due to the war. Often food was rationed by the government. One day, she knocked on the door of the building manager, who happened to be sick. Oscar was treating the man when Muluk walked in, carrying a large amount of food in her hands. She had found it outside, thinking that a tenant had probably dropped it. When Muluk left, Oscar asked, "Who was that beautiful Jewish girl"? He was astonished not only by her beauty but by her honesty, returning food at a time when it was rationed and scarce. This would be the start of Oscar's new life.

Tashkent is now the capital of Uzbekistan, which used to be part of southern Russia. The city had a multicultural society with mostly immigrant Persian Jews who had fled from Persia. They had lived in an oppressive society for years, persecuted first by Islamic regimes, then by Soviet invasions. There were times when Jews were forced to dress in black caps and corded belts to identify themselves. Their shops could not conduct business if the entrance didn't have a lower step to make sure everyone knew they were entering a store run by a Jew.

They were not allowed to own property, and their accounts were not valid in any court trial. There were times when a regime forced Jews to pay taxes higher than those paid by other members of society, and whenever they went to pay their taxes, the Jews were literally slapped in the face, as a means of debasing them. Times would get worse during World War I, which started in 1914. Persia had hoped not to be involved in this war, declaring itself to be a neutral country, but to no avail. The war spread to their land, which became a battleground for Russia, Britain, and Turkey.

There are times when our own comfort and tranquility are greatly affected by events that are seemingly unrelated to us. Extraordinary events unfold on our television screens, but they happen to "other people," not to us. Still, it can make us think: What if that happened here? What if my own life ends? Have I done everything I wanted to do with my life? Is this all there is?

Our trials and tribulations are real to us, but they pale in comparison to what happens in times of war or pogroms. The normal conditions we take for granted suddenly vanish. This was especially true of earlier times, when today's technologies were nonexistent, and there was less at hand to help with survival.

When the Russian Revolution broke out in 1917, this region received the same treatment as any other communist part of the country: the abolition of religion. The Judaism that had kept the Jews together for centuries had to become an underground movement in order to avoid persecution. In the eyes of the world, the Jews seemed to abandon their religion, although the reality was that many would gather to practice Judaism in secret. They continued to conduct their businesses, though they were mainly artisans and merchants.

This region of southern Russia was so isolated from mainstream European Judaism that the Jewish people there were called Bukhara Jews and developed their own language and customs. This region with all its history of invasion from the

Soviets, rebellion by the locals, and history of oppression developed as the land of the fabled fabrics, the place of the Silk Road. Jews developed a type of textile interwoven with thin strands of gold, which became famous and much sought-after in the area.

When there is less direct exposure to the elements and you control your surroundings, you might become slower and less of a planner. You have no true motivation to change. But if you are escaping and on the run, you are suddenly forced to think quickly and act quickly—you have to plan, and must develop a mental agility in order to survive.

Muluk was born in Tashkent in 1928. After the war, Muluk's family could no longer bear the harsh conditions. The closing of Jewish schools and repression by the Russian invaders were too much for them. Her father, Isaac, was a rabbi and when he heard about the closing of a synagogue, he went to rescue the Torah. When he arrived, he was shot in the face and lost an eye. Later he would use a glass eye that would become a holy terror for kids each time he pulled it out of his eye socket.

Isaac decided to move to Persia. At first, Muluk's mother, Frida, did not want to make this enormous journey, especially with her young daughter. Muluk's grandfather played a critical role in making the final decision, as he was a strict follower of the traditions. He told Frida: "You have to follow your husband wherever he decides to go." And that was enough to change her mind.

The trip was very long. They traveled for days by train and walked without food or water in hot weather and with very few belongings. They felt like they were being followed and continued, panicked, stepping up their pace, until their legs gave way and forced them to rest.

There was a feeling of dread hanging in the air, of having something around their necks pulling them back, and it increased with every step. Their dread was founded—the Soviet Army was patrolling the border. Muluk thought she was going to die on that trip. Frida had to scrounge for water for the girl, and she managed to harvest the dew from plants to keep her hydrated. They had all come close to death by the time they arrived in Persia, after many days of walking.

Muluk's grandfather left them at the border of Iran and went back to Tashkent, thinking that he, as a merchant, needed to take care of his business. However, he was soon caught by the Soviets and, after several days without food or water, was sent to prison in Siberia. Meanwhile, Muluk and her mother reached the town of Mashhad on a sunny day in 1934.

At that time, the world was undergoing the Great Depression, and in Persia, major changes were occurring under Reza Shah as the country experienced great reforms.

Reza Pahlavi had declared himself Shah and begun Persia's modernization, separating state from religion, opening schools, and allowing women to go out in public without the veil, or "hijab." The country was developing: railroads and roads were constructed, agriculture was flourishing, and oil exportation increased annually. The Shah changed the name of Persia to Iran and abolished all special rights for foreigners. But throughout this transformative period, Russia and Britain were still involved in the region, protecting their interests—namely oil, and their access to it.

Although Muluk was only 15 years old in 1943, she was so beautiful that men would stop to stare at her. Despite the fact that she was still so young, her family knew this was the time to look for a husband. The chosen candidate would be expected to give the family gifts of money, gold, and land, but what they wanted most was to be relocated to what is now Israel.

By this time, Oscar had become a well-known doctor and had accumulated wealth, but was 52 years old and had never married. He was considered the perfect candidate. The arranged marriage broke Muluk's heart because she did not love him, but she accepted the dictates of her family. With no love between them, she and the doctor wed.

Muluk soon learned that Oscar had a big heart. He was kind and treated her with respect and compassion. She would also come to know that he was beloved by everyone, had many friends, and people would come from far and wide to seek his counsel.

During World War II, Iran was part of the war effort, often referred to as "The Bridge of Victory." Iranians worked in factories to produce trucks for the war, fixed roads to move equipment, and assembled aircrafts and war materials. However, the food produced by Iranians was taken away and exported to support the war. Ships leaving with war supplies were coming back full of runaway Jews and Poles.

Iranian Jews were protected in Europe during the Second World War because their passports did not specify their religion. The Shah had convinced Hitler they were Kalimis, a made up name used to refer to Moses in the Koran, and insisted they were an Iranian tribe.

In 1943, the year Oscar and Muluk got married, the world was in the middle of World War II. These were difficult days—the radio was a steady stream of casualty reports. Not only soldiers, but civilians, too. It was devastating and it fueled both depression and fear. During this historic year, Iran declared war on Germany and was accepted as a member of the United Nations. The Big Three leaders (the U.S. President Franklin D. Roosevelt, British Prime Minister Winston Churchill, and the U.S.S.R.'s General Secretary Joseph Stalin) promised to reaffirm Iran's independence once the war was over and to protect its territory as a single nation.

At the time, Iran had one of the biggest Jewish communities, numbering around one hundred thousand. Thousands more moved from Eastern Europe to Persia seeking protection from Nazi persecution. An Iranian Jewish diplomat was giving passports to Jews in Paris in order to help them escape execution or deportation to concentration camps.

In the midst of all this, the newlywed Oscar and Muluk were starting a new life together. At the beginning of their marriage Muluk was quite unhappy; she had left behind her mother, father, and brothers. Everything was new and different. She had a new house, and with it came new obligations. She had to take care of her home and her husband, and to organize what little food they received. The constant news reports of the war made everything that much more difficult.

Jews were protected in Iran during the Second World War, but times were tough there. In addition to food being rationed, there was preferential treatment so that those who could afford to pay more received more. Many people did not have jobs, many were injured, and entire families disappeared. There was a large movement of immigrants across the country. Once the war was over, the Soviets stayed in Iran until 1946.

Oscar worked hard as a doctor providing for the underserved, sometimes receiving payment in food or services. Iran was under rule of a new Shah, and the Soviets refused to return the territories they'd occupied until there was international intervention, leaving only after an oil supply treaty was agreed upon. However, the oil industry was mainly managed by the British, who took most of the revenue. Nationalization movements were widespread, and in an effort to continue controlling the petroleum industry's assets, the British offered Iran even revenue split. By this time, nationalization movements had already radicalized the country.

Against this turbulent background, in 1949, Muluk became pregnant again; she had already lost two babies and this was to be her first child, a beautiful boy named Doron. His name meant "gift" in Hebrew, and he provided the young family with the bond it needed in order to continue. For Muluk, Doron was a gift from God, and she experienced his birth as a great moment in her life: The moment when her heart opened up to her husband.

Outside the Azarkmans' residence, Iran experienced all kinds of upheavals. The possibility of nationalization of the oil refineries created much controversy; many thought it was due to the Cold War, and that the concept of nationalization was derived from communist influences. To others, the time had come to use oil revenues to develop agriculture and other areas of the country for everyone's benefit. Iran nationalized the oil refineries and the British asked the world to freeze all of Iran's assets outside of the country, and to stop selling any products or services to Iranians. These were difficult times for the nation. Iran needed many imports to continue its operations.

1953 Jerry Azarkman as a baby in his mother arms.

Doron was three years old when Muluk became pregnant again with Yoram (Jerry's Hebrew name), who was born in 1952. Yoram means "God is exalted" in Hebrew. Muluk thanked God for her second child. Meanwhile, Iran had a new prime minister who was elected through a democratic process named Mohammad Mosaddegh, a lawyer who had studied in Paris and earned his doctorate degree in Switzerland. He made enormously important decisions during this period, starting with the nationalization of Iran's oil industry. The new prime minister also created unemployment compensation to make employers pay for the care of injured workers, freed forced labor on farms, and instituted many other progressive reforms. In 1953, Mosaddegh was overthrown by a CIA-backed coup.

When questioned about his birth date, Yoram often tells the story that his Mother claimed it to be November 28, but that no one is one hundred percent sure of the actual date. Muluk wanted another child and gave birth to Sahar in 1955. Sahar means "God hears me" in Hebrew. Later in life, the boys changed their names: Sahar became Ron and Yoram became Jerry, but at the time of their birth they were given the names of Persian kings so that no one would suspect they were Jewish. Doron was Darius, Yoram was Chosro, and Sahar was Parviz.

In Iran, when the three boys were little, the oil industry's revenues began to flow and many changes happened in the land. Speculation increased and the prices of everything went up. Because of the coup, martial law was imposed and no one could be outside at night. Oscar and his wife started wondering if Iran was the right place to raise their three children. Iran's political instability, especially in Tehran, made Oscar search for another city to work in and he began warming up to the idea of a big move.

Struggles inspire thoughts about lost opportunities, as do the failures of ventures you'd thought would change your destiny. You battle with yourself as you struggle to make the right decision: "Should I do it this way, or that?" Your fears breed negative thoughts: "I won't make it, this isn't going to work." This is when your will kicks into gear and makes you try harder, and the script changes to "yes I can, yes I will!" All the conflicting thoughts swirling through your mind are preparing you to become stronger, and propelling you on to your next challenge and to making it happen.

1957 with Jerry Azarkman and his brother Doron, their father Dr. Oscar Azarkman and their mother Muluk Azarkman, the Orfanian family provided this picture.

1959 Jerry Azarkman with his mother and his brother Doron.

1955 Jerry with his brother Doron and mother.

Chapter Two

The World Molding a Character

A ll the events that occur in our lives help shape us. The challenges not only make us different, they make us more powerful and give us the ammunition to respond to future circumstances. Some events will mark us for the rest of our lives. There will be acts that mold our characters the way a piece of art is created and developed. In the same way, our behavior is a reaction to all that is happening around us.

The number of Oscar Azarkman's patients was increasing in Iran. He had a pharmacy and a doctor's office in Tehran. He decided to open a new office in Varamin, in the southern part of Tehran's Province. This town presented a great opportunity for Oscar, as he had one of the few pharmacies in the region and was the only doctor. His services began to grow, so much so that Oscar was operating most of the time out of Varamin. This growth took its toll on the family, because Varamin was somewhat distant from Tehran, and Oscar spent so much time on the road that he decided to stay over during the week. His lengthy absences made Muluk and their three boys miss him more and more.

Muluk started asking her husband when he'd return. The separation was not something he liked either, as Oscar wanted his family close to him. He missed Muluk's cooking, watching his boys play, and the noise in the house. He decided to build a new home in Varamin with separate rooms for each son, beautiful gardens, and a big backyard for the rabbits he used for experiments. Muluk was taken by surprise. The boys loved the place and their new opportunity to play in the gardens. Times were good.

After Christianity, Islam is the second largest religion in the world. When the Prophet Mohammed created it, Islam was a single unified religion, but following his death in the year 632, fragmentation in the religion began. Mohammed had chosen his close companion and friend, Abu Bakr, to succeed him, but a faction decided that Mohammed's cousin, Ali Ibn Talib, should be the successor instead. This resulted in the sectarian division of the followers of Islam. The adherents of Abu are called Sunnis, the biggest group of Muslims in the world. The followers of Ali are known as Shiites, who live mainly in Iran, Iraq, and Lebanon. Varamin was full of Shiites, who believed in the value of martyrdom. In order to survive in this society, Oscar pretended he was a Muslim and a Shiite.

Pressure started building around Oscar to prove that he was really a Muslim. One of the Shiites' biggest traditions is the observance of the Day of Ashura, which commemorates the division between the Sunnis and Shiites. On this day in 680, Husayn ibn Ali, the grandson of Mohammed, was killed. Shiites demonstrate their devotion by marching with self-inflicted wounds, making cuts on their heads and beating the wound with their palms to induce profuse bleeding.

The town's Shiites asked for Oscar's oldest son to take part in the ceremony by opening a wound on his back. Muluk was terrified by the prospect of Doron wounding himself and then repeatedly hitting himself with a chain until his shoulder bled. She could not understand these traditions of people hurting themselves just to prove that they belonged to a particular religion. But she had to respect her husband's decision and allow her son to participate.

Although the oldest of the Azarkmans' three sons, Doron was a small boy. Nevertheless he had to open a wound and make it bleed throughout the ceremony. Seeing her boy in pain and bleeding continuously was a horrifying ordeal for Muluk, and she followed him during the entire ceremony until she was able to take him back home. Even this sacrifice, made by mother and child both, was not enough for some of the Shiites. But worst of all was Muluk's fear of someone claiming they were Jews. There were many Shiites who still did not believe the doctor and kept looking for ways to test Oscar's faith and devotion.

Muluk and Oscar grew increasingly fearful that the Shiites might find out that they were Jews. Their fear of being killed and leaving their kids to fend for themselves, or even that one of their kids might be killed by the Shiites, grew every day. Oscar started planning their escape; they could not look suspicious or alert anyone of their plans. He sent all of their expensive handmade Persian rugs to be cleaned, putting them in a truck bound for Tehran. The next evening, with nothing except the clothes on their backs, they left Varamin forever.

The Azarkmans were running for their lives. The children did not understand what was happening; all they knew was that in the middle of the night they left their warm home and were put into a car, where they slept all night. Their only crime was that of being Jewish. They left behind their beautiful palace with lush gardens and a bedroom for each child, all their toys, schools, their park, and their friends. They were leaving a big part of themselves in this city, a place they would never return to. A city that had welcomed them at first, and, in the end, brought fear and terror from threats, fanatics, extremists, all because of the "sin" of being Jewish.

They were leaving behind their home, the pharmacy, Oscar's patients, and everything else. No time to sell anything, no time to exchange anything, no time to give things to a new doctor. The fear was so intense that they left without even saying goodbye to anyone. They simply disappeared. All the kids knew was that while they were sleeping, their Dad picked them up and packed them in a car. Varamin was behind them now, only a spot in the rear view mirror of their lives.

There is a well-known African expression: "It takes a village to raise a child." One might extend it to say that a village can make an individual. Doron, Jerry, and Ron had been shaped by their early experiences in Varamin, a big home with beautiful gardens, the palace of a very prestigious doctor. Muluk had servants who helped her with all of the household duties and the children. Oscar had an office at home where he'd receive patients. He had a medical degree and treated his patients in their homes during house calls, in his office, or at the pharmacy. And then it was all gone.

Healthcare is seen in any society as a profession of compassionate individuals ready to serve suffering men and women, but also as a profession that produces a high income. When you're sick and need treatment, you'll give anything not to suffer or see your loved ones suffer, and this is the moment when a physician's hand becomes essential. Doctors of medicine are individuals who are keen observers and are expected to have high individual values. Of course, they are well compensated for these attributes. A doctor and his family are expected to have a high standard of living. Jerry remembers that, as seen through the eyes of a child, their home was very close to a palace.

The Azarkmans reached Tehran, but that did not mean their anxiety disappeared. Their fear followed them, as if it could find them any time. Oscar was also well known in Tehran, where his brother was taking care of the pharmacy. When the Azarkmans arrived, the family knew they would not stay for a long time, and that this was it. They would leave all of their relatives, businesses, parks, and friends behind. They had to abandon the story they'd worked so hard to mold. The Azarkmans felt the anguish of being Jewish in an anti-Semitic society, as their ancestry and traditions were not accepted where they lived. They were as human as anyone else but they could not survive if they stayed in Iran.

War followed the path of this family over and over again: World War I for Oscar, the father; World War II for both Oscar and Muluk; plus all of their country's internal conflicts. The persecution of the Jews shadowed them, and all the social upheavals society was undergoing made them come to the end of the road, to a big decision that was going to change their family's destiny. Conclusions that would make them leave their land for a new one, a new home, and a new start: Muluk, Oscar, and the three kids were to leave Iran.

The numbers of persecuted Jews in Iran were rising and there were efforts to convert these Jews to the Nation of Islam. The Shah started to create several strategic changes that alarmed conservative groups. Modernism meant a confrontation with conservatism. Many zealots were upset, feeling this was not the role of the government; there were constant demonstrations in the cities that ended in bloody battles. All of these changes generated a high level of discontent among a majority of the population. The central government began weakening while the clergy gained in strength, causing Jews to fear an outburst of anti-Semitic pogroms.

Iran is known as one of the oldest civilizations in the world. It was previously called Persia, a name given by the Greeks to a unifying land where several tribes lived. Its name was changed to Iran by the Shah; the new name means "noble people." Many Persian archeological artifacts dating back to the Bronze Age reflect the history of this nation. The history of Jews living in this land is very ancient too, and reference is even found in the Bible's Book of Esther. Jews lived there for many years, their traditions passed down from one generation to the next. It felt like home, and a very familiar place where they had buried their ancestors.

When Oscar started receiving threats from the Shiites, he knew he could no longer stay in Iran; they would never accept that a Jewish doctor had taken care of their women or had injected them with medicine. Muluk feared for the lives of her kids and husband. She knew that if the Shiites found out they were Jews, they could all face a terrible fate. She had to convince Oscar they could no longer stay in Iran. He understood all of her reasons and, with a heavy heart, prepared their exodus.

Oscar realized they could not stay long in Tehran either, as Shiites would be able to find him at any time by merely asking around. Oscar's brother was taking care of his pharmacy, which was still open. Oscar was a well-known physician and there was no other way to survive other than moving from Iran. The children did not know what was going on but the entire family felt the tension in the air. Oscar arranged all of the travel papers and, within days, they were flying to Israel. Leaving Tehran, leaving Iran, leaving everything behind again except for their Persian rugs, which were worth a fortune to any Middle Easterner and which Oscar was saving for a rainy day.

The Azarkmans left Iran on the wings of an El Al, Israel's national airline, to the Jewish State. It was 1958 and Jerry was only six years old. These were the early years of a very young nation: Israel had been declared a state in 1948, only 10 years before their arrival. Once in Israel, thanks to a law called "the right of return," they were considered to be a family that had been forced from Judea ages ago during the dispersal of Jews called the Diaspora, and were now returning to the Promised Land, the same land that God had showed Abraham and Sarah.

The Azarkmans were part of an "aliyah" (ah-lee-yah), a wave of immigrants returning to the Holy Land. Through the Law of Return, the Israeli Constitution permitted overseas Jews to relocate to Israel, and the government paid for all of their traveling expenses and for establishing themselves in the new land. The local Jews paid higher taxes to finance the return of these families. Israel needed more people to help construct the Jewish State.

Persian Jews were assigned to areas close to Israel's borders to help protect the territory of the new nation. They were settled in farmlands, which was not what many of them were used to. The Azarkmans were no exception. Their intended residence was located in a very poor area. Once they filled out all of the required paperwork at the airport, the family took a taxi to the place that had been allocated to them. The taxi drove a long distance, and when they neared the border with Jordan, in the middle of nowhere the cab stopped in a dirt road and the driver informed them that this was their new home. It wasn't even a house. The ramshackle place was falling apart. Oscar decided he could not allow his family to live there and asked the taxi driver to go back.

Muluk had a letter in her purse that her mother had sent her. When Frida, her mother, had arranged Muluk's marriage to Oscar, one of the conditions was that husband-to-be would relocate her parents to Israel. Oscar paid for all of their transportation expenses and they were now living in a refugee camp called Hatikva, designated for those Jews coming from Arabic countries who were not assigned any land. This could be for a variety of reasons: perhaps they did not want to work the land or live so far from the city. Many of these refugees were coming to Israel on foot, in cars, or on camels from Syria, Lebanon, Iraq, and Iran.

So, the Azarkmans joined Muluk's mother, who had been living at Hatikva with her two sons in a one bedroom residence for ten years, making a living there by cleaning homes. One son was a soldier, and the other was injured. He had almost lost an eye in the late 1950s, but a transplant from a monkey had saved it. The house was so small that they had to take turns sleeping because there simply weren't enough beds or blankets for all to sleep at the same time.

Communicating with the boys, who spoke Persian only and no Hebrew, was another challenge. Their grandmother registered them in a local kindergarten so they could begin learning some Hebrew. She only spoke Russian and Bukharan Hebrew to them. They understood some of the Bukharan since Persian had some similar words. The home was extremely crowded and it was a big change for all of them.

Muluk's mother was very religious. Her husband had been a rabbi and she wanted the children to follow her in her readings, prayers, and performing of Jewish rituals. She did not cook on Fridays, when no one could work, play, or do most activities, because they observed Shabbat (the sabbath). On Thursdays, she would set up a big pot and cook the food on a low flame throughout Friday, using a cloth to cover it, which they could not touch the entire day. Then she'd remove the food from the pot very slowly so as not to touch it, following Jewish law. The next day, on Saturday, Shabbat, they would eat the meal, which was always delicious.

Grandma taught Jerry how to make her cookies, with nuts and raisins. He'd help her flatten and roll the dough, cut it into pieces and put it in a skillet in the fireplace covered with a cloth, letting it cook slowly. The tradition of the cookies is still a daily ritual for Jerry: cookies must be on his table with tea, morning until afternoon.

Despite all of his sacrifices to become a doctor, after moving to Israel, Oscar's studies were not honored. His degrees were worth nothing here, and the Azarkmans were back at square one. They needed to start all over again, with three small children and hearts full of hope that this new land was going to bring them joy and peace to raise a family. Starting over from scratch, after giving up all of their history, leaving behind all those they had grown to love, relatives, friends, and their entire life story. But they still dreamt of a better place where they could raise their kids without persecution or fear, and with the opportunity to flourish.

Every day Muluk would fill out papers looking for a job for Oscar. But the days passed without finding any work opportunities. They could not live under those conditions much longer. Oscar started selling his Persian rugs, the sole treasure he still had, but who could buy them? The State of Israel was also just starting out, and nobody had much money. Oscar practically gave the rugs away, but he raised enough money for a down payment on a house in Holon. So after eight months of living one on top of the other, the moment came for the Azarkmans to move into their new home.

Holon is close to Tel Aviv. Its name means "small sand," because it is a city built on sand dunes, and is highly populated by relocated Jews originally from Arab countries. Holon was considered to be Israel's second city of industrial development and it became the three boys' new playground. The dunes made a big impression on them; Jerry and his brothers would use pieces of boxes to slide down the hills, sleigh riding and boogie boarding on sand. They loved this place, because it was a welcome change now that they were only living with their mom and dad.

Jerry's grandma registered him in a nearby school where he faced a considerable challenge: He was supposed to enter second grade, but the class was full, so he was assigned to the third grade, where his difficulties began. Jerry still did not know how to read, write, or speak Hebrew, and his teacher was religious. The new pupil's first assignment was to memorize ten pages of the Bible, and the teacher yelled at Jerry, demanding that he repeat what he had memorized. But Jerry knew nothing. He did not understand the language and was just learning how to add and subtract. Wanting to find out what was wrong with him, the teacher learned he had been placed in the wrong class, and managed to work it out so that Jerry was moved into the second grade, where he belonged.

In those days, students were assigned a single teacher for the entire duration of his/her elementary years. Pupils were lucky if their teacher was a good, talented professional, a caring person who would relate to them, and who would go that extra mile that some children needed. But Jerry still knew very little Hebrew and it was hard for him to catch up. He thought he wasn't smart, when, in fact, he simply wasn't getting the attention he needed to grow and develop academically.

Muluk was prepared to go through these enormous changes in her life and the lives of her boys. Since her early girlhood she had already experienced major upheavals, having lived in a territory occupied by the Soviet Army where Jews were not allowed to go to synagogue, and then fleeing from this oppression with her mother. Similarly, Oscar had moved around Iran and Iraq several times, sometimes with his ten brothers and sisters and sometimes alone.

Change was not new for them, but moving to a young nation was something completely different. Theirs was a country born just a few years before that was still finding its way and surrounded by enemies in a hostile, unwelcoming region that did not want them there, let alone to allow them to thrive. The young nation of Israel was a place where war was part of everyday conversation, where countries around them supported rebel forces in an ongoing struggle against the Jewish State. These neighboring nations were investing in order to remove Israel from the community of nations, supporting the Palestinians in their fight to regain the territories in which Jews were now inhabiting and settling.

David Ben-Gurion, Israel's first Prime Minister, had the Herculean task of putting this new nation together when the Palestinian land underwent partition and was divided, with one part left for the Palestinians and the rest given to Israel. He started building the Jewish State from the bottom up, with the motto: "If an expert says it can't be done, get another expert." These were hard times for all of the Jews who already lived in Israeli territory and those who migrated there. Together, they began building a nation. Meanwhile, Israel was in the middle of a war with the Arabs. Ben-Gurion knew the difficulties they were going to have and the strong will their countrymen and women needed to build this country. Many didn't believe they could survive as a nation; many were afraid the war would kill them all. They were in the middle of these convulsions when the eloquent Ben-Gurion declared: "In Israel, in order to be a realist, you must believe in miracles."

Those miracles were needed for the newcomers to survive under such adverse circumstances. The Azarkmans were considered Bukharan Jews: Jews who weren't from Europe but from regions close to Asia and the Middle East, namely Iran. Even inside of the Jewish homeland they were treated like minorities, considered to be less knowledgeable, less developed, and more tied to the old-fashioned ways.

Their Hebrew was different from the language used by Jews from the West. Oscar and Muluk were prepared for hardships—they both knew how to handle this period of their lives. It brought back childhood memories. They knew they had to start over.

When events repeat themselves and you see things happen over and over again, your past experiences guide you to make better decisions, so you can then select which choice is better. Choosing the right course of action might very well change your entire destiny. Those experiences you have already gone through put into your hands a vast panorama of opportunities you can catch or let go. These past incidents are valuable, bestowing lessons and wisdom that will give you support you might not receive from anyone else. These experiences give you the ability to trust in yourself, providing the confidence you need to overcome anything. Your future is in your hands and everything has the opportunity to become better.

The Azarkmans moved from Iran because they feared for their lives amid all of the internal conflicts there, but then they moved to an unfamiliar land where all of the surrounding countries were their enemies, and there was constant preparation to thwart invasive threats. Even children were trained for the military in order to be prepared for war. Belonging to Israel's armed forces was similar to a member of a family becoming a priest in many countries—a source of pride for the family and community. In Israel, it was an honor to be in the military because you were fighting to preserve a homeland for Jews.

Meanwhile, little Jerry had his own internal conflicts. Anything around the lad distracted him from school and homework. Boys just want to have fun! He wanted to play, not do his assignments. He didn't feel any connection to his teacher or feel the need to learn. Since he had trouble paying attention and constantly made careless mistakes in class, the teacher had little patience with him. If any difficult task required him to make an extra effort, Jerry just gave up. School was not his thing. He just wanted to play and learn more about subjects he was actually interested in. The second grader did not understand why he had to learn many of the things taught at school. Jerry's arrival in Israel at the young age of six was an enormous change in his life. He was a stranger in a strange land.

He had inner conflicts all related to school, but had to go because his mom and dad would never let him skip class. Once at school, he forgot many of his daily tasks, such as bringing his homework to class. When he went home, he'd forget to take his homework assignments from school. He was last in his class, which he knew led to even more problematic interactions with his teacher. She would dictate the math test out loud to the class, and although Jerry was good at math and could provide the right answers, due to a grammatical mistake on his test in one of the responses, the teacher flunked him. He would tell her that he did it correctly and she'd argue that everything had to be correct, including grammar. The immigrant kid from Iran just couldn't catch a break.

Instead of excelling, Jerry tried to get just the grades needed for passing. His motivation was nonexistent. He felt like his teacher didn't like him, and that she preferred other students to him. She had a better connection with Jews raised in Israel and not immigrants from Europe. The Iranian-born boy felt he was being discriminated against at a very young age because of the origin of his family. The teacher would call him Sephardic.

Sephardim were Jews who had moved from Jerusalem in the year 586 B.C. when the Temple was destroyed, migrating to Spain and establishing themselves in several towns there, including Toledo. Spain was invaded by the Moors, Muslims from North Africa. Once the Moors were driven out of Spain, the Jews were expelled in 1492. They were not allowed to take any gold or silver with them and had to sell all their property, businesses, and cattle to locals at bargain prices, or exchange them for goods. Many Sephardic Jews moved to Portugal and other countries, including in the Middle East. Many were robbed, killed, enslaved, or died of hunger.

Jerry's destiny changed when he finished fifth grade, and his teacher, having completed her first to fifth grade assignment, was replaced with a beautiful young teacher assigned to teach his class from sixth through eighth grade. From the first day Jerry felt that this new instructor was like a breath of fresh air. She'd smile, ask him questions, and tell him he was capable of doing more than he was showing. She talked to him and gave him history assignments. When he took tests, he scored excellent grades.

Jerry now wanted to answer questions in class, get better grades—he wanted to learn. His entire situation changed from one day to the next and he took advantage of it. From being the last in his class, he became the first out of a group of forty students. Now, despite his attention deficit disorder and being easily distracted, Jerry was able to answer the teacher's questions and do his homework.

Homework became a number one priority for him. He struggled to become the top student, wanting to prove to his teacher he could understand and excel. He felt motivated: he had a great teacher who asked him what he wanted to be and do. He told her he wanted to become a pilot, and she went step by step, explaining to him what he had to do in order to become one. He had a goal and she was guiding him so he could obtain that goal. "You have to be a good student," she told him.

Teachers are remembered forever, especially when they are good and make a positive impact on your life. A good teacher encourages, supports, helps create positive changes in you, and can push you to climb up the ladder of your life. They take you and give you the tools you need to step up one more rung. Jerry had just such a teacher. He now knew that to be a pilot, he had to be a good student and possibly attend a Military Academy.

Jerry was being prepared for his future. He was learning that life needs all your inner resources, and that not even the smallest thing is given to you. It all requires individual effort, desire, and the will to make it happen. He graduated from eighth grade and he knew high school would not be a problem.

By contrast, Oscar was not flourishing. He had arrived in Israel with hope, with a whole new life and future in front of him and his family. What he did not know before uprooting his life was that the Israeli authorities would not recognize his degree in medicine. That all of his efforts to finish medical school and treat so many people back in Iran were not going to help him in Israel. He had to start from scratch. Life was tough and he started selling the handmade rugs they had brought with them from the Old Country. Once they were gone, there was nothing else to sell, but he still had three boys to feed and a family to take care of. The years were catching up with him, and he no longer had the strength he had when he was young. His heart was not as strong either.

Muluk had to step up to the plate. She was young and the only survival option the family had. In Holon she applied for and received a job as a seamstress in an export factory, where all the clothing manufactured was sent abroad. Muluk knew very little about industrial machines and the assembly line process. Her co-worker at the neighboring machine noticed she was extremely slow and befriended her. The fastest worker in the factory, she'd sew pieces together and give them to Muluk, so she would not get into trouble or lose her job for being too slow. Her friend started teaching her how to use the machines and eventually Muluk reached a point where she was just as fast as her friend. Muluk was putting food on the kitchen table, but, unable to find employment, Oscar was staying at home.

Over time, Muluk noticed that she could make more money by subcontracting her sewing to the factory. She discussed the idea with Oscar, who supported her and told her to go for it. But it was not so easy; the contracts were very rigid, and once you committed you had to deliver on time. Muluk's factory friend pushed her to do it and joined her in the venture. They both bought their first sewing machine and brought it to the Azarkmans' home in order to do the work they had subcontracted from the factory.

However, there was no room in the house for the sewing machine, so they had to put the table and set up the sewing machine on top of Jerry's bed. Muluk, who came from the land of the Silk Road, starting sewing and working with fabric. From the time he was a little boy, Jerry saw his mom sitting at the sewing machine for hours, sewing for days on end. He remembers going to bed while his mom was sewing and waking up the next morning only to find her still working on the sewing machine. To this very day, he still remembers the sound of the sewing machine and cannot fall asleep in a quiet place—he has to turn on the TV in order to go to sleep.

Muluk was sewing day and night to fulfill her contracts to make a living, but she could not cook or take care of the kids. She'd sew all day and cook only once a week. The rest of the week they ate only bread, eggs, and cheese, all foods subsidized by the government, and all the meals were the same. Breakfast, lunch, and dinner—only bread, eggs, and cheese. When Muluk cooked, lightness came into the house, and the aroma was everywhere. She tried to cook enough food to last the week, but her cooking was so good that the family tore through it in a couple of days, and, eventually they were back to the despised staples. Jerry became his mom's helper: overseeing the sewing machine, and fixing it when it broke— her little handyman. He started making some money and with his savings bought his first camera. He'd buy products to develop the photos, but Muluk would get upset by the smell of the chemicals, which distracted her from sewing, even though Jerry's darkroom was in the backyard.

Muluk's hard work was paying off and the family moved into a bigger house. Oscar found a job in a nearby warehouse, taking inventory of tools for a construction site. Honest labor respects all who practice it, but for Oscar it was painful; many people knew who he was and it was embarrassing to go from being a doctor to a mere warehouse employee. You could read the sadness in his eyes, in the way he spoke. Oscar was a very educated person who knew French, Arabic, Persian, and Hebrew. He wrote books on natural healing. Sadly, he burned the manuscripts and never published them.

Jerry had always been bullied by his older brother, who would hit him, take his toys and other belongings. Jerry prepared to defend himself, and one day when his big brother hit him, Jerry struck back, hitting him hard with a stick. He ran away to hide because he knew he was in trouble, but a neighbor caught him and told his father. Jerry ran away again and hid in an attic until nighttime came and he had to go home to sleep. Oscar was waiting for him and asked his son which he preferred: take a spanking or stay up all night in the bathroom. Jerry chose getting spanked and still remembers the pain in his dad's face while he was hitting him—after just a few blows, he was allowed to go to bed.

Jerry was twelve years old when he contracted a bad ear infection. It felt like he had a small tumor in his ear, and he didn't go to school for two months. While he stayed home, Oscar brought him many books on astronomy. During his convalescence, Jerry learned all about the planets and stars, and how they moved through the constellations. He pondered over and over how the universe had been created, and the sheer immensity of it all. He pestered his father with countless questions about creation, until, finally, Oscar directed his inquisitive son to the Holy Scriptures.

Jerry began to think that when people couldn't answer his tough questions, they would refer him to religion. Jerry stayed in bed for two months while he was recovering, and had the chance to read many books. He had always been a deep thinker, and he now began formulating some of his early ideas. He saw that a person could be defeated in part due to the influences of society, and that intolerant religions were a major contributing factor. His own philosophy of life began to emerge through questioning what life is all about, how one's character is molded, and how one do actions and reactions to events and the environment craft a destiny.

Oscar was always telling the kids stories and asking them questions about what they wanted to be and to have. He always told Jerry that the sky was the limit: if

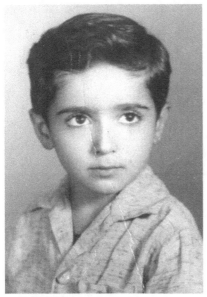

1959 Jerry Azarkmand at 7 years old.

1961 Jerry Azarkman, just
before moving to Israel 1961.

Jerry wanted a ship, it could be the biggest ship, or the biggest fleet of ships—but he had to be happy with what he was doing. If you have everything you ever wanted but are not doing what makes you happy, none of it is worth it.

For so many years, Jerry's father had insisted that there was no limit to what you can do if your will is strong. This was burned into Jerry's mind. Years later, on the flight to New York, Jerry would bring to mind the wisdom he had learned from his father all his life: He had to think big and he had to be strong.

Chapter Three

Military Proud

W hat does it takes for a parent to let go of a child? To let them grow and mature on their own? What is the appropriate age? When is the correct moment? When is it the time for a parent to say: "Go live your life!"? No one has the right answer. Only time will tell. What we do know is that parents provide their children with a foundation of morals for guidance. They are the first to teach them what's right and what's wrong. How well parents deliver and instill these early values will help determine how their children grow and develop into good, decent, adults. But if you remain close to your parents as an adult, and continue to involve them in your life, they will provide many more years of lessons, support, and advice. Jerry was fortunate to have had the strong presence of his parents in his life since he was born. Muluk was a devoted and involved mother and though Oscar was an older father, he, too, was a big part of Jerry's life. They gave him the strength to keep going by the example they set. Even when they could not see a solution to their current situation they kept trying: knocking on doors, filling out papers, communicating their needs and gathering information from countless people, and waiting for the moment when they could see the light at the end of the tunnel.

When the Azarkmans reached a place where they were unable to see even a glimmer of light, without alternatives or solutions, they were still sure, deep inside, that they'd find a way out and that things would turn around. The family bonds ran deep and strong. Despite highs and lows in the life of a family, despite differences in personality and temperament, a cohesive family unit is a priceless and powerful thing. One needn't look very far for good examples and for help in making important decisions.

It was clear to Jerry that if he wanted to be a pilot, he had to go to military school and be a very good student. Judith, his sixth through eighth grade teacher, had worked hard to motivate him to get better grades and to stay at the top of the class. At the end of every school day, Jerry went straight home to study and keep up his good grades. Jerry suffered from attention deficit disorder, though in that era there was no diagnosis and, therefore, no help. It was challenging for him to remain focused in class; any little thing could distract him and make him lose track, which then made it difficult to catch up.

One day, close to the end of his eighth grade year, recruiters from the Reali School in Haifa visited the school, along with representatives from the Hertzelia Military Academy. Judith was the first to remind Jerry that this was a great opportunity for him. The recruiters explained the benefits of their program and how to register. The application was voluntary, and, if selected, all of the recruits' expenses would be paid by the program. Jerry was prepared to go for it. He knew what his goal was and was ready to take this opportunity. He was the first one to line up and apply.

To be accepted in a school of this caliber was very difficult. It involved several stages and this was only the first. The recruiters took the list of those interested in continuing to their high school education program in a military academy and went to the principal's office to review their grades and obtain additional information about them. Most of the students were excited at the prospect of opening up a parallel career while they were getting a high school diploma. Many students in both eighth grade classes participated and the ensuing tests included all the topics one could imagine, from psychology to social studies to math. At the end of the day, following many hours of exams, Jerry knew he had given his all, and that his efforts would be reflected in the answers he had given.

The waiting began. The aspiring cadet came home from school every day to check if there was anything in the mail for him. Days passed and his anxiety grew. Jerry knew that this was it, this was his dream. This military school had huge prestige in Israel, and its selection process included kids from all over the country. Jerry was thirteen, and attending Hertzelia would change his life. This school was essential to him and he needed to be accepted. It was a giant step towards independence, and a way to declare that he was old enough to move to a military base. There were so many things going on in his mind! Finally, the day arrived when there was a letter addressed to him waiting in the mailbox.

Thirteen years old. Was he strong enough to face the news, or would it mark him forever if he failed? Was he mature enough, and capable of facing the challenges if he was accepted?

Military school would be an enormous change for the young Jerry, but he was sure it was his time. He wanted to be more independent, to prove that he was capable. He had arrived early at that age when kids want to put some distance between them and their parents, when they feel like the world is spread out in front of them and anything is possible. As much as he loved his parents, he was going through the adolescent changes that can spark rebellion and a desire to separate. He had also matured emotionally, earlier than most, probably due to the hardships his family had to endure. But the upheaval of going to a military academy was compounded by Israel's continuous battles with its neighbors, which was a fact of everyday life. Jerry's head was spinning.

Jerry tore into the letter in such a rush that he was afraid he'd tear it to pieces. The letter was very short and simple: You have passed the first round of tests and have advanced to the second round of the selection process, which will include 3,600 youths from all over Israel. The letter contained a special message for Jerry: He was the only one selected from his class. Filled with pride, he showed the letter to everyone.

Oscar and Muluk were very proud of him, but at the same they were afraid of what it might entail. His mother was especially fearful of letting him go. She knew that right after the academy, he would have to enlist, and that, given his training at the academy, he would most likely be sent to the front. Her imagination conjured up images of her little boy being injured, or killed. Oscar was patient, compassionate, and supportive of his wife. He talked to her for hours, and explained that children grow up and need space to make their own decisions and confront their own destinies. He reminded her that this was what they, too, had done—left their families in order to pursue their dreams. He stressed how hard Jerry had worked to bring his grades up, because his goal was to become a pilot, and this was his way of moving forward.

Muluk and Oscar knew they did not have many options for their children. They could not afford to pay for college or give them money to start a business. The Azarkmans' options were very limited at this time in their lives, and in any case, the word on military school was not final, and their worry probably premature. At night, when they were alone, Oscar would repeat this to Muluk many times: Jerry still had numerous tests to take and there were lots of other candidates the academy needed to consider before Jerry could be selected.

Jerry completed his final term at school. He studied hard for his finals and got the highest grades in his class. He knew Judith, his teacher, was a godsend who had given him the motivation and support to change his life. Later in life Jerry realized this was the turning point for him, an opportunity to change his destiny and to make him believe in himself. He now knew the sky was the limit. It meant that to achieve his objective would take only a true desire and a strong will. Although there would be other key moments in his trajectory, having Judith as his teacher would always remain a milestone. Judith would no longer be part of his life, but he would remember her forever.

Immediately after graduation day, Jerry was ready to take the second round of tests for the military academy. He went directly to the campus in Hertzelia with 3,600 students from all over Israel. The pressure was felt by all. Every kid was fighting to stay and only the strongest and the smartest, the ones willing to put all of their efforts into taking the tests, those who would not give up, would stay. Jerry knew this. He could not fail or give up. He had to keep going, and remember what Judith had told him so many times: to step up, you have to show what you're capable of doing.

There are moments in life when you don't realize the full impact of your decision until long after the fact. This was such a moment.

The students were bused to the campus, located in a town called Hertzelia. Jerry was filled with pride at being there, especially as the sole student selected from his class. But he knew that being proud wasn't enough—it would take a great effort to go all the way.

Hertzelia Academy was a very prestigious school for the development of officers and army combat leaders. Israel was under constant attack from the Arab countries and the Jewish State's need for new soldiers and officers was an everyday reality.

He got off the bus and the process started. More tests, many of them physical. Jerry was already recognized as an athlete and had participated in many competitions, particularly in middle distance races. His family could not afford to buy him sneakers and he had to run barefoot, but even under those conditions, he won the 1,500 meter race. All his previous training and competitions had brought him here in great shape; he was fit enough to face the tests.

As the selection process continued, the group of 3,600 candidates was whittled down to only 68 students who had made the final cut—and Jerry was one of them! This was the happiest day of his life yet. His joy was even bigger than when he had taken that first test with Judith, and finally scored a good grade after years of failure. But the emotion was different. It was the sensation of a maturing young man who was seeing his life with new eyes. He was on his own.

Jerry now needed to bring the good news home to his parents. They were waiting for him at the door when he got there. He wanted to make the announcement, but his body language gave him away; he was wearing a big grin and had the excitement and air of a winner. Feelings of joy and great triumph visited the Azarkman home, but Muluk was still anxious. What she had feared before was now drawing closer to a reality. No more tests. He was in the military academy and all her worries were real. Her older son Doron was already serving his mandatory three years of military service, and now her second son was leaving home.

At Hertzelia, commissioned officers were trained to serve in different branches of the army, but the most important step at this point was to unify them into one single, solitary, body. The staff needed to tie this group together, and to make them feel close to one another. The cadets had come from all over the country. They were

1966 Jerry Azarkman going to the
Military Academy at age 13.

1969 Jerry Azarkman in
Military Academy uniform.

all Jewish, but their backgrounds were different, although what the majority had in common was that they were born in Israel—except for Jerry.

Life was different now for Muluk: She would no longer see her boy every day after school. She missed his smile, his voice, his company. She missed his help with the machines and how he fixed things around the house. She even missed the smell of the chemicals when he was developing his photographs. She would wait for a letter from him, for news about how her son was doing. Even though it was one less mouth to feed, his absence was a terrible feeling. Muluk was a strong woman, one who had gone from having servants and living in a beautiful home to leading a simple life in Israel, with hard work that she was proud of. She had sacrificed everything for her kids, and for the safety of her family.

Each dorm room at the campus contained four beds for four strangers, selected to room together. All four arrived full of energy, proud to have been selected, and ready to be the best students and the best soldiers. Four kids full of dreams, with their future in their hands, leaving behind their families. They were four boys who shared great chemistry and became fast friends, almost overnight. They didn't know that for Jerry to have a bed without a sewing machine working above him day and night was simply divine. Jerry wasn't feeling quite like celebrating, though, because he was suddenly homesick. He missed his mom, his one-room home, his brothers, and his dad.

Israel was going through difficult times. Egypt was constantly moving its troops to the border, and there were frequent flare-ups. The area was under constant threat of war. Through the years, Israel had organized its military forces and was prepared for any battle, but the country needed any war it fought to be done so in an extremely strategic way. Israel knew that the moment it attacked Egypt or any other country in the Arab world, the rest of the Arab states would retaliate against them. Israelis knew they had to plan not only to attack, but to simultaneously be able to defend their borders from other countries. The operation had to be enormous, and the Air Force was essential: they had to hit hard and make it such a powerful blow that Israel would prevail.

The three energetic boys chosen to room with Yoram Azarkman were Avinoam Shemesh, Avtalion Natan, and Ido Riger. They all had big dreams, all wanted to become officers, and were eager to protect the state of Israel. The training in various military duties was hard, but they understood that everything had a purpose. It didn't matter what their families' economic and cultural background was: they were all separated from their families, and all keenly felt the absence of their parents, home cooked meals, and of home itself.

Training was inflexible. It started early every morning and was rigorous. The cadets ran for forty-five minutes, showered, had breakfast, then took a bus to school. After classes, they ate lunch, changed into their uniforms, and continued their military training. They had classes in Taekwondo, Judo, Krav Maga, boxing, wrestling, and shooting with all kinds of weapons. They got used to aching all over from the strenuous physical exercise, long hours, and exposure to the weather. The days were hot and sunny, and the nights were long and cold. The four soldiers-to-be had to have strong ethics, and be brave, disciplined, and serious about their decision to serve.

They were learning new skills and how to overcome obstacles. They were also being taught to follow orders, and began to have an understanding of military tactical thinking. The four boys took on all the physical challenges the military academy threw at them. They were developing patriotism, and learning how to defend their country. Daily, they supported each other through every task and exercise, growing together and becoming a family.

Egypt was increasingly moving its armed forces through the Sinai Peninsula, where, as part of an international agreement, United Nations troops were posted to serve as a buffer between the two nations in order to prevent them from going to war. Egypt was not enthusiastic about having armed foreigners on its territory where the United Nations Emergency Force (UNEF) had originally been deployed after the Suez Canal conflict of 1956, to ensure that all of the peace agreements were followed. However, during this same period, Arab countries were signing military pacts to join forces to fight Israel. The Arab countries' decision not to recognize the Jewish state, or the "Zionist entity" was a cause for anxiety all over the country. The threat of Pan-Arab unity, of their agreements, their solidarity against Israel, and constant indications of a possible attack meant that Israel had to prepare for the worst. At home every cadet in Jerry's academy was greatly admired by the neighbors and the community. They were the pride of Israel, their future army officers, and they were their own children. Just a few years earlier they'd been playing in the sand dunes, in the neighborhood and now they were being trained in the art of war—how to use weapons and defend their country. Everyone was proud of them, and they knew one day they'd be fighting and willing to give their lives for the Jewish homeland.

When the State of Israel was created in 1948, the land of Palestine had been split in half. Why weren't two countries formed in what had been called Palestine? Cut in half, one half for the Jewish people and the other half for the Palestinian Arabs? There was no independent country of Palestine: All this land was under the control of the Ottoman Empire until after World War I, when Turkey lost and Great Britain took over the region that included Syria, Lebanon, Iraq, and Palestine. In the Palestine area, the British created a country called Transjordan and gave it to the Abdullah family as the Hashemite Kingdom. Jordan's army invaded part of this area in 1950 and took over the country that, at the time, consisted of what is now Jordan and the West Bank.

The West Bank is land that runs along the Jordan River, a natural border that separates it from Jordan. Twelve percent of the West Bank's territory was on Israeli land, but under Jordanian control. Before the creation of today's concrete fence called the separation wall, the West Bank was an open zone for launching terrorist attacks that took place not only on the Israeli side, but on the Jordanian side, too. Since the wall was erected, there has been a significant reduction of terrorist incidents. The West Bank stretches out from the border with Jordan to just fifteen miles from the shore of the Mediterranean Sea, which gives it an additional strategic value. Israel could potentially be split in two, giving the West Bank access to the sea and increasing the possibility of border conflicts. For all these reasons, the West Bank is a highly strategic zone and is essential for Israel's security.

In Israel, military service begins at eighteen and runs for three years. It is mandatory for every young Jew, male and female living is Israel (except for those who receive religious deferments), and voluntary for those living abroad. In addition to military training at Hertzelia, Jerry and the other students had a parallel academic curriculum to adhere to. The academy was known for its high academic standards, and this made the experience even more challenging for Jerry and his friends. They could not "get by" simply on the strengths of their military skills—they had to excel in school, too.

In 1967, the region was experiencing immense pressure. Israel had many confrontations with Syria and Jordan. Bombs were exploding in Israel by Jordanian guerillas, causing Israel to attack the West Bank city of as-Samu, occupied by Jordan, whose king triggered a chain reaction that led to war. King Hussein complained that Egypt did not come to his aid in order to contain Israel, and the Soviets, who were supporting Syria, gave Egypt incorrect information that Israel was invading Syria's border.

Egypt expelled the UNEF soldiers and U.N. representatives and supported Jordan's forces in conjunction with Iraq in order to protect Jordanians from Israel. Egyptians took control of the strategically located Straits of Tiran and established a naval blockade that could have adversely affected Eilat, Israel's only Indian Ocean port. Israel denounced this blockade as a violation of international law. In addition, Egypt moved its armed forces in the Sinai closer to the border with Israel, which Tel Aviv believed was a declaration of war on the Jewish State. A few days later, Israel launched Operation Focus, a surprise air raid that destroyed Egypt and Jordan's air forces. The strategy behind this sneak attack that crippled the Arab ability to fight could be summed up as: "He who strikes first strikes twice", meaning that striking first almost doubles the impact of the strike. The surprise attack felt far bigger than it actually was, and in just six days of fighting, from June 5 to June 11, 1967 Israel dealt a swift and crushing blow to the Arab world.

Shortly after Israel's stunning victory in the Six Day War, Jerry and his classmates toured the captured Sinai Desert by bus. Israel now occupied territories that included the Sinai Peninsula and Gaza Strip (which had been part of Egypt), the West Bank and East Jerusalem (formerly ruled by Jordan), and Syria's Golan Heights. In the Sinai Desert, Jerry and the rest of the cadets witnessed the destruction the Israeli air attack had wreaked on Egypt's air and ground forces. The devastation had occurred just days before and all the wreckage was still visible. Jerry remembers seeing from afar the smoke still emanating from the charred remains of planes and trucks.

The occupied territories had a special value for Israel. While for Syria it only represented the loss of thirteen military camps, the Golan Heights meant farmland for tiny Israel, which would establish thirty-three agricultural settlements, as well as fifteen percent of the Jewish State's supply of water. For Israel, controlling the West Bank meant the recovery of two historic Biblical cities: Judea and Samaria. And Jerusalem, the capital, which had been divided for years, was now whole again.

When the buses arrived at the destroyed Egyptian military camps, the smell of burning oil was still in the air, along with the odor of dynamite explosions. There were dead bodies all over the place, decaying in the sun, amidst the ruins of airplanes and tanks. Jerry saw something unforgettable: A white area that looked like a patch of snow. The bus driver drove closer and the students left the bus to see what it was: The bones of Egyptian soldiers cremated by many hours of intense sun and thermally melted by Israeli air force strikes. Looking at the ashes spread all over the desert, Jerry realized it was one thing to hear the news of victory on the radio but quite another to witness the death and devastation firsthand. The horrific sight made an indelible impression on teenage Jerry, and the experience would change him in years to come.

The bus continued on to the closest city and the streets were full of people welcoming them—the Arabs were friendly and even offered the cadets food. This was the first time Jerry ate Arab food, which was very different from the bread, cheese, and eggs he was used to eating at home. The boys were introduced to the delights of shish kabob, pita bread, hummus, and fava beans, and Jerry thought it was all delicious. This city was named Beit-Lachm, which means "house of bread", and the Christian world knows it as the birthplace of Jesus, or Bethlehem.

The purpose of this visit was to make every cadet understand the importance of their training, how significant every single step had been in preparing them for war and defending their country. It was also intended to be a sobering look at death and destruction: their life or their enemy's life, kill or be killed. This impacted them deeply and made them train harder, and discover the important role of each individual in the puzzle that comprised the troops.

They returned to the camp and their training resumed. Jerry's mind was in a whirlwind; his values were being molded yet again. He still took part in the exercises, learned about guns, and developed his tactical skills, but in his heart he began to believe that these weapons would only bring more violence. He who lived by the sword died by the sword. War meant destruction and death for both sides, and he asked himself if the taking of so many lives would ever bring peace.

Jerry and his roommates discovered that nearby there was a camp for American exchange students, many of them female, so they took it upon themselves to walk the five miles and impress the girls with their combat fatigues. The camp was surrounded by strawberry fields, and the boys thought they'd be even more welcome if they came bearing gifts, so they picked as they walked. They exchanged smiles. Some of the girls knew a few Hebrew words, and the boys showed off their high school English. It was a great adventure.

By the following day the word had spread, and dozens of other boys set out for the camp, strawberries in hand, convinced that it was the ticket to get them in. But the teachers saw a column of soldiers about to invade their camp, and they were promptly thrown out. So much for American girls and strawberries.

In another of their adventures, the four boys walked to a nearby watermelon farm. They were met by a sea of green, sweet, melons, and the sight made their mouths water. They could almost taste the ripe beauties as they began to gather them. No one had noticed an eighty-five year old Arab woman approaching, her fist raised high, shaking with indignation, and threatening to kill them. The boys surrendered their bounty immediately and apologized profusely, but there was no placating the woman. She marched over to their camp, muttering oaths under her breath the entire way. A complaint was lodged with their superiors, followed by a swift punishment: the boys were not allowed to go home over a long weekend. Their appetite for stolen watermelons vanished quickly.

The whole camp was empty except for the four friends. There was no food, and the kitchen was locked. All they found was a box of cocoa powder, which quickly became the subject of mayhem and merriment. Jerry and Avinoam shot cocoa pellets at Ido and Avtalion, and they returned fire by flinging back handfuls of the pellets. Everything was brown—the walls, the floors, the furniture, and the kitchen fixtures, and, within days, it had congealed with the grease on the stove, smelling like a giant, sour, brownie. This time, their punishment was not to leave for a month the camp, but, at least they were left with plenty of food while their classmates were at home.

Yom Kippur is the most important holiday for Jews, the day that falls on the seventh month of the Jewish lunar calendar. Each new moon marks the start of a new month, and the lunar calendar has 12.4 new moons a year. To compensate for the difference between the lunar year and the solar year of the Gregorian calendar, the Jewish calendar has an additional month every two or three years.

Yom Kippur is the Day of Atonement for Jews, a day set aside to examine the soul and to reflect on one's moral fiber. It is the last day to appeal to God, and the final opportunity to change the judgments, to demonstrate one's repentance and to make amends. It is a complete Sabbath, in the sense that Jews refrain from eating and drinking, and from performing any labor for twenty-five hours. Yom Kippur starts before sunset and ends the night of the following day. It's a day of prayer, and synagogues are open morning to night.

On October 6, 1973, Egypt and Syria launched a surprise attack on Israel on Yom Kippur, the holiest day of the year. That year, it happened to coincide with Ramadan, the month when the Islamic world prays, fasts, and the faithful develop their spirituality, humility, and patience.

The Golan Heights and Sinai Peninsula were attacked at the same time by Arab forces. Israel's 180 tanks, 160 pieces of artillery, and 3,000 soldiers in the Golan area were confronting Syria's 800 tanks, 600 pieces of artillery, and 28,000 soldiers. This area was a priority for the country, as it had many Israeli settlements unlike the empty land in the Sinai Desert. Within fifteen hours, the Israeli Defense Force was already battling back.

Egypt attacked 450 Israeli defenders at sixteen posts, with 290 tanks in three brigades at the Suez Canal. The Egyptian offensive included 100,000 soldiers, 1,300 tanks, and 2,000 artillery pieces and was called Operation Badr, Arabic for "full moon." Nine Arab countries supported both Syria and Egypt, while Palestinian fighters were exploding bombs all over, sowing fear in the civilian settlement population.

Israel immediately started to face the enemy and three days after Egypt's first assault, they were counterattacking and began controlling the territories and the war. Meanwhile, tension increased between the two superpowers. The Soviet Union backed Syria and Egypt while the United States supported Israel, which made the world fear the imminent possibility of direct confrontation at any moment. The United Nations got involved and brokered a ceasefire twice in order to stop the fighting. President Richard Nixon was embroiled in the Watergate scandal, so Secretary Henry Kissinger conducted all the negotiations on his behalf.

Once Jerry finished Academy training, he was eighteen and had to immediately register in the army. He told his superiors point blank that he refused to kill another human being. The commander replied that he had been trained for war and that he had to serve under any conditions, but as Jerry kept on insisting that he did not want to kill anyone, he was sent to prison. During the day, the jail was unguarded, and at night the guards told him to go home and return the next day. This went on for several days until a new officer came to the command post and told Jerry that he would be sent to the school of communication. There, Jerry was trained in different communications methods. He had to learn all the codes and passwords, what each one meant, how to answer, and what the chain of command was.

The Yom Kippur War lasted until October 25, 1973. It was the fourth war between Israel and the Arabs since 1948, the inception of the state. Golda Meir was Israel's Prime Minister at the time. While Jerry was at the command post, he handled communications between the battalions out in the field. One message Jerry received reported that a tank had been hit by a missile and the entire crew was killed. Jerry's roommate Avinoam was in the doomed tank and he died on the first day of the war.

After four days of battle, Jerry's other roommate, Avtalion, stuck his head out of another tank to check its structure and a bullet hit him. Avtalion was in a coma for a month. When he woke up, he could not identify anyone or move his body. The only person he recognized was Jerry, who visited him for many weeks, teaching him how to read and write again. To this very day, Avtalion is still in a wheelchair.

Ido Riger emerged physically whole, as did Jerry, but with the psychological traumas many soldiers suffer after combat, even if they haven't received any bodily injuries. Jerry knew he had survived due to his refusal to handle a weapon. Ido moved to South Africa where he became a very successful businessman. He still visits Jerry and they remain good friends. None of the four became officers.

Following the Yom Kippur War, the United States became more deeply involved in seeking peace talks between the Arab countries and Israel. Years passed before Egypt negotiated a peace treaty with Israel, and once they signed it, Israel gave the Sinai Peninsula (land that contained invaluable oil) back to Egypt. In retaliation, Egypt was expelled from the Arab League by twenty other countries, as the League's policy was not to recognize Israel: no agreements, no peace.

The flight attendant began serving drinks to passengers on flight LY7 to New York, but Jerry was so excited about his new adventure that he could not take his eyes off the window. He was imagining his future.

1970 Jerry Azarkman visiting Mount Sinai.

1969 Jerry Azarkman at the Military Academy, West Bank background of Jenin.

1968 At a Military exercises at Sinai,
Jerry Azarkman is on the left with
his best friend Avtalion Natan.

Chapter Four

Finishing Military Service

W hen you witness firsthand the death and destruction of a war, lose loved ones, see the disabled and the wounded, your life can never be the same again. The experience can make you value life much more than before, and family can be the most important part of coming home. Relatives will give you the support and love you need to stand up again. Your spirit is forever injured and you'll need the hand of the people who love you and are willing to hug your heart and soul.

All the material success in the world can't erase one's memory of the pain and suffering witnessed in a war. The face of pain, of the maimed, of the dead, is reflected in the survivor's psyche. Those faces reappear in dreams through the years and when someone dares to ask you about your wartime experiences.

The Middle East is a region of warfare, where destruction and death are in the news on a daily basis. Displaced families move from one place to the other, and have no roof, no home, no sense of community, living with the stark reality that everything is gone. The confrontations between the differences over beliefs, religions, borders, military power, oil, territories, and ancient cities are the causes of constant battle. The region's history goes back to centuries of combat between neighbors, with one people conquering the territory of a nearby tribe, and different religions fighting one another. It's always been the law of the strongest—whoever has a superior weapon, stronger fighters, and better strategy conquers his neighbor.

For centuries the area where Israel is located has been a place where members of different religions meet to pray and give tribute. It's a sanctuary where several religions visit during the year and celebrate rituals. This gives Israel another reason to protect the security of its citizens and visitors.

The Yom Kippur War ended, and Jerry had to continue with his academic process. He had graduated from high school at the age of seventeen, and taken the exams for entering college. His plan was to go to college after the army, but he decided that he could use the time while serving to further his education. He wanted to learn programming, and saw an opportunity to earn a diploma while still in the army. To accomplish this, Jerry would need to leave the army base to attend an adult school, but this was nearly impossible, as no one was allowed to leave the base. However, if Jerry had learned anything, it was that when he had an idea and wanted to make it work, he needed to be persistent and determined until he'd accomplished his objective. He had to plan his approach and demonstrate that his need was real and urgent, and to ensure that his request was emphatic enough.

Jerry knew that the first challenge would be to prove that none of the duties assigned him would be in jeopardy because of his having to leave early each day. He mastered his duties, finishing them quickly and correctly, then organized his tasks in such a way that he'd finish them each day by 1:00 p.m. Knowing his request would not be accepted the first time, Jerry was prepared to persuade his officer. He knew it would take day after day of conversations to convince the officer, and that he'd have to demonstrate his duties could be done on time. He had to show his determination and be somewhat of a nag. It was no easy task to change the rules of the military base, where regulations had been set for years for everyone to follow with no exceptions. For Jerry to challenge one of them required consistency and the capacity to prove his point; the most important part was for his officer to believe, trust, understand, and support him. Jerry had confirmed his dependability to his superiors by being disciplined, always at the top of his rank, and completing every task to the best of his ability.

He had already undergone all of the required routines when he was in the military academy. He did his duties every day precisely, completely, and in the way he was instructed. So the persistent Jerry finally convinced his superiors to allow him to further his education, and his officer let him go to the school. He had successfully shown he had extra time during the day to dedicate himself to completing his programming diploma, and he received a very special permission to leave the camp every afternoon.

Jerry had to demonstrate that he could finish all the duties he was assigned daily with no excuses, and without skipping any responsibilities. He then began to travel to school from his base every afternoon.

Most duties in life can be performed to perfection if each step is repeated over and over again. Repetition brings excellence. This is the power each individual has in his hands to effect change. When one wants to change conditions, one just has to take each of the necessary steps and practice them every day until they are done to perfection. These changes can take one to another level in both skill and confidence. They bring new energy, giving one the ability to confront any superior, and preparing them to demonstrate how well one performs.

Jerry saw that he was wasting hours every afternoon on his motorcycle commute from the base to the school and back again. It would take over two hours in rush hour traffic to return to the base, whereas, if he went directly home from the school, it was a much shorter trip, and he could use the extra time to study. So after a few weeks of this daily trip, he decided to ask for another special dispensation. Now this was an even greater concession, because it meant that if there was a call to action during the night he would not be there to immediately join the forces. Jerry showed that in the wee hours of the morning it would take him only twenty minutes to get to his base from home. The request had a strong logic behind it, for Jerry would be saving time on the road, which he could then use for studying and finishing homework. After several talks with his superiors, Jerry's officer finally agreed to give him the opportunity. He then had two afternoons where he was not attending school and he found a job working with a group of troubled kids in a nearby park. His job was to infiltrate and befriend them, steering them away from gang activities.

Every day after school Jerry would go home, to the delight of his mother. She had her boy, now a young man, at the family table again. Oscar had become a well-known personality in their neighborhood, and every Friday, the Azarkmans' Shabbat ceremony was enormous, with people coming from all over to their home to gather and pray. They'd spend the afternoon sitting in the shade of their backyard trees and chatting. Oscar was a people person. His social skills were a magnet for people who enjoyed his stories, advice, observations, knowledge, and hearing about his experiences. The Shabbat brought families together: Oscar with his companionship, Muluk with her great cooking.

An extraordinary cook, Muluk prepared recipes from a mélange of food Jews ate in Russia, Iraq, and Israel. The Azarkmans' situation had turned around; having already moved to a bigger house with more rooms and space, they rented the small home, where they had started out, to another family. The Azarkman boys were grown up and moving on with their lives.

Jerry finished his studies and military service and started thinking about what his next step in life would be. He'd spent many years in a military milieu—his life was structured around rules and duties. He was already twenty-one years old and had spent almost half of his life in training camps. Now he wanted something different. His future could not be tied to the armed forces. As a pacifist, he held the deep conviction that he did not want to kill another human being, enemy or not. He wanted to live a normal life away from destruction, weapons, and tanks.

During his time in the army, he had taken several exams and filled out all kinds of forms stating he wanted to become a pilot. When he was about to finish his duty in the army, he was contacted by both the Israeli Air Force Flight Academy and the Navy commandos, inviting him to continue his military education with them. However, he was no longer interested in pursuing this career path and declined the offer. It was not easy for the young man to abandon his dream of becoming a pilot, but his moral convictions were stronger. He could never kill anyone just because they did not share the same beliefs or because they were from a different country, or for any other reason. Jerry knew he was never going to be a pilot under the conditions of having to serve in a military force. Recruiters persisted in sending him letters, and he replied to every one of them with a firm no. When he turned twenty-two, they stopped trying to enlist him.

Jerry's younger brother had a job repairing technical equipment in an electronics store, and he talked to his brother about the possibility of opening up a store of their own. It wouldn't be an easy undertaking, because most electronics were imported and taxation for imports was very high. This made the price of the electronics rather high. For customers to be able to buy products with such high ticket prices they had to have credit cards or to have saved up a lot of money. Alternately, stores needed to provide layaway plans so customers were able to afford to buy electronics. It was a luxury and not everyone could afford it, especially in Israel in 1970s, when the nation was less populous and prosperous than it is now, and before free trade zones were common.

His brother persisted in his idea, and the two brothers decided to open an electronics store. When their minds were made up, they went home to talk to their parents. They shared their thoughts with Muluk and Oscar, explaining exactly what it would take to open their business. They had to come up with a plan to obtain all the necessary permits, find a property to rent, and negotiate a contract for buying and building up their stock, and even the day they were going to open to the public. They had a sound idea, were enthusiastic about having their own business, and were ready to go. They found a good location, determine the kind of inventory they would have, but they had no money to start. They had saved up some, but it wasn't nearly enough.

Muluk and Oscar thought hard about how they wanted to help their sons, and decided to sell the small house were they had started out many years before and to split the money equally between the three brothers. Both brothers were ready to use their shares, while Doron pondered what to do with his portion. After thinking about it, Doron decided to buy the house to start his own family someday, and used his share for the down payment on it. Doron got his mortgage, and the brothers got their startup capital.

In the year before going to the army, while he was completing his high school certificate, Jerry had a job at a local community center. These centers were common in Israel at the time. Every neighborhood had one, and it was a place for kids to hang out after school, under supervision. They had activities and clubs, a strong social milieu, and a place to do their homework. There were a number of girls in the group, and one of them stood out. Dina was a polite, somewhat shy girl who was born in Israel, but had spent a portion of her childhood in other countries. Her parents moved the family to Italy when she was five, and then moved again, this time to England, when Dina was seven. Her father worked for El Al, the Israeli national airline, and he had several foreign postings for the company. At age twelve, Dina's family moved back to Israel and settled in Holon, where Jerry's family had made their home.

Dina's father had come to Israel from Hungary after the war, and her mother had come from Bulgaria in the same year. Theirs was one of the first waves of immigration from Europe immediately following World War Two, and was composed mainly of survivors of the Holocaust. They were the lucky ones who had not been sent to concentration camps, but both their families had suffered displacement, dispossession, hunger, and relentless anti-Semitism in their respective countries. Dina's father, Abraham, would tell the story of being stopped on his way home from school by a German soldier, who demanded that young Abe give him a beautiful watch he was wearing. Abraham wasn't about to part with his prized possession and flatly refused. In Nazi occupied Europe, a Jew could have been shot on the spot for a lesser offense, but, miraculously, the soldier shrugged and moved on.

Abraham and Betti settled in the same Kibbutz, where they met and fell in love. Neither knew a word of Hebrew, but their eyes did all the talking.

A Kibbutz, meaning "gathering," is a community of people who come together with shared values and ideals, establishing a settlement owned jointly by all. Most started as agricultural communities, though today many are based in industry, high-tech, or tourism. They are communal in the sense that no one owns personal property, and all co-own the land, homes, and equipment. They rotate jobs, eat in a common dining hall, and their children sleep in a common children's house with caregivers every night. The Kibbutz'niks, as they are called, are known to be hard-working and idealistic people with a passion for the land. The Kibbutz started in 1909 when a group of Jews came to Israel to work the land. They dreamed of owning their own farms and developing more arable land, but this was not an easy task as Israel was mostly deserted. The little that was not desert was hard, rocky earth, or swampland. It was a time of many illnesses—malaria, cholera, and typhus—and it was a land of much instability, where skirmishes were frequent and crops were routinely set on fire by enemies. The settlers thought that if they gathered in an organized fashion, living and farming together, they had a better chance of surviving.

Jews from all around the world collected funds. They created an organization called the Jewish National Fund, JNF for short, for the purpose of raising funds to buy land and develop it in what, at that time, was known as Palestine, part of the Ottoman Empire. The JNF's mission of raising funds and developing land was part of the effort to settle Palestine, later to be called Israel, as the homeland for Jews from all over the world. They began by collecting coins in The Blue Boxes, a donation tin placed in the home of every Jewish family and business.

The first land purchased through the efforts of the JNF brought together a community of nine men and two women. Among the settlers was Joseph Baratz, who wrote the book, *A Village by the Jordan: The Story of Degania*. The name given to the first Kibbutz was Kvutzat Degania, which means "Gathering of God's Wheat."

Dina's parents, Abraham and Betti, stayed and worked in the Kibbutz for a year, then married and moved to their own home.

Dina's father had come from a very religious home, but he himself had turned his back on Orthodoxy when he left home at seventeen, so Dina was raised in a very secular home. Her family was ethnically, culturally, and politically Jewish, but was not observant of Jewish law. However, they gathered for a traditional Passover meal every year at her paternal grandfather's house. As a religious Jew, her grandfather Jacob would never shake hands with a woman—not even his son's wife—and he never ate at their home because they did not keep kosher. At Passover, Jacob frequently tugged on Dina's skirts, to show his displeasure at their length.

Abraham began his career with El Al Airlines as a flight dispatcher, then gradually moved up the corporate ladder. He had always felt cheated out of an education due to the war and his family's poverty, and much later in life he went to college for the first time and earned his degree in psychology and gerontology. After the war, Abraham immigrated to Israel as an idealistic Jew, to begin a new life and to help build the young nation. Before marrying Betti, Abraham fought in Israel's Independence war, and helped build roads. Both Betti and Abraham had emigrated at seventeen, arriving alone and with nothing but their sweat, and worked to pave the way for their families to follow.

Betti came from a non-religious family, which was common in the Bulgarian community. Her father, who had a thriving leather tanning business in Bulgaria, was reduced to working in a lamp factory, assembling parts by hand. When Dina was young, she would ask him why his hands were always black and his fingernails dirty. He took it good naturedly, explaining that the grease from the factory couldn't be washed out. He even showed her how he would scrub until his hands were raw, yet they stayed black. Dina loved her grandfather dearly and came to regret her persistent questions. She could never quite forgive herself for causing him shame.

Grandfather Rachamim, or Dedo Racho, as she called him, was a simple, humble, and uneducated man, content with his lot in life and never complaining. He possessed the kind of wisdom that can only come from hardships and experience, and not from a classroom. His favorite saying was "You can spend your entire life learning, but you die stupid." It took Dina many years to understand the meaning: no matter how much education you amass, there is always more to learn.

After a day at the lamp factory, Rachamim came home and all he wanted was to sit in the kitchen and quietly eat the simple supper prepared by his wife. A favorite dish of his was Bulgarian style custard, and Dina remembers him at the kitchen table, by himself, eating the remnants at the edge of the pan with a spoon, content as can be. Grandmother Oreta, or avta to Dina, was an expert creator of candies, cheese puffs, jams and jellies, and syrupy pastries that were heaven to little Dina. Some were so sweet that they were served with a glass of water—you had to alternate small bites with sips of water or your throat would close from the sweetness. When Dina's father was sent to Italy by the airlines, she entered kindergarten and had to learn the new language. Once, she cried silently during an entire class because they were writing a story about the weather and she couldn't remember the word for wind. She had to mimic the motion with her hands in order to get the right word from the teacher. Years later, Italian was all but forgotten, but she always remembered *il vento*.

Dina was a picky eater and the cause of much grief and battles in the kitchen with her mother. But on landing in the Rome airport, she discovered breadsticks, and thought she had touched down in heaven. Breadsticks became a staple at home. Mom never objected.

On the first day of first grade, Betti took her daughter to school and explained that this year, she would be taking the school bus home. Dina promptly forgot, and at the end of the day, the cafeteria ladies took pity on the little girl who hadn't been picked up and they brought her to the kitchen. Hours later, when the distraught Betti showed up at the school, she found her daughter happily munching on breadsticks. The kind ladies had tried everything in the kitchen to pick up her spirits, but little Dina was not to be seduced by spaghetti marinara or even pizza. Thank God for breadsticks.

Two years later, Abraham moved the family to London. Their first days in London were spent in a rented house with a backyard. It was her first time ever living in a house, and Dina fell in love with the luxury of having her own room, and with the idea that you could go outside when you felt like it and instantly be in the midst of a garden. She would never take having her own house for granted.

In her first year, Dina attended a Jewish school because her parents wanted her to feel less alienated in this strange land. Again, she had to learn a new language quickly and adapt to a different culture. Barclay House was a good school, but it was a long bus ride from home, and Dina didn't warm up to the religious practices, since she had been raised in a secular home. So, a year later, her parents let her attend the public school in their neighborhood. It was literally across the street from their apartment building, which meant she could walk home at lunch and avoid the dreaded English school lunches. Dina was a quick study and advanced from the lower level class to the higher level one within three months. She was bright and bored with homework, and fortunate to be able to excel without cracking a book once she came home from school. This practice worked now, but it would not serve her well in later years.

For the next four years she would have Mr. Bell as her teacher. Mr. Bell was strict but fair and kind. He was thin, impossibly tall, had a delightful British wit and steel gray eyes, and Dina found herself hopelessly in love with him. Sitting in class was never a chore or a drudge, because she had her lovely Mr. Bell to gaze at and hang on to his every word. Life was good.

In 1968, the family moved back to Israel. Dina was in sixth grade and had some catching up to do. Her writing and reading skills in Hebrew were poor, since she had spent her elementary school years in Europe. She caught up with the language skills quickly, but now the bright girl could no longer rely on her wits alone to do well. She somehow coasted all the way through eighth grade, but once in high school, her grades began to drop. She now had to apply herself, but loathed doing any after schoolwork. In ninth grade, Dina's math teacher flunked her. "You are smarter than that," she told her. The sting of those words and the Big "F" on her report card—her first ever—were all the motivation she needed to change. She had to prove to herself and to her teacher that she really was smarter than that.

That summer, Dina took some classes in math at the local community center, and pounded algebraic concepts into her head until it ached. In September, she retook the math final and scored an A plus, but that was only a small part of her good fortune; it was there that she met her future husband.

Jerry was the youth counselor for her grade level at the after-school clubhouse. She was immediately taken by this quiet, strong, young man. He had sensitive eyes, a depth and maturity uncommon in most eighteen-year-olds, and he was very handsome. Dina now had a more compelling reason to hang out at the center.

She flirted shyly with him, but he didn't seem to notice. Eventually, Dina sent her best friend to tell him that she was interested. A few more weeks of these teenage tactics, and Jerry agreed to go on one date with her. It was more of a favor than a date—he was too busy with his studies, she was too young, and a few other such excuses, but Dina didn't care.

The following evening, they met at the movie theater. The movie was a lush, exquisitely filmed story of a married Irish woman who fell in love with a World War I British officer, and it was the perfect backdrop for the initiation of their own budding romance. They began to spend more time together in the after-school program, and, little by little, it turned into a relationship.

Jerry talked to her frequently about the conflict between his military academy training and his newly emerging pacifist ideas. When he enlisted, a year later, he was a staunch pacifist and refused to handle a gun. Dina was frightened for him when he was sent to military jail, but respected him for his convictions.

In the course of the next three years, Jerry finished his enlisted duty, and Dina graduated from high school. It was clear to both of them that they would get married as soon as she was done with school, and in the summer of 1975 they had a small, simple, backyard wedding at her uncle's house. It was very informal: Dina wore a long, cotton peasant dress, and Jerry arrived on his Vespa, in slacks and shirtsleeves.

Within the year, Jerry would graduate from his Vespa to a Citroen Deux Chevaux, a funny looking, inexpensive mode of transport. The car was old and decrepit, sputtering its protestations loudly when the engine was started and Jerry had to hold his breath just to cruise down the block. Nevertheless, it was a car and a big accomplishment for a young man. Much impressed friends could only score rides if they agreed to get out and push when necessary (often), and to pour water into the radiator when the tired old Deux Chevaux came to a convulsive, steaming, full stop. Fortunately, Jerry saw the humor in the situation. He decided to add some levity by painting the car in black and white zebra stripes, much to the delight of the neighborhood.

By this time, the brothers had opened an electronics store in Holon, south of Tel Aviv. They wanted their store to stand out from other similar businesses, and thought the key would be the selection of products. After analyzing what their strategy would be, and how they would set themselves apart from the rest of Israel's electronics stores, they decided to opt for a higher end product and target a different niche than the rest of their competition. They would create a store for sophisticated customers who loved electronics and for gadget enthusiasts; a group willing to spend more money for higher quality and better features. So the Azarkman brothers' initial cash outlay for inventory was very high. These expensive electronics were not found everywhere so their display was very attractive to their target audience of savvy shoppers. The alluring product selection brought in a lot of traffic, but most people came in only to learn about new features and gadgets, not to buy, so sales were low. Not everyone could afford such luxury products.

In the meantime, Jerry educated himself about the procedures for importing electronics, a process bursting with regulations and restrictions, and a language all on its own. The complex jargon was used by customs officers and import specialists and was quite daunting, but Jerry saw only a door behind which were great opportunities, and he was going to open it.

The importation tax on electronics was 300 percent, added to the cost of the product. Israel, like many countries, tried to protect its local markets from losses due to the importation of luxury goods, and one way to reduce the importation was through high taxation. Jerry looked for ways to avoid high tariffs and create bigger margins for their products.

Looking at foreign trade is one way to observe and study a nation's economy—the relationship between importing and exporting requires a delicate balance. When a country imports more than it exports, it should sound an alarm for its leaders and economists, as buying more than selling causes a deficit.

Jerry found that one way to avoid higher taxation was to make at least part of the product in Israel, with the added benefit of generating jobs, and internal production and currency. Jerry had to figure out how to import components of electronics and finish the assembling process in Israel. How could some of the imported parts be substituted and produced domestically, turning them into "Made in Israel" products?

Jerry thought turntables would be the perfect product to introduce under their own label. He took them apart, analyzed and studied them, wondering which part could be made locally—the head, arm, or acrylic cover? The turntable they selected was one of the top sellers at the brothers' store, and Jerry searched for factories that could produce one or more of its parts.

The brothers researched the source of the turntables. They knew they were made in England, but they needed to find out more about the manufacturing process—how they were built, how long it would take to produce a shipment, details about transportation, the port of exit from the U.K., and the port of entry for Israel. They went to England to get the answers firsthand, and studied the entire process of exporting from England and importing to Israel.

Jerry considered every angle carefully. To produce some parts in Israel and assemble those in the country would reduce the import taxes considerably, but they had to make sure the quality didn't suffer. This was essential, since the brothers wanted to ensure that the product line was of the same high caliber. The image of the business had to remain consistent. They knew that if they could sell a high-end product at a lower price their store could eliminate the competition and become the destination place for electronics. These were big ideas and their business plan had to be thorough.

Jerry's investigations around Israel led to the discovery of a company capable of producing the acrylic lid, a see-through box without a bottom, the purpose of which is to protect the turntable and the record from dust. They then found a company to connect the turntable's head to its arm, and another to pack the finished product in brand new boxes and seal them.

They made several trips to the auctions where the turntables were sold. Once they understood the bidding process, they felt confident enough to make a bid. The turntables they acquired needed to be disassembled before being placed in the boxes, and the company agreed to follow these instructions to the letter. There was no problem whatsoever on that end.

Meanwhile, in Israel, the factory was prepared with materials for the acrylic cover, the assembling crew was ready, and the box company was prepared. All were waiting for the container's arrival. Their excitement was mounting. They would only have to pay thirty percent of the original tax, which meant a sizable profit margin and a competitive advantage.

When the container arrived, the brothers went to the port city of Ashkelon to pay the tax and release the container, but, as luck would have it they were assigned the most ornery and unyielding customs officer, who insisted they pay the full rate. They pointed out that that any imported electronic device requiring further assembly in Israel was exempt from the full tax. The customs officer, a stickler for rules and regulations, did not believe it and demanded that they bring him something to this effect in writing from the Israel customs authority, located in Jerusalem.

The following day, the brothers made a trip to the capital to plead their case, and two days later they were back at customs again, this time armed with the rule about the exemption in black and white. Still, the officer remained unconvinced. He insisted that the arm and the head were essentially the same piece, so, as far as he was concerned, the turntable was complete.

These were the days before Google, so Jerry next went to an Israeli university and got a diagram depicting the parts of the turntable and a letter explaining to customs that the product had three components: the turntable, the arm, and the head. No dice. The stubborn officer refused to release the container until the Jerusalem office gave the order, so Jerry headed out to the capital yet again, explained the whole process, got the written consent, paid the taxes, and finally got the release of their goods.

However, weeks had passed while the container with its precious cargo was being detained. When containers are not sent back to the transportation company after five to ten days, demurrage fees—usage compensation for any other costs to the transportation company—are incurred. They could not pay for the transportation until all the papers were processed and this caused hundreds of dollars in expenses for storage and late fees. Due to the endless bureaucracy, the deal turned sour and they had to borrow so much money to pull it off that their big dream was killed.

Jerry had talked to this customs officer at great length, telling him how he had been in the war, served his country, come from a struggling family, and how someone from such a humble background faces so many obstacles when moving up the socio-economic ladder. How could one person be so callous as to inflict damage on a whole company, a family, the future of an individual, even damaging the country, in a way? Jerry told the bureaucrat that his attitude was pushing people like Jerry to leave Israel. The customs officer's reply was, "Go ahead, leave. You'll be back on your knees."

This really stung. It burned Jerry. He loved Israel—he'd been raised there, he had gone to war for Israel, had been willing to give his life for Israel if necessary. Israel was where his family had moved to with dreams of a better future, where he'd gone to school, started his own family and his first business, and where all his relatives lived. But he had been naïve. He'd thought that by educating himself on the laws and regulations and preparing for any eventuality he was going to move the great wall of bureaucracy. What was left out of the formula was that it all depended on who the pencil pusher was, on his own interpretation of the product, and how he'd apply the regulations. This customs officer was the duke of his domain, the king of the jungle, the ultimate word in determining the final result. How could you anticipate something like this?

In the end Jerry was right, but the cost of proving that his assumption was correct dragged their profits down. In fact, the profit was so minimal that it took the fire out of their guts. Their energy was completely drained by that losing battle with red tape. However, this teachable moment showed Jerry that he had the drive to see this immense task through, from inception to completion. One can learn as much from defeats as from triumphs—sometimes more.

This is an example of how someone can have a great idea, research it thoroughly, initiate the processes of an unprecedented change, do everything right, yet still suffer losses. The one big catch in this particular case, besides the customs officer, was the lack of sufficient capital to invest in the prolonged, lengthy process, with enough time to make it happen. This can be a breaking point—preparing ahead of time, evaluating all possible requests and problems that could come your way, analyzing all the processes that you're going to be creating, what your main obstacles might be. But, it is part of your responsibility to study possible consequences if something goes wrong. Having everything ready beforehand is the biggest challenge for thinking ahead—being so prepared that every question asked will have an answer.

Three essential components of success are: preparation, passion, and the ability to adapt. Careful study, analysis and meticulous preparation increase the likelihood that things will go your way. Passion and excitement remove the clouds of doubt and let you focus on what's possible instead of on the roadblocks. But since life is often a practical joker with tricks up its sleeves, when the big curves are thrown at you, tenacity and the ability to think on your feet make it possible for you to see your project all the way through.

Meanwhile, Egypt and Israel were beginning to talk about the occupied territory in the Sinai Peninsula, which Israel had seized during the Six Day War in 1967. Then, as now, Egypt was experiencing dramatic change. When Cairo threw out thousands of Soviet advisers, it looked like an opportunity for the Unites States to forge closer relations with an Arab country, especially since Nixon and Kissinger had been backing Israel and American relations with the Arab countries was nonexistent. High level conversations started and, for the first time after four wars between the two countries, their armies agreed to move—Israel to the east, Egypt to the west—creating neutral land for the United Nations to protect. For the first time since 1967, Egypt reopened the Suez Canal, which had been so vital for the transportation of goods.

Jerry began developing the idea of moving out of Israel, to start at a new place where his imagination could roam free, where the tension of war did not exist on a day-to-day level, and business would be open to anyone. He could start a new life far away from the warfare and constant political struggles, in order to build a new business. He started planning his journey towards a new life.

President Richard M. Nixon's support for Israel during the Yom Kippur War led to an Arab oil embargo, which caused shortages in the U.S. Nixon had escalated the Vietnam War, then reduced the presence of U.S. forces in Indochina and held peace negotiations with Hanoi. During his second presidential term he was embroiled in the Watergate scandal, which began when five men were caught after breaking inside of the Democratic National Committee headquarters in Washington's Watergate building on June 17, 1972. These White House "Plumbers" were looking for incriminating documents inside of DNC Chairman Larry O'Brien's office that could affect Nixon and his campaign for a second term.

The FBI tied payments to the burglars to a slush fund of the pro-Nixon Committee to Re-elect the President. Nixon was accused of covering up the scandal and, facing near certain impeachment, resigned from office on August 9, 1974 as the 37th President of the United States.

While news of Nixon's scandal at Watergate was broadcast on every television and radio station, Israelis were also listening to the mellow harmonies of five boys from Southern California. They were enraptured with the unmistakable American sound, and by everything their music suggested. The Beach Boys' lyrics conjured up visions of surfing, tans, and those famous California girls, all part of the sun-soaked, easygoing lifestyle by the beach. Their music stoked the fires of young Israelis' imaginations and the dream that they, too, could someday day live in sunny Southern California,

These infectious tunes were also playing at the brothers' store, and they helped fuel Jerry's dream of starting a new life in the United States. He was motivated by the idea of being able to pursue a life in a new society, far from the tensions of war and the limitations he encountered every time he had a business idea. Jerry watched as many American movies as he could, soaking in the culture and paying attention to background details no less than the plot, memorizing street names like Sunset and La Cienega. He could already picture himself living there.

The dream was firmly in place and it was now time to make a plan. He began by researching the type of documents required to travel to and open a business in the U.S. If he entered with a business visa, he'd be permitted to do business in the U.S., so Jerry set out to obtain one. With this in mind, he started visiting Israeli companies with products he could represent in the U.S. In the garment industry; his accounts included a leather jacket and lingerie company. In the building materials industry, a company made an electronic device for bathroom bidets, detecting when a toilet was being used so water would automatically flow. Jerry had to learn the ins and outs of these products: pricing, specifications, shipping, operations, and all the information he could absorb in order to sell them.

Obtaining a visa to the U.S. was difficult. Not everyone was approved, and getting one could make you feel like you had just won the lottery. On any given day, hundreds waited in line at the U.S. embassy. Lines formed in the early morning, and you knew you were in for an all-day affair. Jerry knew that the interview would be conducted on a one-on-one basis. The officer would ask him at length about his personal life. Once again, he would be in the hands of a bureaucrat who could kill his hopes and dreams with one, swift, downward motion of his stamp: DENIED.

A visa applicant had to bring all manner of papers and documents to the interview, supporting his or her intent to eventually come back to their own country, and detailing what they were going to do once in the U.S., whether on business or purely for pleasure. If visiting relatives, you had to supply their address and an invitation letter from them. If on a tour, you had to supply the itinerary. The documents for obtaining a business visa were numerous: proof of employment or personal business in Israel, a business plan for the kind of business to be conducted in the U.S., corroborated by the company with which he/she was intending to engage. All these details had to be carefully documented, even including personal bank accounts and properties listed in their names. All this was for a temporary visa—residency was an entirely different matter. During the interview, the officer would look into the eyes of the applicant carefully, watching for signs that they were nervous or lying.

The hopeful applicant had only one chance—once a passport was denied, it was most likely one would never get a visa or that it would take other means to obtain one, such as marrying a U.S. citizen. One had to be prepared with all the required information, look clean and professional, and maintain an air of confidence so as not to divulge their inner state of turmoil.

The giant waiting room was hot and cramped, and stress levels were high. Anxiety is contagious. People looked around nervously, wondering who would get lucky and who would be going home empty-handed. Their fates were being decided.

Jerry looked over his documents one last time, making sure nothing was amiss. When his turn came, he walked over to a cubicle and sat down if front of the officer. He tried to hold on to his composure and hope as the officer began firing questions at him, but he got the sinking feeling that he was going to be denied.

The officer had a hostile attitude. Jerry knew he was just doing his job, trying to weed out inauthenticity, but in doing so he made Jerry feel as if his own answers were being viewed as questionable. His papers were authentic, but the officer was questioning them as if they weren't. Before the visa officer could give his final pronouncement, Jerry made a quick, bold, decision—he interrupted the officer with a request to get more information to bring back. He simply could not risk a denied stamp in his passport and have all of his dreams killed at once. He had to prepare himself better and try again.

Now that Jerry knew what to expect, he set about preparing his presentation. He contacted companies in the U.S. and planned meetings with them, he gathered letters of appointments. He prepared his trip, when he was going to visit each firm, got his roundtrip airline tickets, bought a new suit and briefcase. He practiced questions and answers in front of a mirror until he felt comfortable, and then he went back. This time, he got a different officer and his passport was stamped with a spanking new entry visa.

Jerry had $2,000 for the trip. He contacted a friend from the army who had moved to New York, and laid the groundwork for their arrival. First, he and his wife would visit Romania so Dina could say goodbye to her family before moving to America. Jerry prepared for the trip, packed their modest belongings, and went to bid farewell to his family. He never liked saying goodbye, and told everyone not to go to the airport, but Muluk insisted on coming and seeing him off. They had a tense taxi ride to the airport. They tried to make light, casual conversation, but all three were lost in their respective thoughts about what the future would bring.

When the taxi arrived at the airport Jerry told Muluk he'd forgotten to buy his mother-in-law a gift, and asked her if she could go and pick something up while they checked in. Muluk agreed, although she knew that by the time she returned with a gift, her son would probably be long gone.

Jerry preferred to say goodbye this way to his mom. It was hard for him to leave her and he did not want anything to weaken his resolve now that all he could see in front of him was the great unknown. No time to go back, no time to think about what he was leaving behind. He had to set his mind on his future. Jerry went straight to his flight and boarded without looking back. He had already said goodbye to his mom in his own way.

Jerry and Dina traveled on El Al to Bucharest, Romania to visit her parents before leaving for the U.S. His father-in-law was managing El Al operations there and it was a farewell trip for Dina. They spent a week in the beautiful city, the so-called Little Paris, but Jerry's mind could not stop from churning. Anxiety about what was ahead kept him from enjoying the city, its ornate palaces, grand museums, and beautiful gardens.

Jerry's mind was on one thing and one thing only—America. He was not in the mood to be a tourist and wanted the days to pass as quickly as possible. Still, Jerry wanted to leave a good impression on his in-laws and he graciously participated in the plans, but the days went really slowly for him. For Dina, it was good, quality time shared with her parents, because the unknown was already knocking at the door. Finally, the day came when they started on their course to the U.S. After many hours of flying and changing planes in England, they arrived at John F. Kennedy Airport on August 27, 1976.

Part II

The Survival

The Four "Ds" of Success:
Desire, Drive, Discipline and Determination

Chapter Five

The Journey: Crossing an Ocean, $20 in His Pocket

Anyone can think of an idea for a business: what to sell, how to sell it, whom to sell it to, and where to sell. One can have a really solid idea and a plan for each step of the way, yet, without sufficient capital, it's just a little more than a great idea.

At some point in our lives, we may think about what could be done differently in order to be more successful. Not everyone who wants to start a business is creative enough to come up with all the solutions to implement their idea, so they may seek the advice of someone they respect. If they do have a really smart concept and they may lack knowledge in specific areas of the business they want to launch, relying on a mentor is an option, someone who has already succeeded in business, yet hopefully is not in a competing field and will gladly share their knowledge.

There is always the danger of people looking over your shoulder, and if you don't seize the opportunity, they may jump ahead of you. That's when deep regret sets in and you kick yourself for not having jumped in at the right time. People constantly hunger to know how others make out better than they do.

The Small Business Association reported that 627,200 new businesses opened in 2008; 595,600 of them closed, and from those 43,546 failed due to bankruptcy in same year. The ratio of successful new businesses is just three out of ten; only half of these go on to survive over five years.

Starting a business and making it successful is not an easy task. Keeping it going requires not only enthusiasm but dedication, and a thick skin for dealing with rejections. It also requires paying close attention to others who might try taking advantage of you as the newbie, just starting out, naive, and vulnerable to sharks. It takes a constant vigil over the competition, noticing how they're similar to your operation, and how they differ.

A large part of protecting your investment is creating an overall positive experience for your customers. When they feel that their patronage is appreciated, that they've received a good deal, not only in terms of price, but in how they were treated from the moment they walked into the store or your website, until the end of the transaction, chances are you are creating not only a single sale, but a repeat customer.

It takes the resolve and the understanding that during the following weeks, months, even years, you may not have a day off, or be home on the holidays, and that you'll be working outrageously long hours and probably won't even have a salary. You'll have to dig deep for that discipline, all the way down to your bones. You need self-control to wake up every day as if it's a fresh start, not thinking that yesterday was a bad day, and instead thinking, "I will do better today." It requires determination, so that no matter how difficult it is out there in the cold, cruel world, you can still turn it around and keep going.

This determination, where does this comes from? It starts at an early age, if you're fortunate enough to have parents who set clear boundaries and expectations. Discipline is formed through consistency and structure, and good teachers nurture and encourage it. It can be strengthened by playing sports, or through hobbies, such as collecting stamps, coins, etc.

What drives your mind, body, and spirit to keep you on course? Whatever keeps you going, you'll need to elevate your game to its highest level in order to confront your failures. No matter how good your idea is, there are going to be mistakes and roadblocks, and you'll need the ability to swiftly fine tune your strategy and adapt to new and changing circumstances.

Big desires and dreams alone won't make it happen. In a creative burst of intellectual energy, your brain pounds out business ideas so fast you can barely keep up with them, this is a moment of reflection. You feel an immense need to put your ideas into practice and make them a reality. Stop. Write them down. Go back to them every day and try to develop them on paper before you make a decision based on emotion. Your level of excitement can blind you, and while your desire may be powerful, this doesn't automatically translate into success. You will need to combine your desires with your exponential drive, put your discipline into the formula and multiply it with your determination to obtain not "ds" but your four "Ds". It's time to raise your game.

This is not the "D" you got in school for barely passing. No, you'll need more than a passing grade—you're playing in the big leagues now. If you truly want to have your own business, you'll need to shine. You will have to be at the head of your class, and your four Ds have to propel you to success. You'll need to put all of your effort into making it happen.

In his short life so far, Jerry had already started experimenting with Determination: he was able to convince his officer during his military service to grant him special permission to keep studying and stay overnight at home. He was able to continue serving in the army during the Yom Kippur War without pointing a weapon at anyone, becoming a communications technician in the middle of combat operations.

When a customs officer told Jerry he had to pay full taxation for an imported container bearing parts to be assembled in Israel, he had the Drive to overcome. He did not let go. He brought all the papers necessary to obtain his reduced taxation. After seven years of military training, Jerry had Discipline. He decided that he wanted to go to United States and start a new life for him and his family, and he converted his Desire into a reality.

At various times in his life, he had to use one of these assets: Determination, Discipline, Drive, and Desire. He had proven himself using one attribute or another on many occasions, but now Jerry had to combine them all. He was facing the biggest test of his young life: planning to strike out in a new country where he'd confront the challenges of language, resources, and legalities. He would have no other choice and only one solution: put this formula into practice, or return to Israel in disgrace. How could he face his family if he failed to make it? He knew he had to combine all his strengths, skills, and abilities to mold his future into a success story—his family was depending on him.

His desire had to be of the strongest intensity to quell any doubt he still harbored. Nothing could stop him from starting a successful business in America so he could bring the rest of his family to the U.S. As an extra bit of motivation, Jerry pictured them on the other side of the ocean, waiting and depending on him.

Jerry and Dina arrived in New York on an oppressively muggy summer day. The air was still, and the anxiety of the unknown was hanging in the air. Jerry had contacted Assaf Kimchi, a friend from the Army who assured him he'd be meeting them at the airport. It had been a source of comfort to them on the flight, knowing that a familiar face would greet them in this strange new land, but now Jerry had a flash of doubt. What if he got the day wrong? What if something had happened to Assaf? Assaf had been through the same military training as Jerry, and was imbued with the same principles of honor and respect, but Jerry couldn't still his nerves. He had no other contacts, nowhere to go, had no money to speak of, and virtually no other resources. Jerry tried to pound back the doubts by repeating, "He'll be there, I know he will," over and over to himself. His optimistic heart continued to beat out the message, even as his anxiety ran interference by injecting a millisecond of panic here and there. Another moment of nervousness at passport control: Would their business visa be recognized, and would they be questioned about their entire plan? Jerry had heard horror stories about entrants to the U.S. being allowed only a two-week stay, in spite of a more generous visa stamp on their passports. Fortunately, they were granted unrestricted entry, and went on to customs to pick up their luggage.

To Jerry, it didn't feel like they were actually in the U.S. until they emerged from the glass doors into the "real" New York. It was all he could do to quell his doubts and anxieties by giving himself little mantras of hope until then. He couldn't know then that whether Assaf would be waiting outside was a small matter compared to what customs had in store for them.

Jerry had been thoroughly honest in filling out his customs declarations on the plane; he had indicated that they were bringing silver jewelry, among other products, as merchandise samples to represent several Israeli manufacturers. The instant the customs officer read that line on the form, her demeanor changed from pleasant and accommodating to menacing, questioning his products. Jerry explained the necessity of bringing samples to show his intended customers, to which she barked her next question, "Where are the diamonds?" Jerry half-smiled. He was sure she was just misguided, so he explained, very calmly, that they had no diamonds. The question was repeated, with more urgency and at higher decibels, "Where are the DIAMONDS?" Jerry couldn't believe what he was hearing; it had to be some kind of prank, or some horrible misunderstanding. But it was only the beginning of their ordeal.

After what seemed like an eternity of questioning, Jerry and Dina were taken to separate rooms and searched. First, their luggage was turned inside out, and every single item, including the most innocent one, was held up to their faces as the officer questioned its purpose. Jerry had seen many American movies about crime, and this seemed like an interrogation scene where the criminals were held in a stark room with a metal table, behind a one-way mirror. Only in this case, there was no good cop-bad cop in the script, just one, very angry customs officer.

Then came the humiliation of removing their clothing, reduced to standing there in their skivvies, and Jerry had to close his eyes and pretend he was only dreaming and would wake up soon. Finally, when it became crystal clear that they were hiding nothing, Jerry and Dina were released into a common room and allowed to exit. They looked at each other with pained expressions, shaken by the experience, but determined to put it behind them. Jerry was ready for whatever was waiting next. They walked out into the hot New York day, and there was Assaf, just as promised, with a big grin on his face. They packed their luggage into the trunk and climbed in the back seat, and Jerry noticed a big, round hole in the front windshield. Considering what he had just been through, flashes of gangster movies immediately came to mind. He asked his friend about the hole, and was relieved to hear that Assaf had bought the old car with the hole already there, probably caused by some falling road debris. Smiling with relief, Jerry noticed that he had been holding his breath for much of the past two hours, and began telling Assaf what had just transpired. "Wow, buddy, welcome to America!" his friend joked.

Jerry and Dina stayed with Assaf in his apartment for a month while they learned their way around New York, the capital of the world, as it had been called countless times.

New York was a vibrant city, where the streets were constantly filled with people on the move, day or night. Jerry had never seen anything like it. Skyscrapers that blocked the sky, swarms of bodies crowding the sidewalk, hustlers, street vendors, the glitz and sensory overload of Times Square, the enormity of the World Trade Center—it was all new and wonderful and frightening at the same time. He had to learn how to move around the Big Apple, understand the subway, the busses, and to familiarize himself with the different boroughs. He studied maps of the neighborhoods, memorizing routes to the places where he would go to conduct business. He couldn't afford to waste time wandering aimlessly or getting lost.

Jerry found a small apartment in Brooklyn for $100 a month and the young couple moved in. He and Dina now had a place of their own in America, where all of Jerry's dreams would begin to materialize. Their place was furnished with crates and equipped with only the barest of necessities—they had to make their money last. Every single spending decision had to be carefully thought out.

In the 1970s, Brooklyn was one of the most highly populated areas of New York. Originally inhabited by Indian tribes, Dutch settlers started moving there by 1636, eventually naming their settlement Breuckelen, after a town in Holland. By the time the Azarkmans joined Brooklyn's ethnic mélange, a third of a millennium later, the area had a combination of different ethnic groups: Caucasians, Blacks, Puerto Ricans, and more. In Brooklyn, there was a brewing center for pilsner beer, the first golden beer of the world. Most of the beer was produced in Bushwick. The beer had been brewed there for over 130 years in small pubs at many locations with a homemade style, because the quality of the water was excellent for this type of beer and many European—especially German—immigrants had settled there.

New York City offered world class museums, attractions, and theater. There were beautiful bridges and beaches, clubs and amazing restaurants. Jerry did not have the time or the money to be a tourist, though everything was new and fascinating to him. He walked the streets of Manhattan visiting businesses, offering the products from the companies he was representing. He had to look like he wasn't a new arrival, fresh off the boat. He had to blend in, look professional and clean cut. He had to give the impression that he'd already been in business for some time, a real operator, with years of experience under his belt. Jerry was highly conscious of the image he was projecting when visiting his businesses contacts. He wanted to instill confidence in his professionalism and in his products, and thought that one way of doing this was to rent an office in Manhattan.

Manhattan is the oldest part of what is now New York City, and was settled by Dutch colonists following, as legend has it, their purchase of the island from Native Americans for $24 worth of trinkets, renaming it New Amsterdam, after the Netherlands' capital. Of course, Manhattan evolved into one of America's wealthiest cities, and is considered the world's greatest center of commercial and financial trade. Wall Street, the home of The New York Stock Exchange, has the capacity to determine the direction of an entire economy. In the midst of this awe-inspiring world center, Jerry discovered the perfect place to open his office; it was a very small space, almost a hole in the wall, but perfect for his needs and his budget, so he decided to rent it. The very next day, he printed business cards bearing his new office address so he could make a better impression.

Jerry walked up and down Manhattan's mean streets, knocking on many doors as he tried to market his products. He was able to get his foot in the door. There were many meetings, and people seemed welcoming, but he didn't get any orders, and made no sales whatsoever.

Between the rent for his office and apartment, plus food and transportation costs, he was running out of money, and things were looking bleak.

Jerry made most of his calls on foot, and by December the weather had turned miserable. He wasn't used to the freezing New York winters, and the bone chilling temperatures added to the overall feeling of discouragement. New York began to feel like an overwhelmingly big, unwelcoming place, with its massive concrete structures and hostile climate. Along with their diminishing finances, and very little hope for financial success, Jerry and Dina began to think about moving to Los Angeles.

After five months of pounding the cold sidewalks with increasing frustration, the decision was made—they were going to L.A.

Ever budget conscious, Jerry found an inexpensive way to cross over to the West Coast. Flying was out of the question, and even travel by train or Greyhound was out of reach for them. He had heard about a company that transported cars for individuals who wanted their vehicles to follow them in a cross country move, but didn't want to do their own driving. There was a need for a driver to move a car from New York to Los Angeles, and Jerry jumped at the opportunity. The company provided the car plus $100 for hotels and gas, and Jerry had only a week to deliver it.

Jerry and Dina stuffed as much as they could of their belongings in the small BMW, but much was left behind. It was January and the weather was stormy, with nothing but bad weather forecasts for the road. Jerry decided to drive south instead of west—he knew it would take longer but the weather would be much better. Dina was in charge of navigating while Jerry drove. The trip was long and exhausting. They spent two nights at cheap motels and slept in the car the rest of the time.

On the third day, crossing West Virginia, Jerry sighted flashing lights in his rear view mirror. With dread in the pit of his stomach, he pulled over and watched as a highway patrol officer approached his car. The southern drawl and the cowboy-like hat were foreign and intimidating to them, and their hearts sank when he told them he was fining them $200 for speeding. That was an enormous sum of money to them and a significant portion of what little cash they had left.

After seven days of driving, they reached Los Angeles, the dream city with the dream climate. Jerry had a full five minutes to savor it before being knocked back into reality—now what?

In Israel, Jerry's parents were good friends with a couple who had a son living in Los Angeles near the Fairfax District. The couple had told Jerry that if he was ever in Los Angeles and needed anything, he should go see their son, Isaac. Jerry and Dina looked the place up on the map and knocked on the stranger's door.

Fairfax is in the middle of Los Angeles. It borders West Hollywood to the North and Beverly Hills on the south. The Fairfax District is sometimes called the Kosher Canyon or Bagel District, as it's an area with lots of Jewish businesses and residents. Orthodox Jews often walk around this neighborhood. Married Jewish women cover their heads with scarves and Jewish men usually cover their heads with a yarmulke or Kippah, which means "dome," to remind them of God. This is done in observance of the Torah, Judaism's written law.

Jerry and Dina appeared at the doorstep of this man's home without knowing him but with excellent references. After explaining who they were, he invited them into his house. They were in Los Angeles, the land of dreams for Jerry. He felt that even the air had a different smell; the streets were welcoming, with families strolling around the lovely, manicured neighborhoods. He saw parks and smiling people. He had been in the City of the Angels for less than a day but was already in love with it. However, what was his next step, what should he do? His pockets were nearly empty, with less than a hundred bucks to his name.

Their stay in New York—five months of attempting to sell his products, the tiny office, and the small apartment—had drained all of his resources. Even though his expenses had been very carefully calculated, after five months, Jerry had almost completely run out of money.

He found that Fairfax was a small city within a city; he walked and studied the neighborhood, observing how the Jewish community had created their own little town with kosher delis, restaurants, bakeries, and places of worship and Judaic education. People smiled and were generally friendly. They seemed happy within their own community.

Kosher (meaning "fit or allowed to be eaten") cuisine conforms to the Halakhah, the collective body of Jewish law. In Leviticus 11:1-47 in the Old Testament, God tells Moses which animals were acceptable for consumption, or Kosher, and which they were to refrain from eating. This restriction includes products derived from forbidden animals and from improperly slaughtered animals. Additionally, Kosher law dictates the proper combination of ingredients. An observant Jew is not allowed to mix meat with dairy or eat them during the same meal. Even the cooking utensils for meat and dairy have to be properly separated. The process of manufacturing foods in a plant has to be observed and certified by a rabbinical authority, in addition to local health bodies, to insure that Kosher law was strictly followed.

The Fairfax District had become the destination for most of L.A.'s immigrant Jews, a place to start out. There were around twelve synagogues, and many Holocaust survivors resided there. Produce and many other kosher products were sold at its Farmers Market. A legal aid council operated in the area, helping Jews with paperwork, forms, and law-related needs. It was perfect for Jerry, the right place to start, with people culturally similar to him, although different in a way too, as he was not religious.

When Jerry had knocked on the door of this family friend, they were complete strangers to him, yet his reaction was to invite them into his home immediately and without questions. Who does that? Not many people would, but he was a Jew and Jews have historically traveled the world, often with nothing but the shirts on their backs, extending a helping hand to one another. They followed the belief that "today it may be you who needs help, but tomorrow it could be me."

They felt welcomed and relieved after the exhausting trip, but they didn't want to overstay their welcome. Jerry planned only to rest for a few days, to regroup, and then to look for a place of their own once he was able to make some money. He realized this was it. He had to make it happen. There were no other choices. He knew the Golden State had all kinds of industries and was one of the most prosperous states in the Union. If it was a country, California would be the eighth wealthiest country in the world. Where to start? He now knew that the companies he represented were not very attractive or easy to do business with because he had visited so many places back in New York and had been unsuccessful trying to sell their products.

Several factors were preventing him from closing a sale, including the costs of transporting merchandise thousands of miles from Israel to New York. Transportation increases the asking price of merchandise and distance is a major component in calculating shipment intervals in between reorders. The terms of payment also posed a dilemma, as the letters of intent for banks to process the transaction had too many restrictions.

The cargo would most likely be exported through Haifa, Israel's largest seaport. When an order was placed with a coat factory, for example, the manufacturer had to get a loan from the bank to buy the leather, cut the jackets, sew them, and get them to the ship. At a minimum, it took more than thirty days to complete this entire process. Sometimes payment was released after the merchandise was produced and sometimes it was disbursed only after merchandise reached the destination warehouse.

Payment depended on the terms of the contract. Some companies buy FOB (Freight On Board), meaning the manufacturer's responsibility ends once the product is on the ship and the money must then be released. Others buy CIF (Cost, Insurance, and Freight), which means that the product will be delivered to the door of the company purchasing it. Both agreements require a bank to handle the disbursement of funds and a contract between both parties must be signed.

There is also a third possibility: Part of the money could be sent in advance with the remaining sum released as a simple transfer of funds after the shipment arrives, but this generally took place only after a relationship of trust had been developed. The purchasing company in New York would then have to wait another thirty days to receive the jackets, due to transportation and clearing of customs, before they could begin to display them. But what if it they weren't the right sizes or colors? There were many risks involved for both sides in the process.

In addition to the above factors, there was another key determinant for any negotiation—who was going to be the person responsible for the merchandise and the release of funds? Jerry was the middleman, but how could he be responsible for the American company's release of payment? He could be there and request it, but who in Israel was making it happen? The operation was complex enough and fraught with potential glitches when the goods were only being shipped to New York from Israel. Now that Jerry was in Los Angeles, the process was even more complicated because the merchandise would arrive in N.Y. and then have to be moved via truck or train to L.A.

After a few days at their new friend's apartment, unbeknownst to Jerry and Dina, more guests were expected; Isaac hadn't mentioned that his sister was coming for an extended visit. On the day of her arrival, following a very surprised introduction, Jerry and Dina quietly retreated into the bedroom to give the brother and sister some space. They were already uncomfortable about imposing, and then things began to get really uncomfortable. Through the thin walls they heard the sister complain, loudly, that there wasn't an available bedroom for her. Poor Isaac sheepishly explained the circumstances of this unplanned visit, at which his sister exploded, "How could you let them into your home when you know that I'm about to visit? They're complete strangers! Where am I supposed to stay?"

This went on for some time, in ever-increasing decibels. When were these people leaving? Why didn't he ask? Was he too afraid to ask? How could they be sure they wouldn't kill them in the middle of the night? They might be crazy! She was not afraid of them, she could throw them out. She'd take their things and throw them into the street, because he was too chicken to do it himself.

Jerry and Dina didn't need to hear another word. They packed their belongings and left that night, with hardly any money and with no place to go. They walked the streets for a while but had no idea where they were headed. They sat on a bench in a park and spent the night talking. Once morning came, Jerry left Dina in a library with their bags and went to look around the neighborhood.

He walked for a few hours but could not find any place that would take them in. The night was coming again and the only option they found was a stairway behind a supermarket. Having gone without sleep the previous night, they were so exhausted that they slept as soundly as if they were ensconced in a four-poster bed of a five star hotel. Fearing that while they slept someone would steal what little they had, they rested their heads on their meager belongings to protect them.

The next morning, refreshed, they picked everything up and gathered their worldly possessions into a shopping cart, making their belongings easier to handle. Homeless and without any money, they ate at a local Jewish deli, where Dina stayed while Jerry walked the streets, searching for a place to stay. But he couldn't tell anyone he was homeless because he wanted to find a job, and felt that confessing this fact reduced his possibilities to zero. He looked for an apartment but had no money. Everyone asked for the first and last month's rent, but he had neither.

On their third night of homelessness, Jerry and Dina were forced to return to the rear parking lot of the supermarket, next to the dumpsters. The smell was awful, but they felt secure there, protected by the structure. It was mid-January, 1977, and California was having a mercifully mild winter. There was a definite chill in the air, but as they hunkered down for their third night out-of-doors, they remembered the far nastier weather they had left behind.

Life was sending some mean curves their way, and Jerry felt that he was being tested, again. He wondered how he would fare this time around. There was plenty to fear, but he'd been through enough in his young life to know that, in a matter of hours, the sun would come up and he'd be able to make a fresh start. And always a fresh start.

Jerry was blessed with a dogged persistence and knew that he was not going to give up, but he wasn't alone. He sensed Dina's fear and wanted to reassure and protect her, so he made the decision to keep his worries mostly to himself and to put on a façade of optimism. They would find a place soon, he would find a job, and everything would be fine.

At the break of a new day, there is always a new opportunity. Regardless of circumstances, you can never throw in the towel because once you stop, you are sure to fail. The one bright spot in having little or nothing left to lose is that you have the liberty to be more daring.

As John Lennon sang, "Life is what happens to you when you're busy making other plans." You are forced to confront unplanned challenges. You begin to wonder if the universe has conspired against you, and if an even greater stream of misfortunes is heading your way. When you start thinking about giving up, that is precisely the moment to draw upon all your inner resources, your optimistic philosophy, and the belief that all will somehow right itself. After all, no bad spell lasts 100 years. Somehow, there's a solution to your dilemma. You'll be fine. Only death has no solution. Miracles happen every day. Eye-popping marvels occur regularly. Doors are wondrously opened before us and opportunities transpire, mapping out a future and a life. But you have to do your part.

Jerry did not believe in destiny or that an angel was helping him. Nor did he believe that his mother's prayers, back home, for his success and protection, were going to lift him out of the mire. All he believed was that everything was up to him.

It was now Friday, and Jerry knew that the observant Jewish community would begin to shut down as the Sabbath approaches, which meant he had precious little time to accomplish anything because all work ceases on Shabbat. He reached an old building with a sign in both English and Hebrew that said, "Apartment building manager wanted, free rent." He knocked on the office door and an old man peered out. Jerry assumed he was Jewish and asked about the job in Hebrew, but the man countered in English, asking him if he spoke any. Jerry replied that he didn't. The landlord said he was useless to him without English, at which Jerry shot back, "Listen, I don't have money with me but I can write you a postdated check. You can cash it in a month, but I need a place to stay right now."

The landlord saw the determination in the set of Jerry's jaw. He asked him inside and listened to his pitch. Jerry was a skilled handyman who could help him fix anything in the apartments. He was going to be an asset to the landlord, if he was only given the chance to prove it.

The landlord said he needed someone who spoke solid English to show and rent the apartments, so he couldn't use Jerry as a manager. However, he thought that he might be able to use Jerry to help with the building's maintenance. It was an old, run down structure, with peeling paint and cracked ceilings, a furnace that broke down twice a week, and a trash room that was always overflowing. He told Jerry that he was going to give him the apartment for $100 a month, which was low for the area. For that price, he'd be expected to fix things around the place. Take it or leave it. Jerry knew he wasn't getting a great deal, but in their desperation, anything was an improvement over the stairway in back of the supermarket.

Jerry returned to Dina with the good news that they were no longer homeless!

They climbed a sagging, old staircase and walked to the end of a dark hallway. As they turned the key to the door of their unit, they held their breath in anticipation. Inside was a small, dark room, bereft of furnishings save for an old twin bed and a refrigerator. They looked for a bathroom—there was none. A single bathroom down the hall was to be shared with the residents of the entire floor. It was depressing, yes, but it was dry and relatively safe, and it beat sleeping on the sidewalk.

Now with a place to stay, Jerry felt he could start working on the dream of an import-export business, and find buyers for the products of the three Israeli companies he represented. He had received a second wind and was ready to continue the immigrant marathon to make it happen. He knew he had to turn his life around because he'd already signed a check from a checking account he'd opened at Chase Manhattan in New York that no longer had any money in it. He had to make money for rent, food, and transportation. The pressure was immense. He needed to survive.

Jerry realized he had to face his inability to speak English, so he registered at a nearby school offering free classes. There he met someone who told him about a company that was hiring. After school, they both went to apply and Jerry was hired to sell Rena Ware, a line of pots and skillets, door-to-door. The company was founded by Fred Zylstra, an immigrant from Holland, and the products were designed to cook without water. It was a superior product, priced accordingly, expensive and very hard to sell. He tried for days, but no one seemed interested. Dina went a few times with Jerry but she had less luck: she couldn't even make it past the front door. Jerry also continued to search for buyers for his Israeli products, but was making no progress.

At the end of the day, returning to the depressing room, Jerry would find Dina fairly despondent. The building housed a few unstable residents, and they frequently heard a low, moaning sound in the hallways. He'd try to comfort his wife and tell her everything would change and reminded her of her own dream in coming to America, to attend college and study psychology. He promised her that as soon as everything turned around, he'd help her accomplish her goal. Jerry tried to hide most everything from Dina. He feared that if she knew how low their reserves really were, and how dim the prospects were for an immediate income, she'd want to go back to Israel. He'd wake up in the morning, tell Dina he was going to work, and on the way back, bring a couple of dollars' worth of food. They subsisted mostly on steamed rice and potatoes. There wasn't any money for seasonings or oil. A thirty-cent loaf of wonder Bread and a tub of Alpha-Beta sour cream provided breakfast for a week.

Jerry examined the yellow pages and, using a map, determined that the majority of places where he could sell his imports were located in downtown Los Angeles. He visited the area to learn what was manufactured and sold locally. There were warehouses galore, a garment district, and many kinds of retail outlets holding clearance sales. He went to each place, studying what type of merchandise they had, and where it was produced. His Rena Ware training had given him a good foundation for approaching people, but now he needed the right product. Rena Ware pots and pans were a specialty item and not for a working class neighborhood. The principle was to find the correct product, one that wasn't so expensive, brought value to a family, and could be paid off in small monthly payments.

Jerry knew that time was catching up with him. Even though he had his return tickets, he had no intention of giving up on the American dream. It wasn't easy, and he'd known right from the start that it was not going to be easy. Without contacts, connections, and friends, he had to start on his own from scratch. The pressure was colossal, especially at home, where he sidestepped conversations with Dina as much as possible. In order to avoid revealing any details he always pleaded that he was too tired to talk. He could not share with her what was really happening, but, in a way, the pressure he felt to make good made Jerry try even harder.

Jerry combed the downtown garment industry but was unable to find anyone interested in the Israeli companies he represented. In this area, he saw many variety stores, selling a hodgepodge of items, including clothing, household goods, furniture, and electronics. He was drawn to the electronics because of his past experience with them. In Israel, profit margins for this sector of the market were low due to the high importation taxes, but he felt that he had to at least look into this field. He felt confident walking into these types of stores. He started analyzing the brands and prices and discovered that they weren't nearly as expensive as they had been in Israel. Products that were prohibitively expensive in Israel were priced substantially lower here. He began to imagine selling these products, but he had a major limitation—with only $20 in his pocket, he could not afford to buy much of anything.

He walked down a block on 11th Street that was full of electronic stores. One in particular grabbed his attention, with its drawings of an endless variety of electronic gadgets dancing on the big sign: Midtown Electronics. The door was locked and he peered in to look at the marvelous display. To be admitted, you had to present yourself at the door, ring a buzzer, and wait for the owner to look you over and decide if it was safe to let you in. After giving Jerry the once over, they buzzed him in.

Inside, he found many brands that were familiar to him, and a few that were new to him. In particular, he noticed a floor display of a curious gadget. He picked it up and studied it from all angles, analyzing it. What really grabbed his attention was the price tag: $12—this he could afford.

This gadget was different than anything he'd seen before—a device you hooked up to a TV set so you can play right on the screen. Entranced, Jerry spent a long time playing with the store demo, thinking, "I think I've found it! I think this is it. People would love to own one of these." Envisioning a big opportunity, he made a quick decision to attempt to sell it door-to-door. He was sure he could find the market for it.

There was a slight glitch, however. This was a wholesale outfit, not retail. You had to buy at least a dozen units to get them at twelve dollars apiece. Midtown Electronics didn't sell to the general public; buyers had to have a store and a resale permit. Jerry had nothing—just the fabulous Four Ds, the Drive, Desire, Determination, and Discipline to start a business.

Jerry began by trying to persuade the salesperson that it would be in the store's best interest to sell him just one, because if he had a sample to demo he'd be back to buy many more units. If he left the store empty handed, there'd be no future purchases. He explained that he was trained at sales and knew exactly how to market it. This meant breaking the rules, as the store wasn't licensed to sell at the retail level. But the salesperson saw the determination in Jerry's face and decided to take a chance on him. Jerry left with a big smile and a product in his hand.

Where to sell it? He knew from his Rena Ware sales training that the world was his oyster—he could just go knock on any door and show the product. While he could not explain how to use the gadget in English, he knew there were lots of Latino people in some areas of Los Angeles.

Although he spoke no Spanish and they knew little English, he had a hunch that this leveled the playing field. They were in the same boat, and would be more amenable to communicating with non-verbal cues and gestures. Moreover, with a terrific product on hand to demonstrate, the task was easier to accomplish.

Tomorrow will be a new a day, he thought. He'd start knocking on doors and make people fall in love with it, just as he had.

Chapter Six

Credit, the First Step
for the American Dream

When you have nothing at hand, no prospects or resources, and a string of failures behind you, it's easy to get discouraged. You can let yourself be seduced by the voice that tells you to stop fighting, to just give up, and that nothing's going to change. You can sink into apathy, functioning at a rock bottom level, just to stay afloat. That's what happens to most people when a situation is bleak beyond belief.

Conversely, that's when you can mobilize all your inner resources and make a decision to persevere! You can believe all is lost, or choose to persevere despite seemingly insurmountable odds. That's what Jerry decided to do, faced with empty pockets, no knowledge of the language or culture, no help from without, nothing but an unbelievable drive. Jerry had complete, unquestionable faith that nothing could stand in his way if he mobilized his drive, coupled with a tremendous effort. "No" means nothing.

He would re-invent himself: one-on-one retail instead of import-export.

Jerry was of the mindset that nothing can limit what you decide to do, provided you see your limitations as a challenge, not a closed door. He subscribed to the notion that you, "argue for your limitations and they're yours," as David Bach wrote in his book, *Illusions: The Adventures of a Reluctant Messiah*.

You're blind? That does not mean you can't pilot an airplane or drive a boat. At the age of thirty, Miles Hilton-Barber became blind because of a genetic disease. He said, "I became a victim of my condition, living a mediocre life," until his brother (who was also blind) used speech-output technology to navigate from Africa to Australia by himself. Miles changed his attitude towards his situation, saying, "The only thing holding me back now is five inches: the distance between my ears." He had to fight his fears: fear of failing, and the fear of all the negativity surrounding him.

In the book, *Inspire: Courageous People of Our Time*, Miles who became blind, has set many world records climbing the Himalayas, Kilimanjaro, and Mont Blanc to mention some. He scuba-dived in the Red Sea, hot air ballooned over the Nevada desert, man-hauled a sled over 250 miles across Antarctica, set the world lap record for a blind driver on the Malaysian Grand Prix Circuit, circumnavigated the world using more than eighty different forms of transportation and is still setting records, flying airplanes and the like, although he's completely blind. If Miles can do all this, what's holding you back from making efforts to change your destiny?

This is what made Jerry walk the streets of Los Angeles with the determination to sell, not only a product, because anyone could do that. No, he was selling value to these families. He wanted to bring items that were special, unique enough that they would create a positive change in the homes of his customers. Something uncommon, not found in the corner convenience store, that would delight and excite his customers, and that would bring families together.

These were the days when electronic arcade games were in their infancy and not widespread. Pong was one of the very first. This was a tennis game, designed as training or a warm up exercise with scorekeeping and sound effects. It had different angles and velocities for the ball to return. When the player missed the ball, he/she needed to reset the speed in a limited time. The company saw the potential for a home version and created Home Pong, which would operate on a regular television screen. After a few minutes to connect the game to the set, you were off and running. Home Pong was still in its very early stages and just beginning to gain popularity as the first video game.

Jerry selected a predominantly Latino neighborhood that seemed to house mostly new immigrants. He walked to the very top of a four-story building and began making his way down the halls. The first few doors were opened a sliver, and closed quickly. But as he continued to make his way through the building, he found enough residents that were receptive to his little sales pitch. He was dressed very simply, did not look like he was any more successful than the families he was visiting, and his manner was mild and non-threatening.

Jerry was bringing entertainment and technology to families. He was right there explaining to them how to install, use and play with it, and he was providing Home Pong to them with credit lines that most of these families—who all lived in a world of cash only—didn't have. Most of them did not have traditional jobs, and most worked on a cash only basis, with identification documents from their home countries, only.

It worked for both parties. Jerry was giving them a product with a down payment that almost covered his cost. He was looking directly into their eyes when he left the product with the family. They knew it was Jerry and that he was going to be there tomorrow, selling to a neighbor. Both were engaged now: one by giving the best service with a good quality product, and the other by obtaining a product they would have not even dreamt of being able to buy. This caliber of service was essential for customer satisfaction and was the most important part of the sale for Jerry. It was the reason he was able to keep selling. Jerry was giving value and warranties to these families.

Jerry remembers selling a TV to one of his customers, who asked him how long the warranty was for the TV. Jerry said that the warranty he wanted was for five years, and he wrote a five-year warranty into the receipt. The customer bought the set immediately. This opened up the biggest opportunity for repeat customers. If anything happened to the TV, Jerry would repair it and give that customer another opportunity to buy something new from him. This gave the customer the feeling of security, which he/she is not on his/her own. Once you bought something from Jerry, you felt safe, your investment was secure, and by buying it on credit, Jerry created the opportunity to return to that home to offer another product.

If the product could not be repaired, Jerry would then use a formula, deducting the time the product was used from the overall sales price. Credit was given to the customer for the part he had already paid in order to buy a new product. By always thinking that this was another opportunity to sell and to continue building a trusting relationship with the customer, Jerry was giving them a service.

He was a good observer. During each visit he made to a family, Jerry went inside their home, looking for opportunities to be helpful to them, to give more, to build trust, to go that extra mile so that the customer would remember him forever. For instance, he would carry TV antennas around with him. If he visited a home and found that the TV had bad reception, he'd pull out an antenna and set it up for the customer for free. Once the TV looked perfect, the customer saw the extra service Jerry was giving to that family. The antenna cost Jerry one dollar, the value he gave that family was priceless. Now they could watch TV with the best reception and he had opened an additional opportunity to keep selling to them.

Every time Jerry visited with a product, a new request was added to the list and more products were needed to fulfill the customers' needs. Jerry created a catalog with cut and pasted pictures. His inventory increased to include TVs, stereos, blenders, and other electronics. His clientele even gave Jerry a nickname, "Senor de los Stereos," the man of the stereos.

Jerry always gave his customers an unexpected gift each time he delivered a product they'd bought from him. He gave alarm clocks that he'd set up in the customers' rooms. He not only gave them the alarm clock for free, but he'd set it up for them. Jerry knew it was difficult for some of them to understand the instructions. He never used the gift as a condition to buy from him—it was a surprise.

Every customer who saw him in the neighborhood would greet him, and ask about additional products, features on products, recommendations on brands, and many other questions, including where to pay their bills and what school they should put their kids in. One time, he sold a product to a lady, and when he came back for her payment, he saw that she opened a box full of cash. Jerry asked her why she had so much cash. She explained to him that she was making pillows and selling them at a swap meet. He told her that she could get robbed and insisted that she open a bank account. The customer said she did not know how to do it, and Jerry took the time to go with her to the bank and helped her fill out all the forms. She became his customer forever.

When customers saw him knocking at doors in the neighborhood, everyone was friendly, because they knew it was Jerry. He was nice to everyone, leaving a good impression with everyone and making lots of friends. They'd refer him to their friends and families. He came to deliver a product or collect a payment and people would open up their apartments—he did not need to knock on their doors because they were waiting for him. Jerry had become one of them.

In many cases, these immigrants were starting a family. Many couples get together and start their life together simply, although money restrictions are at the top of the list of concerns for many.

How do you start? Many will live in their parents' homes, with friends or rent a room. Having a job is the main point where one begins to climb the ladder. And, of course, the reason why many of these couples are getting together is that they're going to have a baby. Even more challenges for starting that family.

Beginning a life together implies having your own stuff: a bed, a mattress, and furniture. Here's where it gets complicated. Saving money in many cases depends on family tradition. Some families educate their kids from the time they are little to save, while some don't. But if the poor don't have access to money, how can they save? How does this culture of saving money get developed? Some people don't have the opportunity to become educated. They're born organizers. Kids who save money when they are little will most likely grow up to be organized with money.

Jerry identified with this community because he didn't have any savings when he arrived in America. He even had to borrow the money to pay for his ticket to come to the United States. He knew he had to keep selling in order to survive. He knew he had to pay his supplier—he was buying the products he was selling door-to-door with cash. He had no co-signer, no references, no credit card, and no documents.

These struggles had a face: The face of a man with twenty dollars in his pocket and his heart full of hope, walking those L.A. streets, knocking on doors in a community where no one wanted to be found, where a knock at the door could be the *migra*, asking for the correct residency papers. Jerry had a strong commitment in his mind and was dedicating all his efforts towards making it happen. Immigrants like him, real people with under-the-radar jobs, were his customers. One could actually say that, for some of them, nobody knew who they were. The only identification paper they might have brought with them from their country was a birth certificate that had worn out.

In many cases, the names they used were not their birth names. Some were even using names of relatives or friends, and made up ones, too. Most had jobs that paid them in cash, people with years of work, yet no basic credit history. Immigrants who move from different countries because of war usually bring nothing with them. They were walking long distances, hiding as squatters from the authorities and even from other immigrants, always on the run, searching for a safe spot to relax and to get more energy to continue their journey. This is the beginning of many of the families who came to start their new life in America and who Jerry was reaching with his products.

Jerry came from Israel, after years of attending the military academy and of service. After training at the academy, he had to fight in the Yom Kippur War between Israel and a coalition of Arab countries, led by Syria and Egypt fighting for occupied territories. More than 2,000 soldiers died, over 7,000 were wounded, and this was only on the Israeli side. The Arab casualties were never made public but estimated by many sources to be more than 16,000 killed and more than 35,000 wounded. Jerry saw death with his own eyes. He saw destruction, and the pain of the injured, and felt the pain of all this destruction on a personal level.

Every time he met an immigrant in an elevator, a parking lot, or a mall, he felt their pain. Pain for leaving loved ones back in their countries, leaving his/her home, town, church, and/or playground. The pain of losing stories they'd constructed together with their parents and that today exist only in their memories. Many immigrants won't ever go back to their homelands, not even for funerals, and not even to see their parents for the last time. Some of these immigrants were running away from oppressive countries, places with long histories of war.

Many of these anonymous people who have started a new life in the United States (helped by relatives, friends, employers or even starting their own story by being children of those immigrants) have needs. Every single family needs a job, a place to live, furniture, and electronics. Without speaking any English or Spanish, Jerry started knocking on their door with a familiar sound—a sound that would not alarm them or make them think it was the police or U.S.

Immigration agents. He knocked with the sound of a friend or relative. He wanted to communicate the feeling of a familiar, caring person even before a family would open the door to see who was on the other side. So he created a special way of knocking on the door.

Jerry would never look into a new customer's eyes. He wanted him/her to feel that he/she had the power over him, and that he was in total submission. In one instance, a family opened a door and thought he was a neighbor complaining because the TV was too loud. They invited him inside and told him to lower the audio as he wished. When he explained that the reason he'd knocked at their door was to sell them a product, they all started laughing.

Jerry would always give them a sincere smile and a friendly look, ensuring he was not pushing a sale. When a door opened and a woman was in the doorway, she'd usually say her husband wasn't in. Without being pushy, Jerry would respond that he'd return and would create an appointment to do so when her husband would be in. Once he came back, they felt familiar and comfortable with him, and now it was not a cold sale.

Many of these immigrants came to the United States after walking for days and nights. If they were lucky enough to reach the border, cross over, and have a counterpart who would receive them, they were then ready to start a new life. It became the last link in the chain, their real and biggest challenge to start a new life as undocumented aliens in America. Many of these immigrants are people who are hidden for days from authorities in the desert with little water and food, but with a lot of fear.

Once on the other side, they start a new life in the States looking for a job. Many of these immigrants end up having two or more jobs to raise sufficient money to bring their loved ones to live with them, and to support the rest of the family in their home countries.

Many will start by sleeping on couches or in garages until they have enough money saved to move into their own places, with the help of all their *padrinos* until they become eligible for their first credit. This is the same as any couple starting out. This is the moment when the first step of the American dream starts. In the majority of these apartments, several families live together in order to reduce the cost of rent and to help each other. Immigrants are hardworking people with one goal in mind: to make money to support their families and each other. This is the moment when saving skills will help them to organize their money and make it go further.

Jerry started by giving credit and products to a mass of immigrants who were ignored by all of Los Angeles' established credit institutions and retailers. Jerry would offer a product and would sell it on credit with a down payment. He'd also offer a customer the opportunity to work for him if he/she did not have a job. The next day, Jerry would come to the same home and there were ten new families for him to show his products to and get orders and collect down payments from. He always gave a percentage of his sales to the family that hosted the sales meeting. This same family would collect the money each month for him and that family kept part of the sum. This created a profit sharing model, helping the family that became his representative, plus an opportunity for him to collect the monthly payments. He'd train these people to be able to sell his products and thus become his sales force.

Once a customer finished paying his debt, Jerry would create a certificate saying that this customer had paid all his credit line and had done so on time, and declared him a preferred customer. Jerry would visit this home to try to sell them more products and he'd find the certificate he gave them framed and on a wall near the entrance. They felt proud; in many cases these were the only certificates they had ever received, since most of these newcomers never had any formal education.

How do you get a car, an apartment, a phone line, utilities, etc., when you are starting your new life in the States? This requirement begins with savings: the first step to getting your own apartment, your own things. How about credit? When does credit become an option? Credit is a big word when you are just starting out.

Even with cash in your hands, being able to prove that you will be able to pay, and/or obtaining credit is not so simple. You have to prove how long you've been working at a job, that you've been making payments, and that you're on a path of financial stability. The formal workplace can provide a reference, but what if you are working informally, or are working under the table? How will you be able to prove it? It gets even more complex when you cannot prove that you're living where you say you reside because there is no utility listed under your name.

Jerry was selling so many Home Pongs that the storeowner asked him what he was doing with these electronic games, and he told the shopkeeper he was selling them door-to-door. The vendor was so amazed with Jerry's story and how many games he was selling that the storeowner opened a line of credit for him, right there on the spot, with no co-signers, references, or down payment. Jerry immediately negotiated a volume price.

Most families are living on a paycheck, month to month, or on cash. Once you move to your own home, then you'll be able to show utility bills plus confirmation as to how long you've been working, and your identity. The longer the length of time for these three minimum requirements, the less of a risk you are, and your score will be higher for the credit houses. But what if some of this information is not available? This is when it gets complicated and credit lines are less available.

Jerry provided his first credit line to this immigrant world when he was walking the streets of Los Angeles. He was one-on-one with these people in their homes, looking at them, where they lived, and looking into their eyes when he was giving them merchandise. This form of buying is very common in Latin America. Salespeople knock at your door and offer products you can buy with cash or on credit. Once you buy by credit, they come every month to collect the money and to sell you more. You could hide but they will still return to knock on your door as many times as necessary in order to collect the debt.

In Jerry's case, he was selling and collecting apartment by apartment, and, using his customers as collaborators, he was able to increase his range of operations. Electronics were a big hit in Latin America, although all imports were highly taxed. Products like TVs and stereos were extremely expensive and unreachable in many cases. But Jerry made them affordable with convenient monthly payments. He created a plan to be paid in four payments that was like paying cash with no interest. Jerry brought their products to their homes, installed them, and gave them a personal guarantee. With a big smile, he came to collect their monthly payments.

Jerry operated on the principle that if your customer is receiving value above their expectations, they'll always feel obligated to pay you in full. They would not want to miss another opportunity for Jerry to bring them into such a convenient, trusting relationship that benefits both parties.

When you live with a salary or on commission, you earn money with each paycheck and pay what you need to for your utilities, rent, etc. At the end, all you have is food money, which competes with your additional needs. What's left each month is usually not planned. When you live on a very strict budget, at the end of the month, you're waiting for the next paycheck. Credit then becomes a way, or an option, to get what you want and cannot buy. It's an option if you're a smart shopper and careful credit holder.

Jerry used credit as a tool to serve an underserved niche market of families who did not have any other option for obtaining a television, a blender, and many other products he added to his line. He adapted the model as he was going to serve every type of buyer and circumstance. Family refers family—this was a way to protect his initial investment. By creating a specific down payment program that represents the cost of the product, Jerry was risking his profit, determining the risk of the person he was selling too. Jerry started using his neighbors as helpers to make the right decisions on credit lines and the amount of products to sell to each family so as not to overwhelm them to a point where they could not pay their debt.

The neighborhood began to change. People were able to watch television, they had the opportunity to inform themselves, and they had stereos to listen to their music. Kids could be entertained with electronic games. The families felt they were progressing, that little-by-little the American Dream they had almost given their lives to obtain was paying off. Jerry felt the loyalty these customers were developing each day for him, his products, and his services. The repeat customer was the norm; they looked for him and waited for him to come by.

Jerry became a pioneer in word-of-mouth marketing to this niche. Families visited each other, saw the new television sets, and asked, "How did you buy this TV?" Jerry was mentioned all the time, and soon his operation grew and many employees were working for him. Jerry developed catalogues to sell. He had his niche and it was growing. By being the best in your specific field, you do not need any additional marketing efforts. You have a unique niche that responds with loyalty.

The principle of delivering more than what you promise gave him more benefits by yielding a higher customer satisfaction rate. Paying attention to your customers, carefully observing their expressions, and listening to their comments pays off. This gave Jerry more opportunities to increase his line of products, and gave him other options for services. His collaborators frequently provided feedback that made him take the right sales approach and operation strategies.

Jerry was successful because he loved what he was doing, and enjoyed working with people, knowing them, and assisting others. That sense of service gave him the fiber for the business he was doing. Jerry had goals: he could not go back to

Israel, and he had to pay his debt in order to survive. He needed to be able to take care of himself and bring his family to the United States. He had financial goals, social goals, personal goals, health goals, and family goals. For him to achieve all his objectives he had to be successful—there was no other choice. Failure was not an option.

Jerry had a million reasons to resist that will. He did not know how to speak the language and had little resources, starting with just twenty dollars to buy and resell products. He did not understand the language of his customer. He knew little about the product he was selling and he knew nothing of closing the sale. But his will was stronger than all the obstacles standing in his way. He understood himself well enough to take on the role and work it out.

He started to learn words in Spanish and carried candy for the kids, He always had a screwdriver with him, and if he went to a home and saw a table that looked like it was falling apart, he'd started fixing it on his own while he talked to them about products he was selling.

He learned where they came from, where they worked, how long they were in the country, the names of the kids, and their birthdays. All of this inside information gave him the power to know how much to sell to them. He learned how to play Home Pong at an expert level, gaining him respect among the kids and families in general, because he could always show them tricks.

He knew about the product from the eyes of the customer. He practiced all of the benefits the product offered, the electronics' various features, so he could explain the difference between one and another and from one price point to the other. He always showed the catalog with three options, as he did not want to confuse the customer with too many options. It was very clear to Jerry that the customer would not buy a product due to its features, but because of the benefits it gave them.

There are many distractions that can make you lose focus, but the power to come back and continue your efforts in order to meet your goals makes you accomplish them and succeed. Where there's a need, there has to be a will. When Jerry was walking the streets of Los Angeles knocking on doors, it was tough. Everything went wrong. People did not open up when he knocked, people were not interested in what he had to offer, and people would slam the door in his face. But then he'd touch his back pocket and remember that he had his return ticket to Israel. After a particularly hard day of knocking and knocking on doors but not selling anything, Jerry was riding the bus and pulled out his airplane ticket and said to himself, "By having this option to give up and return back home, I make myself not try harder." He tore it into pieces and said, "Now I have no excuses for myself. I make it or I make it."

Jerry got off at the next stop and rode a bus back to the last neighborhood he had visited. There was a huge apartment complex with more than 100 units. The place was dark, with trash all over the halls and a terrible smell. He started knocking and knocking on doors, and went on to sell $6,000 worth of electronics that day. Jerry did not give up. He discovered his crutches and how this was holding him from walking on his own two feet. That airplane ticket was in his way, and by getting rid of it, he had to fly on his own. By closing any opportunity to give up and return to his homeland, Jerry now had to do whatever it took to succeed. He had to make it on his own. At that moment, you step out of the circle of excuses that are holding you back. All those scars and fears that have built up since childhood hold you back from a better future. Why did Jerry destroy his only chance to go back? That airplane ticket was his excuse for not trying harder, and he had a way out—returning to the same life he had left behind, the war zone, the permanent battle zone where he had lost his best friend, the place he did not want his children to be raised in, under permanent military training. That was not the future he wanted. He had already left it behind and, by destroying that ticket, there was no turning back.

1976 First days at Los Angeles, Santa Monica beach.

In order for him to accomplish his goals, Jerry had to leave out all of his scars and problems and concentrate on only one goal: becoming successful. He trashed his airline ticket and eliminated any options of going back to where he had come from. He had to make it here with what he had. He needed commitment, dedication and the willingness to sacrifice.

Chapter Seven

The Only Way, Credit

How do you think people measure your attempts in life? Does the way you live reveal how many times you have tried and failed? The place you live for example will never reflect the truth of how many times you've stood back up again after getting knocked down. The only witnesses to your efforts will be your mind and your heart.

Family, friends and people around you might tell the story of how many times you've gone out there to make a difference and to pursue your success. Most likely they will, they will only refer to the results of success.

How resilient a person can be, even while taking stock of failure, refusals, rejections, negativity, seizing the impossible to turn it around, and not having a mark, scar or rupture. You are able to rise again and recover. Or maybe you never recover: you just learn how to cope and live with this. You might find yourself starting a new day without, in some cases, having fully recovered, yet still with the desire, the energy, to start again and keep trying, against all odds.

Do humans need an inherited gene in order to reach a level of resilience so that nothing makes them drown? Is it a muscle that's been exercised since childhood in families with lots of children, without the time to give enough attention to any of the children, who learn to sink or swim almost on their own? Is it a mindset developed by exercises? Do you learn it by reading or listening to older folks? Could it be that it develops at school, when you get bad grades and need to study more to get better scores? Is it because your mom or dad gave you attention when you were little? Does a good work ethic require dedication, quality time given at particular moments by parents, grandparents, aunts, uncles, or friends? How do you develop resilience to endure your failures? Is it the exposure to adversity and the positive adjustment that each individual develops to adapt to each situation? How can you stand after the storm passes and has left you with nothing?

Jerry confronted his reality and did not give up. He went out and knocked on doors with a sample in his hand, a real product, so people could immediately understand what this gizmo was all about. Perhaps they'd seen their neighbor's kids, friends, or cousins using it. In any case, he could demonstrate how it worked right there. Some had never seen this electronic game but now they understood how to play it and were able to buy it. They took a chance. He was able to ask for a down payment and come back to collect the rest in small payments, giving him the opportunity to sell more products and better understand his customers' needs.

Midtown Electronics had small appliances and TVs, and Jerry added these to the growing line of products he sold door-to-door. The box for some of these products bore the address of an import company in Marina del Rey named Century. So without knowing what he'd find, Jerry took a bus to Marina del Rey, thinking he might discover a way to buy directly from the importer without having to go through the wholesaler. But perhaps his attempt to cut out the middleman would have a catch. Maybe the quantities per purchase order would get bigger, instead of the small quantities he was able to buy from Midtown. He had to take a chance in order to find out.

What an opportunity, Jerry hoped. It was probably the warehouse where all the products are shipped to from, and it might have other items he could not find at Midtown Electronics. This new possibility conjured more and more ideas in Jerry's mind to increase his small operation. What if he could get a better deal, a lower price for his purchases, thereby increasing his profit margin?

Jerry found the place in Marina del Rey, and he was right! He discovered tons of products, new ideas, and new opportunities, from small appliances to electronics. One of the products that immediately attracted his attention was stereos, which he was familiar with due to his previous turntable business in Israel. Jerry knew people loved music and he instantly realized his customers would want to buy this line of products.

The importer's price for the stereos was $150 each and, quickly calculating the math in his mind, Jerry immediately knew he could sell them for $399 on small monthly payments. Then he noticed a pile of reconditioned speakers, and he thought that this was perfect to add to his offer—with the purchase of a boom box, the buyer would also get free speakers as part of a package deal. This extra enticement would make it a one of a kind deal, creating more value for his offer. Uniqueness was a tool for beating out the competition. Customers couldn't compare the price to anything because it was different and he was giving his buyers more, adding value to his sales offer. More bang for the consumer's buck.

Century had a mini alarm clock that looked like a stereo. Jerry used this as a surprise gift for anyone who bought his line of products, and for any person who recommended a new customer. People love freebies, and he was opening up more opportunities with his gifts. In particular, he was gaining new customers. He'd started his business with new clients from cold sells, but getting new customers through referrals was making his operation multiply and exponentially grow. For him, a recommended customer was much more valuable than just another knock on the door. This new customer came with a referral, someone who already knew him or her, and for this reason, Jerry felt like he was taking less of a risk. He was able to make better decisions regarding how much he was going to give as a line of credit to this or that family and which kind of products they'd be able to buy. Is life a marathon where resilient people go to the front, with weaker people relegated to the back of the pack? Is it a drinking glass? Does life depend on the size of the drinking glass you're measuring your accomplishments or success with? What kinds of drinking glasses are you using? The smallest the glass the more full it looks. Or are you measuring yourself with a big glass and telling yourself its half empty? This is one way of looking at yourself, of viewing how you project yourself to others. It will be your philosophy for life, your way of seeing life and confronting situations.

The more you try finding a new job, or developing your ideas for your own business, the more you will figure it out. All of the events you're part of, and all of your experiences through life, will help you learn your way. In life, you are unique because of what you know and the experiences you. There's no one else quite like you, and all of your past has molded you to become who you are. All of these experiences that life has put in front of you are forcing you to adapt to your circumstances. They're making you become part of a positive adaptation, looking at things through a different view, accepting yourself, acknowledging your abilities, and patting yourself on the back when you accomplish a step. After all of these experiences, you're gaining confidence and reducing your vulnerability to failure.

Viewing the things you undergo as experiences and not as failures is your first step in learning how to navigate the often-stormy sea of our complex society, and it is no easy feat. Turn it around, evaluate your steps, figure it out, make sure it was not an impulsive decision, understand what could have gone wrong, and think about what you left on the table, what step you missed, and what you need to correct on each and every step towards success. You'll always need methods for measuring your improvement and to set your goals up in a way that helps you obtain your desires.

Have you tried and the results have not been the ones you expected? Is your idea doable, are you trying the right way? Only time will tell if you went on the right path, but nothing should stop you from following your dreams. The philosopher Joseph Campbell said, "Follow your bliss!" What is your vision? Secure a path to accomplish it, secure the process and steps, take small steps to build the procedures and route to get there, and with perseverance time will show the way. All you need is to keep trying, work every day consistently, stay disciplined, and you will accomplish it.

Jerry developed his own system, creating a catalog of products to offer door-to-door. He also offered to hire his customers, thereby giving his clients more confidence in themselves and boosting their self-esteem. Imagine being unemployed, trying to navigate how to provide for yourself and your family without a job. Sometimes, the tunnel seems so long and the other end is so far away that success appears to be impossible. It's all in your mind—you're probably carrying baggage from bad experiences. Then, suddenly, a stranger knocks on your door, shows you a product and tries to sell it to you. When you tell him you can't buy it because you don't have a job, he answers, "Work for me." What a kind gesture, signal of confidence, and act of trust.

To the unemployed people he offered jobs to, Jerry gave a spoonful of self-confidence, wellbeing, care, and support. He created relationships. Even though they could not, at first, buy a product from him, the next time they saw him they had resources, and would definitely buy from him.

Jerry saw himself in these people. He remembered how he looked desperately for a job for several days, struggling to take his wife and himself away from sleeping in the streets of Los Angeles. These people had traveled a long distance like he had. They were immigrants like him. These strangers in a strange land needed a hand exactly the same as he had needed one, when the other side of the tunnel had seemed to be unending.

When you go back to any age and start measuring your accomplishments, there are always questions: Have you tried enough? Have you obtained the results of your efforts? Are they what you expected? Are you satisfied with your results? Would you do it again, or would you change something in the formula that might have taken your life in a different direction?

Life goes on, and if you earn your livelihood from a salary or commission, you generally make enough money to pay for your basic needs, like rent, utilities, food, medicine, clothing, and transportation. If, for any reason, one's monthly expenditures exceed one's paycheck, many people are likely to charge additional expenses to a credit card, which will take care of the difference, enabling one to pay in monthly payments.

Jerry was working in the cash world—he had no credit, he had to build it, and to develop trust among suppliers—first to get better pricing for volume purchases, then for purchasing terms. He had to build confidence among his suppliers in order to obtain a line of credit and to negotiate terms. The conditions of this line of credit were essential to him: if he could pay in thirty days, he had time to get new sales and collect monthly payments. In a way, he was turning his money around. He'd receive a profit for several months from the moment he collected a down payment. He had to calculate how he was going to be able to survive while still financing all of the customers buying from him.

He had no computer for keeping records of all transactions per customer, per item, per address, and for classifying sales in many different ways. With computers, formulas are already included; all you do is input data and the software calculates everything, including the monthly payments, margin, interest, etc. But Jerry had to write everything down on paper, and organize them by names and addresses. He'd always note who had recommended a customer. This way, if for any reason the client was no longer making his/her payment, he could go back to the reference source and ask the whereabouts of the purchaser, and the reason for their late payments or at least send them a message.

Jerry had created his own system; his catalog had a form where he would write the name of the customer, address, product selected, purchase price, minimum down payment (most likely the cost of the product), the monthly payment, and the day the payment would be collected. Jerry started to become a symbol of economic stability for the neighborhood. When they saw him coming with boxes in tow, all eyes were upon him as neighbors watched to see who bought what. This meant they had jobs and were able to acquire goods. It created a certain status from one family to another, signifying they were progressing and wanted to now own the same product as their neighbors. They were keeping up with the Josés.

Credit becomes an option only for those who are able to prove they can repay it, and when you are not planning your expenses correctly and have no savings, credit houses qualify you as a high-risk individual who most likely won't qualify for credit. Immigrants are considered to be in a high risk category. Some work in jobs where it's hard to trace their income, and they have problems with identity documentation, such as social security numbers. Their references are often from people who are considered, in many cases, to be unreliable because they're in the same boat regarding documentation. Although this is widely known, what's left out of the equation is the fact that most immigrants repay credit and loans in a timely and reliable way, and are loyal to those extending a hand to them.

Jerry was creating a model intended to enable him to understand and decide the line of credit he would extend and risk for each family. By now, he had walked in this neighborhood for years; personally installing the TVs they were buying. The door-to-door salesman knew their neighbors, relatives, friends, hopes, and dreams. He understood, step by step, how to qualify them for their credit line. He knew who they were referring and who had referred them. After all of their countless conversations, he knew which city they came from, and learned about their culture, customs, and food. He started to create a system wherein he had copies of his customers' documents, and he began to understand what each paper was called. For example, he knew that *cedula* was the identification card of many Latin American countries. The foreign documents provided a guarantee that it was the real name of the person, not a fake document some used for work. He had to add a line in his form for their "also known as," or "aka," name.

Now they were in the United States of America and their first credit line was helping them to start building their own American dream—credit given to them by another immigrant who'd experienced the same conditions and had the same limitations as they did.

In the 1970s, immigrants came from many countries, especially Mexico, India, the Philippines, and China. Altogether, there were more than 9 million foreign-born residents living all over the United States, with immigrants representing 4.6 percent of the entire U.S. population. By 2010, the estimated number of immigrants calculated by the Census to be living in the U.S. was 6.5 percent of the population of the whole country, or 20 million people. Immigrants mainly migrated to California, New York, Florida, Texas, Pennsylvania, New Jersey, and Illinois.

These countries represent seventy percent of all of the immigrants in the U.S. today. Many immigrants come from Mexico. Being in close proximity to the U.S. gives its residents easier access that is relatively convenient, with existing transportation mechanisms—but it's still not easy. In the past, it was a matter of merely walking across the border, but now all of the increasingly dangerous regulations at the border have forced immigrants to look for more difficult areas of access, like deserts. Mexicans are now about twenty-four percent of the entire immigrant population.

Another country of origin for immigrants is China, which has greater distance and transportation barriers for its immigration flow. China is a country whose political situation has prompted many to look for another place to live, the top choice being the U.S.A. Despite their long costly travel across vast distances, China comes after Mexico and the Philippines with the third largest group of immigrants, having 5 percent of all transplants to America from all over the world. Both groups of newcomers are composed mainly of men who come to work in agricultural, construction, service industry, hospital, and other (mainly blue collar) jobs.

In addition to Mexico and China, other countries with high numbers of immigrants to America are from: India 4 percent; Cuba 3 percent; El Salvador 3 percent; Vietnam 3 percent; Dominican Republic 2 percent, and in smaller numbers Colombia, Jamaica, South Korea and Guatemala. Most immigrants come with a bag full of dreams but empty pockets, wondering what the U.S. really has to offer them, with many thinking that life is going to be easier, and that all they need is a job. Nobody ever immigrates in order to make their lives worse.

What contributions do immigrants make to the U.S? They bring population growth, cultural diversity, traditional cuisine, music, different languages, and job creation. Immigrant job creation is an interesting subject. Very simply, they fill gaps in operations by being complementary workers who take low-wage jobs that few U.S.-born Americans would do. These low-wage operations could be sent abroad, but by having a low-wage work force available to them locally, companies stay stateside and hire supervisors, managers, etc., and give job opportunities to locals. Like others, immigrants also need places to live, utilities, food, and clothing, and thus an employment chain reaction starts.

What other contributions do immigrants bring to a country besides taking citizens' jobs away from them, as some critics claim? They pay federal and state taxes (although, ironically, undocumented workers are often not eligible for the government benefits they are forced to pay for, such as social security). Immigrants make a big contribution in terms of cultural diversity, skills, and innovations, bringing many traditions that enrich their adopted country. But one of their main tasks is sustaining the standard of living of American society, by working in the jobs no one else wants to do and are no longer willing to try. America is an immigrant nation that has always been enriched by the art, sports, music, and even philosophy of newcomers.

Jerry had a small operation which had started to grow. He continued to have orders that took him a long time to deliver. He had to collect monthly payments from several customers. Once the sale was made, Jerry had to take the form he had created for each sale and buy the product. He'd go to his supplier the next day to buy the product for delivery. Jerry would keep the form and follow up with collecting payments. He started to feel like he needed help to sell products and collect payments. So he hired his first sales agent, Mario Romero. Who was Mario?

Mario opened the door in one of the apartments that Jerry was selling to. He had emigrated from El Salvador. All of his extended family had already immigrated to Los Angeles years ago, even before El Salvador's civil wars. Very proud of his country, he was the only one who'd stayed behind, thinking he didn't need to leave. But by the 1980s, El Salvador had started experiencing many internal problems between the military-led government and the Farabundo Marti National Liberation Front (FMLN), a coalition of leftwing guerrilla groups. It was a time of violence in an overpopulated poor country with intense class conflict.

All his brothers and sisters had migrated to California and were working in Los Angeles. He started feeling intrigued about how they were able to find jobs and make it in *los Estados Unidos,* even though they knew no English. Mario also began feeling the pressure the military forces were exerting on the population; many Salvadorans were murdered by the military or kidnapped by the FMLN. The civilians were in the middle of the battle, and anyone could get killed. Although the war was undeclared, tension was everywhere.

Mario challenged himself to come see his brothers and sisters and find out how they were able to survive in El Norte. He traveled north to Mexico, arriving at a city called San Felipe in Baja California, a remote desert area around 125 miles south of the border, between California, Mexicali, and Calexico. The locals' main activity was fishing. He knew he had to get closer to the border and moved to Tijuana, a border city with the United States near the well-known border crossing of San Ysidro, located in the southernmost section of San Diego County, California.

Everyone told Mario that all he had to do was blend in, and once he was at the border crossing, just walk through like any local Mexican living near the borderline did, as if he was just going to purchase something at the markets or work in the United States' border cities. There are agreements between countries to let their citizens at the borders move in between their boundaries. This still exists but nowadays a written permit must be obtained at the border and proof of local residency is required. However, back in the 1980s, Mario just had to make everyone believe he was Mexican, and without carrying any bags, papers, or anything, walk across the borderline.

The border between U.S. and Mexico is the most visited one on Earth, with 350 million legal crossings per year and countless crossings by undocumented people. The Mexican border touches four U.S. states: California, Arizona, New Mexico, and

Texas. The Golden State has the shortest border while the Lone Star State has the longest. South of the border, Mexico's states have similar characteristics: Chihuahua has the longest stretch of borderline with *los Estados Unidos*, while Nuevo Leon has the shortest border. Baja California shares a border with California and part of Arizona; Sonora abuts part of Arizona and New Mexico; and Chihuahua touches parts of New Mexico and Texas. The smaller Mexican states of Tamaulipas, Nuevo Leon, and Coahuila only border Texas.

The U.S.-Mexico border stretches for 1,954 miles, and as of this writing, the reported number of border patrol agents is 20,000, who have the ability to control only about 129 miles. There is a sort of natural border control area: the Rio Grande and the desert. Due to the intensification of border control, many undocumented immigrants make more perilous crossings through more difficult areas; many die in the process, often left behind by "coyotes," who are paid large sums of money to take the so-called *ilegales* across to the other side.

But during the 1980s, he did it; Mario was able, as the Doors sang, to just walk "on through to the other side," with all of the guards believing that the Salvadoran was a local Mexican. The Romero family was waiting for Mario in a car across the borderline. He arrived in Los Angeles where he soon had a job. The underground network of immigrants would amaze any corporate head hunter; they can find a job for a friend or relative within days of his/her arrival, despite the fact that many do not know the language or even have the proper documentation.

Mario's job wasn't fulltime. He had extra time for another part-time or even fulltime position. He needed money—his wife and kids were still back in El Salvador. This situation is very common among immigrants, who often hold down several jobs in order to finance two homes. So when Jerry knocked on Mario's door, he found a receptive audience. They communicated mostly through sign language, since at that time Mario did not speak any English and Jerry didn't know Spanish. Yet the two ambitious immigrants both spoke the international language of commerce, and they quickly agreed upon terms. Mario would gather neighbors, family, and friends at a specified time and place where Jerry would sell his products. Mario would receive fifteen percent of any of the sales resulting from this meeting.

Literally a go-getter, Mario invited his neighbors to a meeting the very next day with Jerry, and their business relationship started. Jerry now had his first employee.

He gave Mario a catalog with the minimum down payments and the form for the customer to fill out with all of his/her relevant information. On a map, Jerry showed his new employee where to go, which neighborhoods to canvas. Mario would now sell and receive fifteen percent of any monthly fees collected. This sounded like a win-win situation for both of them. With his family still living in the Old Country, Mario felt confident he could now make it, and that this was the opportunity he was waiting for. He knew he had to earn enough money to send to his family in El Salvador, save enough to pay for their transportation to Mexico, and then pay a coyote to bring them across to the U.S. side so they could join him in L.A.

Mario's family wanted to come to Los Angeles. He had fallen in love with the City of the Angels and already decided to stay and make his home there. Meanwhile, the situation in El Salvador was worsening. As depicted in Oliver Stone's Oscar-nominated 1986 movie *Salvador*, there were lots of human rights abuses by soldiers, who could barge into anyone's home, declare him/her to be a communist, and then disappear him/her so they'd never be seen again. The general feeling was that soon there would be an all-out war in El Salvador.

Mario went into the neighborhood apartment buildings, knocking on doors, and selling his catalog of products to his own people. It was easier for him to explain their benefits, since he was talking to people who came from the same place, and they all spoke the same language. Mario was using the same sales technique as Jerry, who trained him regarding the products' benefits and their monthly payments. Whenever he sold a product, he had to return to that client's home to collect monthly payments and ask for new customer referrals.

There were many challenges in the operation. For instance, there might be a picture of an item in the catalog, but when Jerry went to buy the product, it was sold out or discontinued. Matching it to something similar was not always possible, making them slow the sell. They had to go back to the customer and try to convince him/her to reselect a different product, and in some cases, they lost the sale.

After his first month selling door-to-door, Jerry knew he and Dina could no longer stay in their apartment, which was so small it didn't even have room for a double bed. They had to move to a larger place in a better location. After looking for several days, they found an apartment at Laurel and Fountain, still close to the Fairfax District. Now they had a one bedroom apartment for $175 and their situation was turning around. Jerry would work the entire day, from morning to night. His operation was growing, and he had several sales agents working for him. Suddenly, he received a phone call from his mom.

Muluk informed Jerry that his dad had already been ill for several days, and that she had tried for days to take him to the doctor, but he'd refused to go. She had asked her husband if he'd go to the doctor if Jerry came home and went with him, and Oscar said he would. So Muluk called long distance to L.A., pleading desperately with her son to come back to Israel. This was a shock for Jerry. How could he leave now that his business operation was moving in such a positive direction? If he left, who would go and purchase the products and collect the monthly payments? He was a one-man band. Although Jerry had people helping him, he was still the main man.

But he could not take the chance. What if his dad grew more ill? He would never forgive himself if something happened. Jerry talked to his helpers and explained his situation to them. They promised to continue collecting the monthly payments and sell products while he was gone. Mario Romero was put in charge.

What a momentous decision it was for Jerry to leave the new business he'd been operating for just two years. He knew that old saying, "When the cat's away, the mice will play." All of this was pounding in his mind, but Jerry had no option. He knew that Oscar was pushing ninety. He had left Israel not too long ago, and even though he knew he was leaving a mark on his father, Jerry was not prepared yet for his father to pass away. His mind refused to even consider the topic.

Jerry left for Israel. It wasn't a nonstop, direct flight from Los Angeles to Israel, and he had to travel longer than it took to fly to Europe. First he flew to New York, where he changed planes for a flight to France, and then he flew to Israel. It was a twenty-four hour ordeal. He just wanted to arrive as soon as possible, just in time to take his dad to the hospital. If only Oscar could hold on until his son's arrival, Jerry kept saying to himself, "hold on, please hold on until I arrive, please."

Jerry finally landed in Israel and his dad looked pale, and so skinny. He was eighty-seven years old, but it was impossible to tell his actual age, as the former doctor had taken such good care of himself over the years. Oscar was extremely sick. He told Jerry he felt dizzy and that he had been waiting for his son. Jerry took him to the hospital that same day where the doctors took all kinds of blood tests, as Oscar had been rapidly losing weight, and they didn't know why.

After they finished the tests, the doctors decided to give Oscar a blood transfusion and release him from the hospital so he could go home. Jerry took him there and stayed at his bedside for the following ten days. That was the amount of time he'd planned to spend in Israel, totally dedicated to his father. He had the joy of watching him get better and better. Oscar was eating and sleeping better and Jerry would talk to him all day long, about his trip to United States, the cities he had visited, all his travels from New York to California, the cold winter, and all about his business. He saw his father become more balanced and Jerry was able to help him with everything.

The tenth day came, and Jerry had to return to L.A. He had to say goodbye to his dad. His heart was beating extremely fast—he did not know if he was ever going to see him again. He always hated to part and say farewell, but this one was the hardest and worst of all. With his heart in his hands, he left his father sitting in his backyard in a chair under the tree that he loved so much. That would be the last time Jerry ever saw his dad. Three days after he arrived back in Los Angeles, he received a phone call from his brother, Doran, telling him that he had taken their father to the hospital for some X-rays. Oscar called Muluk from the hospital, thanked his wife for all she'd done for him, and then died from heart failure.

Jerry felt for him. Although he had the opportunity to be with his dad one last time and to take care of him, this did not change his pain, as they had been extremely close. Now he knew he'd have to live with this pain in his heart for the rest of his life. How do you cope with the death of a loved one, and especially of your parents? Are there any words of comfort that will change your suffering? The ache is so deep, and there are no words to describe the grief and sense of loss. The recovery has an unknown path—how many days, months, or years it will take can't be predicted.

You will try to imagine his face by closing your eyes, holding his image in your mind, and trying to keep it forever. A parent symbolizes a mentor, the person who guides you in life, someone inside our own self, and an extension of yourself, like an organ of your body. The feeling of abandonment will immediately show on the surface. It will hurt, and hurt profoundly. It's part of the life cycle of any living creature; humans know that we are born, grow older, and finish that cycle by dying. But are you really prepared for this? How do you accept it? Will you ever accept it?

When do you go inside yourself and tell yourself that this was the expected path? And in the back of your mind, you know that it will eventually happen. You know there is that possibility all the time, but you want loved ones to be next to you the rest of your life, and they will be—at least in your heart.

Jerry was far away in a new land, and he had just left his father a few days before. He could not go back to Israel again for the funeral. This was only a formality, but it made him extremely sad to not be able to hold his mom in this difficult moment. His pain was hard to explain. He could not share it with anyone. He didn't want Dina to become sad, so he kept working hard. He just kept going and going, holding his grief inside of himself.

Bayron came from Guatemala to Los Angles and knocked on many doors looking for a job. He knew no English. He was extremely young looking, and people would tell him he should go to school first, but all he wanted was a job...

Part III

Seven Steps to Success

Success? Only with a thick skin to resist rejections and challenges.
With time, your fiber will develop and make you thrive.

Chapter Eight

Family Arrives

G rowing a business is a tremendous job. Making it develop on its own without an infusion of capital is even harder. It takes longer to make a profit and you're more vulnerable to situations, such as lack of liquidity. It's a risk not everyone can handle, and a real moment of truth. Being subjected to pressure when there's a shortage of money shows the fiber a leader must have in order to navigate these waters and find the clarity to keep on going.

Capital provides stronger negotiating muscle. It provides the strength to go to your suppliers, buy more volume, and, use your bargaining power to get a better rate. This gives your company a bigger profit margin without having to raise prices. At this point, you'll have the power to ask your suppliers to help you expand.

Weeks after Jerry returned from his trip to Israel to see Oscar, one of his helpers disappeared. When Jerry left, he'd arranged for assistants to keep his operation going in his absence, one in charge of each of their zones, with Mario Romero overseeing them. Mario had done his job perfectly, and Miguel Aguilar—another of Jerry's first helpers, also from El Salvador—had completed all his tasks.

Jorge, a salesperson from Guatemala, was very sharp and helpful, but had mysteriously vanished. Jorge told Mario that his wife was sick, but what no one knew was that he'd collected payments from customers on behalf of the company and had not turned them in. The following week, once Jerry was back, he went to collect the payments in Jorge's area, only to encounter many customers claiming they'd already paid for their latest installment. They produced receipts, signed by Jorge, to back them up. What a shock! Jerry was not prepared for this. He had trusted Jorge, as he had done with all of his customers and employees.

The situation was painful. When a customer said they'd already paid, Jerry initially thought he/she was lying and could not believe what he was hearing. But as more and more clients told him the same story, Jerry realized they couldn't all be lying. How would he know the truth, who had really paid and who was taking advantage of the situation? Some customers claimed they paid but had no proof of payment. These receipts were very specific. Each had a box in the bottom listing the amount of the purchase, the down payment, and then four lines detailing the monthly payments and their dates, with three copies per receipt. Jerry kept the original, and one copy was given to the customer. Jerry kept the books, organized them by building or address, and used them to prepare the collection routes.

Some customers in Jorge's territory trusted him and paid in good faith. Being naïve, they didn't ask for any proof that they'd paid their monthly installment or down payment for new merchandise. Jerry started receiving complaints from many customers that they'd given down payments for products but had not received their merchandise. Jerry estimated the loss was $16,000—a very big amount for a small company like Jerry's Interex and very hard to swallow when you're just starting a business.

Any small business loss can turn your operation completely upside down, to the point where many companies fall apart. Employee theft is a major problem for any company, and it's estimated that twenty-five to forty percent of all employees steal from their employers. The U.S. Department of Commerce estimates that employee theft—of merchandise, property, and cash—may cost American businesses $50 billion annually.

Even small businesses with owners who create a family-oriented atmosphere, where all employees are known by their first names, aren't immune to these thefts. Employers believe that creating this familial environment protects the company because workers will feel like they're part of an extended family, but the employee might not see it the same way. Any misunderstanding between the boss and the staffer may provoke retaliation, not merely by stealing, but even by destroying merchandise.

In small businesses, assigning multiple responsibilities to the same employee is very common; however, this increases the probability of the employee committing a crime. Owners believe that by creating a close relationship with their employees, they're increasing loyalty, while the employee might see stealing as an additional payback or unofficial compensation for their work. In many cases, employees who don't steal know who is stealing but won't inform on the culprit, due to social pressures and because they move in the same circles.

Companies believe that by creating a policy or a list of rules, they are controlling these actions. However, many studies show that employee theft is one of the biggest challenges companies face. Many small businesses go bankrupt because of internal losses that aren't caught in time, or regulations that aren't specific enough. Many companies find the employee stealing and let them go without bringing him or her to justice, thus setting a poor example for the rest of their workforce.

Jerry had to put on a brave face and keep going. He had to maintain his good reputation as an honest businessman in the neighborhood. He analyzed each customer's situation case by case, asked for receipts, and if they didn't have any, he did not honor all of their unproven claims. Based on their track records, Jerry made good on the claims of trustworthy customers he'd known for years and who'd always paid on time, even if they didn't have the documentation to prove it. In the case of new customers, he said that although they didn't have any record of the down payment, he was going to recognize only half of what they said they had paid and get them the product, if they were able to pay more money for a down payment. He individually worked with each customer, trying to handle the situation the best way he could, He attempted to reduce his losses to a minimum while still retaining their loyalty as customers.

Jerry's company was named Interex (International Export) and was located at North Laurel Avenue and Santa Monica Boulevard in West Hollywood. It was very small, with only 500 square feet. The whole purpose of the office was to have a mailing address and warehouse space. Because he was a door-to-door salesman, there wasn't any retail space.

Jerry was starting to learn Spanish, and the first word he learned was *mañana*, which some customers used when he came to collect a payment. He figured it out because the person would tell him mañana and stay still, instead of going inside to get the payment. With their hands, they'd make a gesture indicating that they would pay later. He heard mañana often, and soon he was repeating it, too.

The word mañana does not refer to a Swiss Band of the '70s, the name of many songs by Latino singers, the name of a tango, a German Rock Band, a Hawaiian isle, an island near the state of Maine, or a Spanish newspaper; it is not even tequila or a restaurant. It means tomorrow. The mañana culture is similar to the mañana attitude, in United Kingdom the term refers to the irregular practice of workers' when they lose interest in their jobs. The mañana culture consists of leaving for tomorrow what could be done today. Understanding and identifying this cultural characteristic was important for Jerry. In order for him to communicate better with his customers, he had to learn to comprehend their culture and language, so he could organize his resources. He knew that the money he was collecting enabled him to pay his vendors and workers, and also provided for his own needs.

When you're taking your first step toward opening up a business, make sure you know who you're going to target, what your niche is, and the segment of the market that you'll be offering your products or services to. Jerry visited his customers, observed how they lived, how many kids they had, what kind of toys they had, where they worked, and where they came from. Always courteous, helpful, and informative, Jerry was creating his brand: a way of doing business molded around his customers and their needs.

His personal presentation was very important to him. He was clean cut, his clothing washed and well ironed. Having been trained by the military for so long, his appearance and that of the people who worked for him remain essential components of his brand, and this is still true today. Jerry made sure that he always projected a professional persona, enhancing his customers' perception of his trust and confidence. He has always required that his salespeople look and smell clean, and that they dress and act professionally.

What are the seven steps that turned Jerry's twenty dollars into an actual business? We'll share them one by one throughout the pages of these chapters. The first one was identifying who he was going to sell to. When he started knocking on doors and finding his customers, he observed them as he went from home to home, apartment to apartment. They all had similar social and economic characteristics and, in particular, a need for the products he was selling them.

He immediately smelled the opportunities this group of people had for his business model, and knew he had to continue offering different products. He knew their needs. He was building his brand; he was being identified by his customers by what he sold and how he sold it. Jerry was building a brand identity. Costumers knew what to expect when they did business with him.

It's interesting and flattering to hear people say your product appeals to everybody, but this doesn't mean you really know who your customer is. It could even cause you problems down the line, especially when you start advertising in the media. You might lose your investment because you are targeting the wrong demographic. Businesses invest in advertising all the time and wonder why their results are not the ones they expected. Is your message clear? Is your offer aggressive enough? Is your advertising platform directed to the right target, the right niche, the right segment of the market?

Jerry's best advertising tool was word of mouth, unsolicited personal referrals from customers recommending him to their families and friends. His service was convenient, the product was of great value to his customers, and they did not need to go anywhere to buy the products. He would come to their home. Free advertising is often the best kind.

One of the apartment buildings Jerry visited was extremely dark. The halls were scary and spooky, the lights did not work, and the only light came from the building entrance. Furthermore, the halls were full of trash and smelled terribly. Jerry was thinking twice about knocking on doors in this building when a guy came out of nowhere, and asked him what he wanted.

At first, the man, who was named Raul, scared him because he looked dirty, hadn't showered in days, and his breath smelled of liquor. In a low tone, Jerry explained that he was selling TVs and stereos door-to-door for small monthly payments. As Raul took him to his apartment, Jerry feared he was going to be assaulted. When Raul got to his apartment, he opened the door, and the place was empty; he was sleeping on the floor and didn't have any furniture in the rooms. Raul wanted a TV, asked Jerry how much it cost, and gave him cash for it. The next day Jerry returned with the television and, as Raul did not have any place to set it up, he told Jerry to put it on the floor.

Just as Jerry had left behind his life in the military, Raul, too, had his stories of war and destruction in a small country in Central America. The confrontation between the social classes and the military government were changing the history of El Salvador and its people, including in the small town that Raul was from. One Sunday he had a few drinks, but was ready, as usual, to go to work on Monday and start his week. Once he arrived at his job, Raul was told he was fired, and that there was no more work. When he asked why, he was told the guerrillas had taken the owner and killed him, and no one could run the business except for the owner.

Raul went back to his home—if you could call his one room house a home— where, from the inside, he could see the outside because of all the slits in between the walls. The wood did not match and holes were everywhere. There were no options for him now. He had a family to take care of and no job. His neighbors were preparing to go to El Norte to look for a job in the States.

He decided to join them in this desperate adventure because there were no choices open to him in El Salvador. In his home country, the internal strife caused by the civil war was killing everyone. The confrontation between the rich and the poor pitted the military-led government against the Farabundo Marti National Liberation Front. The FMLN was an umbrella of leftist organizations which created a guerilla group organized as a military front. All of these violent confrontations made many run away for safety, as there was no alternative: you were for the guerillas or you were in favor of the government.

Every day, the army (and well known death squads) went into neighborhoods and took anyone that looked suspicious away from their homes and then disappeared them; nobody knew where they had gone. Anyone could be accused of distributing propaganda for the guerillas, and the military would come and take the suspect away. In some towns, guerillas came and forced everyone to join them. There was no choice. You could be killed on the spot if you didn't cooperate.

A month after asking the U.S. government to stop supporting the El Salvadoran military, and one day after asking Salvadoran soldiers not to follow their superiors' orders to kill more innocent people, Archbishop Oscar Romero was killed while saying mass in a small chapel at a cancer hospice in San Salvador in 1980. During Romero's funeral a week later, the military posted snipers in buildings around the National Cathedral and the Gerardo Barrios Plaza, shooting and killing fifty mourners in a massacre.

The United States supported the El Salvadoran government, since President Ronald Regan saw the guerilla as the possible start of communism in the region, with the possibility of bringing it closer to the American borders. Meanwhile, the FMLN received support from Cuban leader Fidel Castro. The estimated amount of people killed in El Salvador's civil war was 75,000—more deaths than the Six Day War and the Yom Kippur War combined. The guerillas were destroying bridges, and burning down factories and coffee plantations. Many workers lost jobs every day.

Raul had no money or food to take with him, but given the violence tormenting El Salvador, when his neighbors decided to flee, they convinced him to join them and he started the long journey north. It took them many days and nights to walk to the border to Mexico. Once there, they hopped a freight train and traveled on the roof. Everyone was from the same town, and they shared the small pieces of bread and little water they had. Once at the border of the United States, the real battle started. They couldn't hire a "coyote" because they didn't have money. Instead, the villagers followed a man who had been deported several times and was heading back to the States and knew his way around. They had to walk during the night, as it was more secure. At night, it was harder for the border patrols to find and detain them.

Many Salvadoran citizens moved to Los Angeles and were living in downtown L.A. Most were able to make it after days and nights of seemingly endless walking, with little-to-no water or food, and the hope that on the other side, there would be a helping hand to offer them somewhere to stay and a job.

These were the people in the neighborhood where Jerry had been knocking on doors when he met Raul. After setting up his TV, Raul took Jerry on a tour of the entire building, going door to door with him until the entire neighborhood was buying products. Jerry worked in these buildings for several weeks with Raul close to him every day. Jerry told the Salvadoran that he had to clean himself up, stop drinking, and cut his hair if he wanted to work for him. Raul was forty-five years old and his hair had already turned grey. He was an extremely nice individual, willing to help everyone. Although he was intimidating at first, once you got to know him, he had a profoundly deep and charming personality. People in this neighborhood loved Raul. He'd cook rice and beans, put them on his plate with cheese and tortillas, and share with everyone. He loved to eat with others instead of alone.

Raul listened to Jerry, accepted all of the good things Jerry suggested, and started changing by cleaning himself up. Once he became an employee, he started saving money in order to bring his wife and three kids to L.A. He knew that if he drank any liquor Jerry would send him home, so he started controlling his drinking problem. He became Jerry's bodyguard, driver, salesperson, warehouse guard, deliveryman, and electronics supervisor. People followed Jerry's lead, admiring his intelligence and perseverance.

The product sold by Jerry and his employees had to be delivered to the customers home. When the merchandise was big like furniture or a big TV you needed at least two people. Raul was the delivery man. In many occasions, Raul will go by himself, even when it was a big item he definitely knew he needed help with. He'd ask the customer that was receiving the delivery to help him take the unit up the stairs or carry it into the apartment. With his charm, Raul would always get a "yes" from people, and this reduced the cost of the delivery for the small company.

Jerry saw an opportunity to sell his business. He thought that by selling Interex, he could raise some capital and then start a bigger company in another city. He placed a free ad in the *Recycler*, an advertising magazine of classified ads for individuals and businesses. The day after Jerry posted his ad, a Filipino businessman came to make him an offer.

The Filipino opened a briefcase to pay with cash and Jerry sold Interex for $20,000. Jerry gave him all of the catalogs he had created, introduced him to all the people who worked for him, and gave him a map of his territory in Los Angeles. However, Jerry shrewdly did not sell the inventory he had on hand or the account receivables of all of his customers. This way, Jerry could start his new business in other areas where he could sell to the same type of customers, but under another company name.

Two weeks after selling his business, Jerry got a call from the now third owner of Interex, he had bought the company for $500,000 from the second owner.

Jerry was amazed by these negotiations; he wanted to understand what they were doing and the gentleman explained it to him. Their goal was to qualify as investors in order to secure a U.S. visa. They had to prove they had a business in the U.S., which is why they bought Interex from Jerry.

Obtaining an E-2 Investor Visa requires proving a substantial investment in a business in the States; it's a nonimmigrant visa it's considered to be a trade visa. In the information you could read from the USCIS - United State Citizenship and Immigration Services for this kind of visa, the amount of money needed to qualify for an E-2 is not disclosed. It is usually between $100,000 and $150,000 at that time, and the money invested in the business needs to be committed for the business only.

The country of the person asking for the E-2 Visa must have an appropriate treaty with the United States in order for its people to be eligible for this trade visa. The U.S. consulate in the country of origin reviews all of the paperwork, and if it's granted, the visa holder receives a green card for himself or herself and his or her family.

The business in question must demonstrate that it can provide sufficient resources and revenues to support the investor and his family, and that it will create jobs for American employees. The business presented by the parties seeking the visa has to be in operation and documentation must be presented to demonstrate solvency. Furthermore, the foreign investor has to prove that the money allocated for the business is his own. The bureaucratic process requires lots of paperwork and has to be presented to the U.S. embassy in the country of residence for the person applying for the visa.

Jerry learned that the new owners were planning to move from the Philippines to Los Angeles. The new owner asked Jerry to help them run the operation. But several days later, he called back to say their visa had not been approved. Meanwhile, Interex's salespeople were frantically calling Jerry to tell him that the sales had not been delivered, that customers needed help; they did not know what to do and were asking Jerry what was going to happen to the business. Jerry had to come to the rescue!

Jerry felt an obligation to his people, and knew that the new owner was not going to operate the business. His employees and customers needed his help. He contacted the new owner, who told Jerry that he was not interested in continuing

March of 1978, first office/showroom in West Hollywood.
So small that we could take pictures only from the outside.

the business. The new owner signed a document allowing Jerry to continue to run Interex.

Jerry started his business operation again and moved to an apartment in Burbank. Dina was studying psychology and his mom came to visit him in the U.S. What a great moment for him! Now Muluk could cook all of his favorite food and would be great company for Dina.

Muluk was single and still very healthy and full of energy. Jerry told her that he knew how much she loved his dad but that she couldn't stay by herself, that she must open up her heart again and find a loved one. Company was essential at her age, and living alone was not healthy. He told her that all her kids were grown up and living their own lives and she had to give herself another chance at love. She had shown loyalty to her husband all of her life and this would not change anything about her past. It was going to be a second opportunity for her.

Under Jewish law, Jews are allowed to divorce, which is recognized as a fact of life. Jews believe no one has to live with another person if that person is not right for them. It's an unfortunate situation, but divorce is a reality. Where there is no love or connection, there's no reason to continue the relationship. At the same time, divorce eliminates bitterness among partners. In the Jewish religion, the divorced parties are allowed to remarry, and in that same way, a widow can remarry, too. However, divorce is not accepted in the Catholic religion, and anyone who'd remarry following a divorce could not have an actual religious ceremony in the Catholic Church—although a widow could. In the Muslim religion, widows are also allowed to remarry.

All families that follow the Law of Judaism are obligated to extend respect and love to the spouse of their parents, and likewise for the new spouse towards the stepchildren. The stepparent and stepchildren must follow the Hebrew proverb *ve'ahavta* (you shall love). It's the framework for the new family to make their relationship work and to find benefits for both the children and the new spouse. Rabbis always recommend that the children and new spouse need to look for acceptance in order to enrich the families. In addition to all of these Torah recommendations, the new spouse must respect the memory of the deceased spouse.

Muluk remained full of life, and her conversations with Jerry opened up ideas in her mind and heart that she had not explored before. She had learned to love Oscar and their family. They had passed together through so much; all of their struggles had united them and made them a tight knit family. She had been next to Oscar during all of his sickness, serving him with love and kindness. Now it was time for her to think of herself, and she really didn't want to stay alone. She did not know what the future had in store for her, but she knew that her son's recommendations were right.

When Muluk returned to Israel, Jerry took her to LAX and told her that she should open her heart and to remember that he'd always look after her and respect her decision. Whenever she was ready, he'd help her find the right match. She agreed with him and left for Israel. Jerry knew there was a widower in New York who'd lost his wife several years ago and was the perfect match for his mom, but he'd wait until she agreed to remarry. Nothing would work if it was forced and not by mutual agreement.

Muluk went back to Israel with the idea of finding someone to marry. One night, while she was sleeping, thieves broke into her home and stole all of her valuable rugs and jewels. The next morning she woke up to discover the terrible news. To this day, she believes that the thieves made her breathe in something to make her sleep deeper so that she wouldn't hear them inside the house. This was a warning, she thought, of what could happen to her if she continued living by herself.

Friends and neighbors introduced her to Jacob, a decent, charming man who was an entertainer. He played the tar, an instrument with a long neck and double bowl shaped body believed to have been invented in the 18th century. It's an instrument that is very common in Iran, where the word *tar* is Persian for string. Some consider it to be one of the origins of the guitar.

Afraid to live alone, Muluk was in a rush to find a companion after the robbery, and soon she and Jacob fell in love and got married. Muluk went to live with Jacob and rented out her house. Within a few months, they decided to live in the United States near Jerry, and they moved to an apartment building in L.A.'s Fairfax District.

Jacob's relationship with Muluk was always very controlling. He was jealous of her. He'd never been married before and didn't let his wife do anything. Muluk was a pleaser who wanted to make everyone happy. But one day she showed up at Jerry's house and told him she felt like a slave and couldn't handle it any more. Jerry talked to Jacob. He and Muluk got divorced and the musician went back to Israel.

Jerry started his new business under the name of West Coast Catalog, using the catalogs of UNIDEN, a catalog company that sold at wholesale prices with margins of forty to fifty percent. This was perfect for Jerry because it had a variety of products and the pictures in the catalogs confirmed that they had the product in stock. This reduced the challenges they'd encountered earlier of selling products that were no longer available or discontinued. The profit margin gave them enough money to still pay employees their fifteen percent commission. The operation was conducted in Burbank at San Fernando Road and Palm Avenue in the Golden Mall. It was a beautiful store, with enough space for both retail and a warehouse, but mainly used to display products and train salespeople.

Jerry bought a car. A lime green Pontiac that he loved, which reminded him of all the American movies he'd seen in the past, before coming to California. The Pontiac was designed by General Motors to compete in the market with Chevrolet Camaros and Ford Mustangs. GM started manufacturing them in 1967 and several versions were built throughout the years. Jerry's car was from the second generation of Pontiacs, and it had a distinctive nose. Jerry also bought a Volkswagen van, which contained samples of his products plus catalogs. He also used the minivan to bring his salesmen to Burbank for training sessions.

One of Jerry's customers owed him $150, and when Jerry went to collect the monthly installment, he said he had no money. In lieu of cash, the client offered him his motorcycle. Jerry checked it out, discovered it wasn't working and would need to be repaired, but that it was worth more than the $150 debt. So, Jerry agreed to take it instead of a payment and brought a truck to pick it up. He worked on it and fixed it, then gave Mario Romero a big goal to accomplish. After Mario achieved his goal, Jerry gave him the motorcycle as a bonus.

Jerry's brother's business in Israel was not going well. Cash flow was very low and Ron was at the edge of bankruptcy. All the money he had inherited from his parents was gone. Jerry flew immediately to Israel to see if he could save the business but it was too late and it was time to shut it down. At this point, Muluk asked Jerry to help his brother. Jerry wanted to alleviate his mom's concerns so he offered Ron not only the chance to come to America but also fifty percent of his company.

The rest of the Azarkman family back in Israel started visiting Jerry in Los Angeles. His brothers saw Jerry's life in the States and wondered about living with him. Now Muluk was in L.A. by herself, giving them another reason to move to America. They loved California: the weather, the food, the beach, and all of the opportunities they might lose out on by staying in Israel.

Jerry had convinced his brother Ron to move to the U.S.A. He arrived with a tourist visa, so Jerry recommended that he modify it to a business visa. He had to sell the business in Israel before coming to the States, but the economy in Israel was shaky—the wars had left great instability and it was hard for them to recover.

Jerry had already created his corporation in the United States, named Adir International Export, and he had worked with two DBAs (Doing Business As): Interex (he had recovered all his papers back from the Filipino) and West Coast Catalog. Jerry modified his already established corporation in Los Angeles to add his brother as a partner with fifty percent of the company not asking for anything in return.

Jerry was extremely happy to have his younger brother coming to live with them in California. Ron and his wife moved close to Jerry, in Burbank. He started his own stereo speaker business, building the speakers from scratch in his factory and working on everything on his own.

Doron, Jerry's older brother, decided to request residential papers before immigrating to the States. Therefore, he took longer to come and join the family, but was the first one to have the correct papers for living in the U.S. He started a movie rental business, buying a movie on Betamax or VHS for fifty dollars and renting it out for two dollars per day. He did not like help from his brothers and wanted to do it all on his own. Once, when the brothers bought some movies for him on his birthday, Doron got very mad.

Doron had been a fearless soldier on the Yom Kippur war. He was a sniper, shooting at his targets from tankers. When the tanker would stop working, he would fix it from parts of other tankers and continue shooting the enemy. He even crossed the Suez Canal to Egypt.

Doron kept his movie rental business and decided he wanted to also open a 99 Cents Only Store between Catalina Street and Pico Boulevard in Los Angeles. Before opening day, in the last hours of remodeling, Doron was working at his new business when he suffered a heart attack. He died that same day at noon, leaving behind his wife Lea, a son Ami, and a daughter Betty.

Muluk could not accept what happened. Nature's way is for the offspring to deal with the death of their parents, not the other way around. It was extremely hard for her, and she felt sorrow, pain, and anger. Blaming herself, she kept saying she'd done something bad and that was the reason why God took Doron from her. He wanted to punish her. It was an unexpected situation for all, but especially for her. When she'd lost her husband, she knew something like that could happen, as he was thirty-seven years older than she, even though she never thought about the age difference. But not her son. It was too much for Muluk to lose her own son at such an early age, when he was ready to start a second business, and was so enthusiastic about all of his work. She'd seen how successful he was with his operations. He was leaving behind his family, a wife and two kids.

Jerry got the call telling him that his brother was being taken to the hospital in an ambulance from one of Doron's employees. One of Jerry's toy vendors arrived at his place and told him he was there when it happened and that it took the paramedics forty minutes to come, while Doron was lying on the floor. Finally, they took him to the hospital but he was already gone. Minutes later, the hospital called the family to tell them they had to come and identify him.

It was devastating for the entire family, especially for Jerry, who loved his big brother immensely. To this very day, Jerry still has all of his brother's videos, the original movies he used to rent in his business. Doron was a heavy smoker and drinker of Turkish coffee, with high cholesterol who always complained about not sleeping well, and he passed away because of clogged arteries. Another reason for his failing health was the stress brought on by the war. When he moved to the U.S., Doron had borrowed money from Jerry, and a week before he passed away; he had paid every single penny back to his kid brother.

When they had been kids, their mom would assign Doron to play with his brothers as if he was their father, to help her out with the three of them. But what Muluk didn't know was that Doron would beat them up and treat them like slaves, too, so in those days they were not close. It was only after Jerry went to the military academy that Doron started writing letters to Jerry and they became really close.

Now they knew that they had to be very careful. This was a real eye opener for the entire family—heart disease ran in their family. They would have to check their hearts regularly to avoid any other fatal deaths in the family. Jerry knew he would take care of Doron's family, and they'd be part of him more than ever.

As a mother, Muluk knew this feeling of loss would never leave her heart; she loved Doron, her oldest son, whom she had chased in between the crowds, following him, when he had to represent the family for the Day of Ashura, back in Varamin, Iran. She could still see him in her mind's eye with that stream of blood running down his shoulder and back. She remembered him playing, when she took him to school. She would never forget him.

Jerry decided to sell his business in Burbank to an Armenian immigrant for $60,000 for the same reason the Filipinos had bought it: he was seeking an E-2 Investor Visa. Muluk was already living near them in Burbank, between Glenoaks and Magnolia Boulevard, very close to the store and Jerry's apartment.

A New York relative of the Azarkmans was getting married. The father of the groom was a widower who lived in Canada. He met Muluk at the wedding and the following week he sent a messenger to Jerry because he was interested in marrying Muluk. His mother told Jerry that it all depended on his character. She was not interested in money, only that he had a good personality. The match was perfect and they soon got married.

Meanwhile, Jerry had made enough money to open his new business. He asked his brother to join him, with nothing in return and they rented a small showcase for Fisher and Sanyo electronics and Bulova watches. The location would be at 1605 West Olympic Boulevard, in front of a Bank of America. Mario Romero was extremely happy, as they were closer to where everything had started for Jerry. It was a Latino neighborhood and now his salespeople lived only blocks away from them.

1978 last quarter in Burbank Golden Mall. This was Jerry's second store after selling the first one in Hollywood.

Chapter Nine

Growing a Family

C ustomers are always looking for a good deal, always checking prices. They look for what they want or need to buy, but in reality, the best price and quality determines their purchase. Sometimes it's not even what they want to buy or need to buy, it doesn't matter where they can get it either. They are looking for the best deal. Customer loyalty is very hard to keep. Nowadays, keeping your customers and making them come back to you for more is an everyday task that's harder and harder to accomplish. In a competitive society, like the one we live in, everyone is competing to grab the public's attention and bring them into their store or to purchase their services. Retaining customer loyalty is becoming an everyday quest for the answer to the eternal question: "What is in it for me?" Customer loyalty is turning into an extinct species.

It's a free ocean where everyone has a rod and fishing is the daily mission—especially in our high tech, wired, online age of e-commerce. It doesn't matter if the fish is already hanging from someone else's hook; your fishing line could still be stronger than your competitor. Or you can still steal a fish from your competitor. All businesses are trying to capture the customer's eyes in order to make the potential patron take a risk on them. Once in your store or on your website and they notice what you have to offer, they might discover something that they didn't know you carried—but if they don't buy, at least they'll keep you in mind the next time they shop.

What makes customers become repeat customers? What propels your store or service to the top of your customer's list? How can you keep the traffic rate growing all the time? How can your traffic rate to transaction ratio stay consistent (at least from year to year) or even grow? Every business, no matter the size, has to track these elements in order to understand fully what they did last year on the same dates. This allows the business to create similar activities that continue bringing traffic and increase daily.

Jerry had created his own brand. He was very well known in the neighborhood, and customers would come back for repeat purchases. They'd purchase more and more merchandise with the credit he provided. He had created a way of doing business that gave his customers reliability and trust. Creating this relationship with them had to be done not only by him, but by his employees, too. Jerry had to transmit this ethos to his employees, training them for even the most basic elements in order to keep consistent with the brand he was creating. Some examples included: the way to talk to customers, the tone of voice to use when approaching them, how to explain features and benefits, how to give details clearly as to what was included in the price, as well as always appearing clean and well dressed.

He had specific ways to demonstrate the product, calculate the down payment, and collect payments. His employees had to have many things in common, starting with being extremely helpful to the customer, being able to connect with the customer, and making the customer feel that they're in the best hands. Jerry also created competition among the employees—a contest of good manners, friendly sales, and of well-groomed associates. Some of his door-to-door salesmen had the challenge of revisiting customers whose negotiations had begun with Jerry, and it was harder to sell to them. The customers would ask to talk to Jerry, who they preferred to buy directly from.

Jerry would explain to each employee his beliefs about what customers mean to him. For Jerry, a business' *raison d'etre* has to always be, first and foremost, the interest of the customer. Putting the customer's needs first keeps that business in the consumer's mind. Any company that puts the customer first will keep expanding its rate of customer loyalty.

Customers who continue buying products or services signify that you're doing something right. Customers have options and opportunities everywhere. Jerry's customers had only one place to obtain credit, but that doesn't mean that they didn't have cash; they could save money and purchase from some other business. They returned because the service they received exceeded expectations: they found additional value for their purchases.

What makes your store different than the store next door is not only the color you paint the walls or the way your products are displayed. You might have the exact same TV set your competitors have. What makes the difference in your customers' eyes? Your employees make the difference.

Jerry would explain the importance of good customer service in his training for new employees. They had to look for solid interaction with the customer and a relationship that would last forever. How can you keep your customers and make them come back and buy again? He'd always tell them his theory about creating a connection with the customer. It was like giving each customer an engagement ring. Why do you give a ring to a woman when you want to marry her? And why does a woman accept it? The act of giving an engagement ring is a formal agreement for a future marriage. The ring is worn on the finger containing the *vena amoris* or vein of love, believing it's the finger closest to the heart.

This is an act of love that they'll both remember forever, reminding them of their love and promise to each other. The ring becomes a symbol of love and care, and a reminder that their relationship must last. There is a connection between both parties that has to work. There will be exciting moments in the relationship and not so exciting ones, but in the end, a lasting relationship will show how strong the connection is.

How does Jerry tie this analogy to credit? His belief that giving credit to someone is similar to giving an engagement ring is because both represent lifelong relationships between people. Jerry was giving his customer the credit to buy products in four installments and was providing the goods they needed. The customer now would have the product and the need to pay for it. Why the need? The customer knew that it was an opportunity for them because if they continued paying, their credit would continue to be good and their line of credit would eventually increase so that they could continue to buy more products.

In this relationship, both are trying to do everything perfectly. In the case the product is defective, for example, the customer may never do business with you again, and the rupture could be forever (especially if he or she doesn't feel properly compensated). On the other hand, the customer still has needs to be fulfilled with the next purchase. For both parties' needs have to be satisfied and the relationship to work, both sides receive the benefits of their agreement.

How does a customer need to be treated to feel happy to return again and again to your business? We are all victims of the term customer service. Sometimes we're happy about it and sometimes we're not. The often heard definition of this word is, "Customer service is a series of activities designed to enhance the level of customer satisfaction—that is, the feeling that a product or service has met the customer expectation" (Turban, Lee, King, & Chung, 2002, p. 87). Customer service will affect the income of any business; it plays an essential role in customers continuing to do business with you. If you fail in fulfilling any of the customer's expectations, guess what? They'll look for another place to buy from and give their hard earned money to a competitor. One must never underestimate the value and importance of timely, respectful customer service that treats people like human beings.

In Jerry's environment, his customers had strong needs and they could only receive credit to obtain products from Jerry. They were an underserved, neglected segment of society; financial institutions were not offering any other options to this group of people. This could have been an excuse for Jerry to do a sloppy job because, hey, they needed him anyway.

But Jerry wanted customers to keep on buying and buying from him. His enterprise was growing and needed to have new customers, and these customers needed to be loyal customers who referred additional new customers to the expanding business. Jerry and his associates had to be courteous and helpful, always giving patrons more than they expected. He was creating great customer service experiences that gave satisfaction to his customers and meet their standards.

Jerry had moved his operation to downtown Los Angeles and was now working with his brother, at Olympic Boulevard between Union and Beacon. The building was owned by two Jewish partners, Harry Bain and Paul Feder, who had built it and bought all the surrounding properties. Their plan was to create the Olympic Union Center, with a walk through area across a property full of gardens. Feder bought out his partner and became the sole proprietor of Fab Enterprises. The ninety-two year old has two sons, Don and Steven, who still own properties in this area.

Their outfit was in a very small location, smaller than 2,000 square feet, in between two major financial institutions—Bank of America and Crocker National Bank (the latter was eventually bought by Wells Fargo). This was a busy metropolitan area with great natural traffic; Jerry went on to create events to attract customers during weekends, when the building's offices were mostly closed. He'd buy a twenty pound sack of onions in downtown L.A.'s produce market for a dime, slice the bulbs into rings, and fry them in a large pan with olive oil; once the onions were caramelized, he'd add hot dogs and cook them for a while. The smell would travel for blocks, serving as aromatic advertising. Jerry then put the onions and hot dogs into buns and served them with fruit punch to customers visiting the store, giving them free meals every weekend.

Saturdays and Sundays were like parties; speakers were placed outside of the store and Latino music was played as loudly as possible. The food, the smell, and the music made a great combination that boosted foot traffic. Many people shopped on weekends. Car stereos and audio boxes were sold for $169, and it included free installation, speakers, and an antenna—and all the hot dogs you could eat! The only day for installations was Sundays. Jerry remembers doing the installations by himself, and the line of cars on Sundays became so long that he had to ask his door-to-door salespeople to come help him back at the store in order to be able to finish serving so many customers.

They sold so many products from the store's audio line; including car stereos and portable boom boxes, as well as TVs, that the store looked empty on Mondays. Customers came especially for the stereos—one of the hottest products for the store. Salespeople competed to sell the same amount as Jerry, and they'd watch how he treated customers on the floor and his selling strategies.

The Azarkman brothers had searched all over the Olympic Boulevard and Alvarado Street area in Downtown L.A., where they really wanted to open their operation, but there were no spaces available there. The building at 1625 Olympic Blvd. was the only location they could find, so they signed a one-year lease. However, they started getting complaints every week because of their weekend activities: the building management would complain about cooking on the premises and loud music. In addition, the store did not have any parking for customers, which is a major issue in urban L.A., with its car culture. The brothers had no option but to start looking for a new space.

Within walking distance they discovered a sign on 1313 Olympic Boulevard for a space to rent. The owner wanted to open a restaurant but could not get the permits from the city to do so. Jerry spoke to him but he kept changing the price on the lease, so Ron told Jerry to let him deal with the property owner. However, when Ron spoke with him, there was no chemistry between them, and now the building owner did not want to rent to them at all. It was a difficult situation; they needed a space but there were no rentals in the area. The only one available was the one they were currently in. Jerry called the owner again and they agreed to renew negotiations. He came back with a five-year contract and they moved the store to 1313 Olympic Boulevard with 8,000 square feet.

All of the struggles Jerry and Dina had gone through had taken their marriage in two different directions. Jerry concentrated on his business, while Dina focused on her studies. Life took them apart and they divorced but ended up remaining just friends.

How do you know when your marriage is going down the drain? What are the symptoms of a troubled marriage? What are the areas you must pay more attention to? There are many recommendations from experts on this topic.

When the main symptoms of a future break up emerge, if the parties do not act aggressively to correct them, the relationship starts to die and there is no way back. Cathy Meyer, a Marriage Educator and Certified Divorce Coach, frequently mentions in her writings there are seven warning signs any couple that wants to stay together needs to analyze and determine if these things are happening.

The first symptom is living in silence, with no common topics or activities to share with each other. The second is when one of the spouses sees the other's defects all the time, watching and criticizing every act the other one does. The third is when one of the spouses is the last one to know what the other wants or does, a spouse who hears about it secondhand, perhaps from a mutual friend. The fourth is when there's a lack of interest in dressing (or undressing!) to attract the other spouse, gaining weight, and not taking frequent showers, etc. The fifth is looking for distractions from the real problems. The sixth one is arguing over the same subject without any resolution; they feel the marriage is standing still or dying fast. And the seventh and most important one is intimacy with one another, particularly sex.

Jerry had worked so hard putting his business together and worked from morning to night, seven days a week. Meanwhile, Dina had dedicated all of her time and energy to accomplishing her dream of starting a career in psychology. Time was an issue for both, one dedicating so much to making the business successful and the other one attending and studying for a college career, and they had less time to spend together. Both had different interests, and their lives diverged onto separate paths.

Patricia was a Latina who lived in the same neighborhood that Jerry worked in. One of the door-to-door associates knocked on her door and showed her a catalog. She knew her father's birthday was coming up and she saw a cigarette holder that captured her attention. It was the perfect gift for her dad. She gave the salesperson the down payment and waited for the gift to be delivered the following day.

However, once the order was placed with Jerry, he found out that this particular product did not exist anymore. The salesperson went back to Patricia and told her she had to reselect another item. She got furious and told him, "You sold it to me, now you go get it." Jerry found substitutes and gave them to the sales associate, who brought her three different types of cigarette holders the next day. But Patricia insisted and insisted that she had paid the down payment and they had to find her the exact same cigarette holder she had preselected.

She didn't stop there and decided to go talk to the owner. After being introduced to Jerry, she demanded that she get what she had paid for. She had given them the down payment and she wanted that cigarette case. Jerry tried to explain to her that some products are bought as one shipment and when they are gone, they're gone, but she kept telling him that it was in his catalog and he had to be responsible for what he was selling. Patricia was so persistent that Jerry told her he would find it for her, even if it meant walking to the end of the Earth.

What a promise! Jerry schlepped to all of the wholesalers in downtown L.A., looking for that particular cigarette holder, but knowing that cigarette case had been discontinued. He continued looking for it until he found a very expensive one that was very close to the one Patricia had chosen. Jerry decided to buy it so as to end the problem with the persistent customer. The following day, the salesperson delivered the cigarette holder and she was happy. Keeping your promises is part of your brand, of your image as a company, and there will be circumstances when everything turns out wrong. You have to be prepared for the chaos, and to always have a plan B. Your customer's satisfaction is in your hands and is your number one priority.

In this case, the customer was not going to let go of her pre-selection. She wanted the store to honor its commitment and she was stubborn. Patricia wanted what Jerry was offering in the catalog. This meant an obligation from the company to fulfill its commitment. In cases like this, when a product is no longer available, a conversation with the customer is the only way out. You have to listen and try to reach a compromise, which could be an agreement for a reselection or a discount on a future purchase. You want to end on good terms, because the damage due to negative word of mouth is worth more than the discount.

Customer service can cost you money if you're not well prepared. In Jerry's case, constantly updating the catalog was necessary. This was his bread and butter, since he did not carry inventory, and was selling from his store's displays. There was no warehouse backup and the catalog featured many products just to show that the company was strong or had a variety of items for sale, though that did not actually mean all of the products were sitting in their store. This model of operation could cause a lot of customer discontent due to discontinued products, last units, product shortages, and so many other reasons related to product supply.

The following week, Jerry went to a show at the Convention Center to sell watches in a booth when he suddenly saw Patricia. Worried that she might make a scene in public, he said to himself, "Oh no, what happens if she did not like the cigarette holder?" Instead, Patricia had come to the trade show to personally thank him for the kind gesture of going out of his way to get the gift for her dad. He asked her how she had found him at the Convention Center and she told him she'd gone to the store, where the associates had told her he would be there.

Your effort to please a customer can go really far; Jerry had invested more money than the original price of the product. Like Indiana Jones in search of the Lost Ark, he had to dig through many places to find a similar substitute, but now this gesture had produced a customer who would value his good service, become satisfied with her experience, and tell everyone around her how supportive Jerry had been.

Patricia had emigrated from a small village in El Salvador named Chapeltique, which had no more than 3,000 inhabitants. It was twenty-five minutes from San Miguel, sixty-three miles from El Salvador's capital, San Salvador, and seventy miles from Tegucigalpa, the capital of Honduras; both main cities are remotely located in between mountains and volcanoes. Chapeltique is thirty miles southwest of the Pacific Ocean, in the middle of the jungle. The town has one of the oldest Catholic churches in the region, which was built in 1821.

While she was only nine months old, Patricia's mother suddenly left the family, leaving her daughter with her father. Patricia was raised by her grandparents. Since she was a little girl, her grandmother took care of her, playing with her, setting the table for tea and bringing a pot full of water to role-play with. Her grandmother, Lucila, came from a wealthy family in San Miguel. She had moved to Chapeltique because her family was sure Lucila was going to marry the town's Coronel. Instead, she fell in love with Patricia's grandfather, who was very handsome, with brown hair and green eyes, but did not know how to read or write. From him, Lucila learned about poverty and not having any food to eat. Her husband would take the little money they had and party all night with his amigos. Lucila would suffer, missing him on nights when he went out partying and would lay awake, waiting for him to return home.

Patricia remembers that her grandmother had a lot of class, wore Louis XIV shoes, and was always nicely dressed. Patricia did not miss her mom when she was little because her grandmother always took care of her, and gave her quality time and lots of love.

Every day, Lucila sent her to the mill with corn to make dough for fresh tortillas, but she hated to go and carry *el guacal*, a special pot for the dough. The mill owner was her *madrina*, or godmother, and she had a son. One day, he was talking and not paying attention when his hand was caught in the mill and his fingers were cut off. Patricia was present and saw the whole gruesome event. Every time she went back to the mill, the entire scene would replay in her mind.

Patricia's father moved to San Salvador and married Vilma, and they had children. Meanwhile, Patricia still lived with her grandparents in Chapeltique.

Her grandmother got sick and both Lucila and Patricia came to the capital to see the doctor, where they received bad news—she had pancreatic cancer. Patricia stayed by her side until she died. Lucila passed away while her granddaughter held her hand and begged her not to leave her. She was only eleven years old. She cried and asked, "Who will sew my dresses now?" Her aunt adopted her and Patricia remained in the capital, living with six kids who were all raised together.

Vilma, her stepmother, had moved to California to search for a better future for the kids. She traveled all the way from El Salvador to Mexico to Los Angeles by bus, and started working really hard in a house in Beverly Hills near Rexford Drive. After working for several years, this well-to-do family paid for all of Vilma's residential papers and, after five years, she was able to bring her husband Enrique and three kids, Eduardo, Cecilia, and Enrique, Jr. to El Norte. Patricia and Rafael stayed behind in San Salvador, living in a small house on an acre of land where Patricia's grandfather and her aunt lived, a pioneer in the region, had developed a small farm. Her father was raised there.

Vilma legally arranged for Patricia's father to have U.S. residency papers, and he immediately requested a green card for Patricia and Rafael. According to bureaucratic regulations, as Patricia was still a minor, the U.S. immigration service asked for the mother's permission for her to migrate, too. When Patricia went to the U.S. Embassy, she was accompanied by her aunt, whom she called mom, because she had taken care of her since she was little. However, the birth certificate they turned in did not match the identification card of her "mom."

But her biological mother had to give Patricia permission for her to legally move to the United States. Now they had to find this woman and confront the mother who had left Patricia behind and her reasons for abandoning her family. Patricia and her aunt went to the neighborhood where she supposedly lived and asked around for a woman named Maria Eugenia. They found out that five years earlier, her mom had died, so with her death certificate, Patricia was able to obtain her green card to migrate to California.

Once in Los Angeles, she started taking English classes at the well-known Evans Community Adult School, where she met other immigrants in the same boat as she was in—no money, no English, but a great desire to work hard and be successful. One of the friends she made at the school was Elizabeth, who cleaned offices in downtown Los Angeles. Patricia decided to take a job working for the same company, cleaning buildings at Figueroa and 9ᵗʰ Streets. She'd start at 7:00 in the evening and work until midnight, every night.

Patricia needed to buy a gift for her father's birthday, and the only way was with credit. But no one would extend credit to her, until Elizabeth—who was teaching her the ropes and showing the newcomer around all the places to go in Los Angeles—told her she had a friend who sold products door-to-door. That amigo was Manuel, one of Jerry's door-to-door salespeople.

Dina remained in California, taking care of their son Daniel, as Jerry started a new venture with his new partner—not only in business, but in his personal life. Patricia had started as a customer—and a very difficult one, at that—then became a friend. Little by little, she started to fill up Jerry's loneliness.

Having a family is essential for any individual and having children is a gift of God, a gift that brings out the best in any person. Learning how to respect them and protect them is a big job—a job that fit Jerry like a glove. Jerry has three kids: Daniel, who graduated from the University of California, Berkeley, with a major in interdisciplinary studies; Erick, who studied computer science, software developing, and mathematics and graduated from the University of California, Santa Cruz; and Ilanit, who is, as of now, in high school. They are Jerry's sunshine, who remembers that when he was young, he wanted a big family and dreamt of having twelve kids. He wanted to have a close relationship with his children, more of a friend than a father. He'd talk with them, even when they were little, about all his thoughts on life, how he saw society, religion, relationships, etc. He emphasized that they shouldn't be just another book in the library, but unique individuals.

Jerry likes to tell a story that his mom and uncles have repeated many times. When Jerry was little, one of his uncles and his brother, Doron, fell asleep on a rug close to where Jerry was sleeping. Suddenly, the uncle felt liquid splashing his face and he immediately woke up to find Doron holding a knife to Jerry's throat. Jerry was so scared that he urinated in his uncle's face. His uncle proceeded to save him from this dangerous situation.

During his childhood, Jerry had to struggle with his older brother Doron, protecting both his brother Ron and himself. He remembers thinking that when he had his own kids, he didn't want them to ever have this kind of conflict between them; in his lifetime, he wanted his children to be very close friends with one another—and with him. Long lasting relationships with siblings are common, but the challenges in making this bond work can generate lots of discord, and even hostility. Parents must not only provide equal treatment for their kids, but every brother and sister needs to perceive that they are all treated the same. It's necessary to dedicate special attention to each one in order to reduce conflict and jealousy. The older children will usually sense the extra attention the younger ones receive. We all know babies need more attention, but having a balance is the first step.

Making the older child cooperate and help with the younger ones will help all of them develop more social skills, and this will assist them with their peers once they grow, although it's always essential to have adult supervision. Brothers and sisters with hostile relationships can have a hard time getting along with their peers in life. However, it can be a great role-playing scenario to practice social interaction. Conflict between siblings at a young age is a great opportunity for parents to talk to their children and help them understand themselves.

Bestselling author Dr. Nancy Samalin, internationally known as a parenting expert, writes about several steps for parents to resolve kids' conflicts. Dr. Samalin provides insightful tips on what she calls the "fairness trap," when children are treated according to a parent's fairness beliefs. The first tip is that parents who repeatedly tell their children "life is not fair" eventually succeed in making their kids believe it is mom and/or dad who is/are not fair. The second suggestion is to give kids permission to disagree. While parents set up the rules and generally have the best judgment, that doesn't mean kids will always agree with them.

The third one is to make a list of rules that are fair so children can navigate following guidelines on their own, such as setting times for TV or computer use. The fourth tip is to be funny. When there's a complaint, make the child laugh. The fifth one is that sameness isn't always the best policy. Children love their 15 minutes of fame, but must also learn to enjoy their sibling's moment in the sun, too. The sixth recommendation is to relinquish fairness as a goal. When children complain about equal treatment, what they're really asking for is an extra hug. Parents need to read between the lines and learn the feeling and intent behind the spoken words.

Ever since Erick and Daniel were little, they have been close friends and great play partners. Once, Daniel told his father that he wanted to know what kind of work he did and that he wanted to experience it. When they were on vacation from school, Jerry brought both boys to the purchasing department and gave them to one of his longtime associates, Delma Marin, to work on any task they could complete.

Delma asked them to create a report and review its elements to ensure it matched another report she'd given them. She remembers that Daniel was very dedicated, checking and checking the reports, while Erick was more preoccupied with trying to play with the computer. Delma overheard Erick urge his brother not to "try so hard. Dad will pay us the same if we make it or if we don't." Today, Erick is a computer software developer and mathematician, and Daniel has studied nine languages, speaking five of them perfectly: English, Hebrew, Spanish, French, and Portuguese. He's also a contributing writer for Tablehoppers.com. Erick currently heads his own e-commerce business.

Jerry remembers that he gave Erick a floppy disk with some programs for children when he was around six years old. Jerry promised he'd put the disk in the computer for him, but he was so busy that he kept forgetting to do it. One day, he came home to find that Erick had figured it out on his own and was already playing the disk on the computer. As a teenager, Erick would sneak out to go see his girlfriend, so Jerry began using all kinds of security devices to keep him inside. However, Erick was able to deactivate them and still left the house. There was no way Jerry could keep him, the tech maven, home. Once, Jerry bought a computer to work on at home. One night, upon returning from the office, he discovered that Erick had taken it apart and separated it into pieces. He got so mad that Erick had to rebuild and reassemble the computer; it took Erick several days, but he did it.

Daniel, on the other hand, was always studying. Jerry would tell him, "I want you to get a B, and I want you to go out with your friends!" But, he knew that would never happen, because Daniel was a straight A student in all of his classes. Studying at Berkeley was a great opportunity for him, especially having the possibility to major in interdisciplinary studies. For Daniel's thesis, he had to find a faculty member who would support his topic, which was "The Self as Linguistic Construct." He stated his hypothesis in sixty pages, arguing that it is an illusion that the self is one thing, and that it is instead a billion different things—language taught you to be one. This thesis is an interpretation between using languages not only to express ourselves, but to unify us as individuals. We are truly different, from our thoughts to our organs to our cultures to our ancestors and to our environment. What brings us together is our language. Daniel had to incorporate the worldviews of many leading philosophers into his research, finding Immanuel Kant and Friedrich Nietzsche to be his favorites.

Daniel attended Berkeley, a highly prestigious alma mater with the highest number of distinguished graduate programs ranked in the top ten in their fields by the U.S. National Research Center. Daniel loves to travel and learn how people live—especially what people eat and how their language is related to the particular food they eat. He believes traveling is a privilege, constantly teaching him how small one is. Daniel is currently studying in San Francisco at the administration of food services.

Jerry dedicates quality time to his kids and they often travel together to many places; when Erick and Daniel were kids and Patricia was pregnant with Ilanit, they went to Costa Rica. They were invited to one of the unique beaches that only had access by boat and where they had to camp out on the sand. There was no electricity, no phone, and no water. However, the night was full of stars, and they talked around a fireplace. When one of the Azarkmans decided to go to the bathroom, he turned on a flashlight and discovered that they were surrounded by crabs. Their screams were heard all the way in Los Angeles! Due to exhaustion, they were able to sleep, but all night there were all kinds of noises surrounding them, as the city slickers were in a true jungle. This priceless experience was one of a kind and among the best times of their lives.

The second of Jerry's steps that turned his twenty dollar investment into a multimillion-dollar operation was listening to his customer, then delivering and exceeding beyond expectations. (Indeed, this tenet even earned Jerry a wife!) During his visit to the very first home, back when he was selling Pong, Jerry started listening to what his customers were asking him regarding other lines of products. During his next visit, he was already offering small appliances and TV sets. Always prepared with a gift for the kids on the day of delivery, he had an additional surprise for the customers, an unexpected gift. He always gave them a pleasant surprise.

Chapter Ten

Leading the Way

I t is not easy to become a leader in society. Everyone is watching and checking what you're doing. They may also be using it to benefit themselves. The more you try to innovate, the more it becomes an exercise that companies around you try to follow, as well. Innovation leads to imitation. Everyone around you observes your success and wants to have it, too. Innovation is the big word that will take your firm to a different level. By making your place of business look fresh, you're provoking an immediate reason for your customers to want to come and see what's new.

Creating excitement with your product requires your creative input. Finding new ways to sell the same product with a new look is a constant challenge for any business. This relates very strongly to being consistent to the brand you are creating, as you ask yourself the questions: Is this who I want to be? And who I want my customers to see as a business? Brand consistency is something you'll have to analyze through the years to ensure the right decisions are being made—

modifying logos, changing slogans, rebranding yourself as a company. All of these need to be carefully reviewed.

These decisions happen sometimes when you move the operation to a new location, or when you hire a new management team to run your business. They might want to mark the starting point of their new ideas. For example, the clothing retailer Gap used the same logo for twenty years, from 1990 to 2010. Suddenly, on October 5, 2010 Gap announced that it would be changing its logo. Just like that—without customer involvement, renovation at the stores, creating momentum with a new line, adding a new brand or style of clothing. Gap announced that this logo change would be only the beginning of all the alterations it will be making in the future.

You might think your customers are not paying attention to what you're doing, but you are wrong; your clientele often see your business as their own investment too. The more they buy from you, the more invested they are in you as a business. Your brand equity is connected to your customers, who feel it also belongs to them. Your business provides a sense of comfort for your customers. It is a familiar place where they receive pleasant results after buying products they need and want from you.

Gap's customers created a blog and communicated their disappointment through it. Thousands of people wrote about their dissatisfaction, while only thirty said they liked the new logo. For years, Gap's logo had been a blue box with the company's name inside of it. But the new logo put the name by itself with the box on one side; the explanation Gap gave to the public was that the clothing company was "more contemporary and current," said Marka Hansen, President of Gap North America. However, consumers were blogging their own interpretations regarding what the updated logo meant to them, saying that Gap was moving away from them, that they were not going to be targeting the same consumer, and that they felt left out. Only seven days after launching its revamped logo, Gap had to trash its new emblem of self-identification and go back to the traditional logo. What a fiasco! What matters far more than whether your logo is nice or not is the identity you're giving your business. Through the years, customers' eyes will be visualizing this symbol every time they have contact with you. They'll identify with it and your logo will be the badge reminding consumers of your business.

Now and then, every enterprise needs a facelift, and to renovate itself, which was what Gap was trying to do, starting with a logo change. Was this a move in the right direction? Yes, it made their customers mad, but at least the switch created heaps of free advertising and media attention for its brand. A year after this corporate fiasco, Gap closed 300 stores. This indicates that the firm was trying to reengineer itself in order to avoid these closings. However, Gap's approach was not the correct one, and its internal changes were not enough to keep a fresh look, renovate its stores, maintain their customers' excitement, and increase sales. Gap needed to make its shoppers continue patronizing all of the stores, especially with the economy suffering a downturn. This was the biggest task Gap faced in order to avoid the closings, but it failed to do so.

A year after Jerry's company moved to 1313 Olympic Boulevard, the owner of the place offered to sell the property to them so he could raise the money to open a restaurant. The proprietor started out by asking for $1 million and after many rounds of negotiations, they agreed on $750,000. The owner was a very tough negotiator, and after agreeing on the $750,000 figure, he demanded immediate payment. Jerry told him, "Okay, let's go to an Escrow office." In those pre-cell phone days, Jerry went to the public phone on the corner, leafed through the *Yellow Pages,* and found a nearby office. He called them, and as the office was open, Jerry and the owner went there. Although the place was not supposed to do the paperwork for business loans, the escrow agent saw that if he didn't help with the transaction, the owner would change his mind regarding the sale. Furthermore, Jerry was determined to buy and needed to close the deal.

The escrow company did home mortgages, and had never done a business loan deal, but it handled the case in a similar fashion and asked Jerry to give them a down payment towards the purchase. He had a blank check with him. It was a Friday, and now he needed to give the escrow company a $10,000 down payment. Jerry knew his bank account did not have that amount deposited in it, and the escrow agents told him he had to come up with the money by Monday. That weekend, the brothers worked hard collecting down payments and monthly payments that clients owed them in order to come up with the $10,000 and deposit it in the account for the escrow company. Monday came and the money was deposited.

Every week at the store, they'd turn around all of the products on display. This made customers feel that the outlet was bringing in new goods every week, although it was just the same items rearranged to give the impression that the store looked fresh and new. Every time they moved their inventory around, a new idea came to the brothers and sales associates as to how to sell the products. Moving them around made the brothers analyze why a particular item was not being sold— was it the price, quality, or brand? It was like a laboratory with each product being reevaluated by sales scientists.

The way you set products up at a store is essential for connecting with your customers. The layout of merchandise must not be inconsequential for the business operation, but arranged to enhance the flow of shoppers once they're inside the store. Renovating this distribution once a year for big operations, and at least every six months for smaller operations, is a must. Customers need to feel that there is something new, even if it's the same product. By changing the layout, you refresh the eyes of buyers vis-à-vis your place. Putting signs all over your establishment stating "Open during remodeling" will intrigue and attract people driving or walking by to come in and see what's new—even if there really isn't anything new being offered for sale. The changes could be the tables you use to put your products on, the color of shelves, lighting, floors, etc. These renovations should be in your plans every year.

When you have a destination department (a product everyone looks for and that your consumer will go directly to, such as milk is for a supermarket), it's never placed at the entrance of the grocery store. Supermarkets place milk in the farthest corner in order to make shoppers walk all over the place. In this way, the markets showcase their store by making purchasers walk all the way from the front to the back for their destination product, past all of their other products. As with real estate, it's location, location, location for retail outlets, too. Many of these salesmanship ideas are common sense, but retailers hire experts in the matter to guide merchants in making the best layouts. At Jerry's store, there weren't any resource for that, so ideas and execution all derived from in-house creativity. Always concerned with appearances, Jerry was continually involved in how the store looked.

Jerry implemented a sales strategy for each product by creating a step up program, which used the principle of good, better, and best. The price reflected this process in a very simple way. He'd set up three thirty-two inch TVs side by side that appeared to be the same type of television. The same, yes, but they were different brands with differences in features and prices. Jerry's plan was to arrange the TVs in such a way so that the brand that was most attractive to the consumer would have the highest price, while the most inexpensive brand would be his starting point. People would come to buy the least expensive one, but this setup allowed for a moment when the skilled salesperson would explain the difference between the sets and why there was more value in the most expensive one.

The human element in any company makes all the difference in the world; any company can have products, but the distinction is definitely with their employees. Employees are the face of the company, and the ones transmitting the firm's message. The products will not determine the success or the failure of the company—only its people will. The work of the company is largely done by people, with their weaknesses and their strengths. It's a people's business, and your salesmen and work force are your gold. This is the third reason for Jerry's success and what it takes to go from twenty dollars to $200 million.

When Jerry walked the streets selling Home Pong, he brought technology to his customers, but he bore something even more valuable to them. The product was the opportunity for him to open communications when the customer opened the door, but Jerry himself made the difference. He was the face of the sale—the one giving the warranty for the product, providing a guarantee that it would work, and the one standing behind it. This guarantee was contained in its price; his customers did not need to pay any extra money for it. It was part of buying from him. Jerry was selling himself and his brand of friendliness and reliability, along with his goods.

Companies invest in operating systems, remodeling, uniforms, etc., but the most important investment should be in their people. The image of a company is managed by its people. The more knowledgably every sales associate is about the philosophy of the company, its credit lines, and details regarding products they're selling, the more customers can tell right away how reliable that company is. Through this, a trustworthy image is built. Knowledgeable employees will immediately translate into a customer's trust.

A salesperson can serve his customers like a Swiss watch, explaining every single detail to clients, but if there is a mistake in the product's chain of delivery, the whole company suffers. What happens if the product delivered is the wrong item, wrong color, or wrong size? The image of the company is hurt. No matter how excellent the salesperson or how well he or she has done his job, if the weakest link breaks, the whole chain fails.

When Jerry started out, he was selling, taking down payments, doing deliveries, installing devices, and making his rounds collecting monthly payments—a one-man band ideal for a small operation. But once you take your business to a higher-level, you want to make sure you're making the right efforts and that, at the end of the day, customers feel that you have over-delivered, surpassing expectations.

Any company that sells products or offers services must have its whole chain of command synchronized. This means all of the processes, from the point of sale to the delivery of the merchandise, must be analyzed and secured so that there isn't a missing step, or a gap that could cause failure. The failure of one part of the chain will cause the downfall of the whole company.

What empowered Jerry to convert his twenty dollars into a multimillion-dollar operation? The third step for his success was his employees. As his mom-and-pop shop evolved into a complex, sophisticated enterprise, the workers were the ones on the frontlines, talking to customers, preparing displays at the store, delivering to homes, on the phones following up on orders with clients, and calling to remind them to send in their payments. Selecting his people and putting together the right team was the most important part of the winning formula.

The salesperson becomes the entire expression of what you want your company to be, and this is evident in the first handshake. The sales people have to reflect correctly the brand and what it stands for, the essence of your company and to do it properly they need to be trained to understand the way you want them to treat a customer, how to sell them the product and services but essentially how to establish the relationship you want the customer to develop with you and your company. If a sales associate overpromises to a customer, this could easily result in expectations not being met.

If the salesperson promises the customer that the product will be delivered the next day and for any reason it can't be, you're already failing in the eyes of the purchaser. In many cases, the customer needs to take a day off of work in order to be there at home waiting for delivery of the product. Alternately, a good salesman or saleswoman can reduce customer expectation by offering to deliver in five days. This is a better option, with more possibility for an on-time delivery, and there's even the chance of being able to deliver prior to the expected day, thus exceeding expectations.

Repeat customers happen when they are satisfied with the service, and when your company is the first option they think of the next time they need to buy something. Implement processes in the sales force: make this process strong enough, develop it to a level everyone believes in—this facilitates the execution of a sale. Making sure everyone in the chain knows exactly what the customer's needs are is the most important task your company's customer service team must accomplish. This includes verifying before closing the sale with the customer, going over and confirming what they want. Jerry always tells his salespeople to make sure they are monitoring delivery, and calling customers to make sure they are completely satisfied.

The Azarkmans already had an 8,000 square foot space, so their first step was to gather all of their door-to-door employees and contract them to sell at the store permanently. It was a difficult conversation, as the associates had to be convinced because they were no longer going to earn fifteen percent of the entire sale. Instead, the commission was going to be decreased down to nine percent. The brothers' reasons were very simple: Now the store was going to have more expenses. They had to fill it up with products and operation costs would increase. The salespersons would now have a schedule to stick to and they had to show up at the store, instead of being out on their own pounding the pavement on the streets. The biggest change was in how the nine percent was being calculated. Previously, it was on the entire sale, but now the percentage would be solely from the profit. This was going to be a reduction of their salaries and, for some, a considerable amount. Many questions came up, especially how they would know what the profit was—they just had to believe and trust.

Explaining to the sales associates was not easy. It was difficult to make them understand that now they'd sell more because customers would come into the store and feel more confident, as they were now buying and taking the product away with them instantly. Most of the sales force stayed, but the first one who left was Mario Romero, who had been so close to Jerry since the beginning. There was no way to convince him to stay.

Jerry would stand at the door of the new location, greeting customers and talking to the ones leaving, especially those departing with nothing in their hands.

He'd take them aside and offer them gifts, while asking what they were looking for, and if the store didn't have it, he promised to have it available the following day. That next day was a shopping day for him, walking down the streets of downtown L.A. where wholesalers were located, looking for the specific products customers wanted. That same day, Jerry would call his customers and invite them to come to the store because he had already bought and was stocking what they were looking for.

Jerry was involved in the hiring process of all salespeople; he wanted to ensure they weren't shy, as sales associates needed to be outgoing, ready to follow up with the customer at all times. He'd explain that they could never stop the bridge of communication or be afraid of calling clients to verify whether or not the products they'd bought arrived at their homes with total satisfaction. This follow up call after the delivery was essential in order to complete the circle of the sale, as well as another opportunity to offer the extended warranty. It was also a chance to close the conversation with, "Next time you need anything, here is my phone number. Don't hesitate to call me if you have any questions." They were creating and cementing a relationship between the salesperson and customer that was close to the point wherein if the client needed to buy anything else, he or she came looking for the same associate.

During the door-to-door days, Jerry created a system of calls. He'd ask his route two employee to call the route three customers, and vice versa, asking simple questions, such as: "Did you get the product you ordered? Was our employee helpful? Did he explain the features and benefits? Are you satisfied with your purchase?" This was a way to cross check each other to make sure the customer was served properly, as well as to ensure the salesperson stayed in line, because customer complaints could cause them to lose their jobs.

Recognition of a job well done took place as soon as the month was over. Jerry met with the sales force frequently to keep them motivated, calling out the name of the top salespeople, which made the rest wonder what they had to do to be on top of their game, too. These meetings with sales associates brought awareness to the best sellers, and influenced the others not to lag behind in their sales. These were motivational meetings, emphasizing the principle of trying harder and harder. In addition, it gave renewed energy to good performers and hope to the ones who didn't accomplish the same numbers—a new month had started, and the competition was on again.

If there was a mistake for any reason, the most important action was to have a conversation in private with that particular salesperson. Jerry would never call attention to or speak about the error in front of the rest of the sales staff. He didn't like to embarrass anyone, and always wanted to show respect to the associate and for his work. With his even tempered personality, Jerry spoke calmly in a very soft voice, reviewing the whole situation and making the steps clear to the employee in question to ensure he understood what he was doing wrong, and how it was going to affect the company and his own sales.

When a mistake was made, Jerry asked group leaders and supervisors to look for the appropriate moment to talk with salespeople. It was essential to never deal with a situation when one was mad or out of control—you always had to come back and speak when both parties were able to talk. Once all parties were in the mood to talk, they'd address the situation by first letting the employee explain his or her side of the story. Then the process would be reviewed to see what was lost in communication, what accounted for the error, or what was taken the wrong way. Evaluating the overall situation presented an opportunity to train the salesperson for this to never happen again.

Jerry loves his family, and the part he loves the most is being a father to three individuals. Erick wanted to study computers and selecting where he was going to study was very simple—close to Silicon Valley. The computer world's mecca is located in Northern California, inside of the Santa Clara Valley. At the southern part of the San Francisco Bay, Silicon Valley is home to countless high tech companies. The Valley's name is derived from material used for semiconductor parts, material that transmits electricity; silicon is used in these computer parts.

Erick Azarkman went to the University of California, Santa Cruz, just south of San Francisco and just fifteen miles away from Silicon Valley. UCSC is well known as a modern research university; according to SCI-BYTES magazine, UCSC is ranked number two in the U.S. for academic research impact in the field of space science, behind Princeton University. UCSC is very close to the world of computers and even offers an extension program in Silicon Valley.

The UCSC Department of Computer Science, where Erick earned his degree, is part of the Jack Baskin School of Engineering. Here, he fulfilled all of his desires to seek knowledge in the computer world and mathematics. In Erick's thesis, he worked with algorithms in order to create artificial intelligence. His research was on solving N-puzzles using the shortest routes in the least time possible. Erick's hypothesis was a close analogy for solving Rubik's cubes; for example, one could solve it in twenty-two steps or it could take hundreds of steps. Using this principle, computer software would be able to perform the least amount of steps in the shortest time in order to get to the desired outcome.

This software could be used for flying planes or for computer search engines, such as Google. The top usage of this software could be utilized to reduce the need for computer memory, thereby making responses as quick as possible. Erick asked Ira Pohl, a professor, to evaluate his research. Professor Pohl had worked for NASA and Google and was a great inspiration for him. Erick made his presentation to Professor Pohl and received an A-plus for his dissertation.

Erick believes that his dad is responsible for opening up the world of science to him. When he was little, he remembers that his father would always bring puzzles home to entertain him. Once, Jerry gave his son a very special gift: his first microscope. When Erick put saliva on a slide and was able see bacteria, it blew his mind. Erick feels that his dad is his best friend, as well as his teacher. Because his father encouraged and trained him to always ask questions and not take things for granted, Erick would probe and dig deeper to understand the reason why something was happening. He developed analytical skills; enabling him to go from surface to substance, appearance to essence—key skills for scientists.

Jerry talked to his employees to train them not only in sales but in the way they conducted their lives. He'd start his training by explaining that they all had goals: financial, educational, social, personal, health, and family goals. He'd provide lots of examples to make the topic easy to understand. He made his training sessions fun by bringing treats, and whoever answered his questions correctly would win a bag of candy.

We all know financial goals go hand in hand with jobs: how do I make more money tomorrow than I made today? How do I reengineer myself to get a raise? We think we deserve a raise because we've been with the company for a long time, but on the other hand, the firm asks, "Why should we have to pay more to receive the same quality of work?" Educational goals can be put on the table to improve your job performance and to demonstrate additional benefits the company gets from your contribution.

Social goals involve our society, the community, and are very important for spiritual reasons, to network, to help each other, renew your energy, and to have a balance in life. We all have personal goals: to get a new car, buy a house, or to get a new look. It could be anything you want. Health goals are important too—to have regular checkups, any medicine you need, to go regularly to the dentist, and so on. Family goals could, for example, be to get your kids through school, to work with them to accomplish the highest scores, etc.

Deciding what your goals are is essential for everyone. Otherwise, life will soon catch up with you and you'll look back and see what you missed. Write down what your goals are, go back to them every month, see how much of them you've achieved, and what you need to do to make them happen.

Jerry had one goal in mind when he started selling his electronic game—he had to survive and make money. This meant selling products in order to pay for rent, buy food, and pay for the products people were buying. He had a focus that helped him through. Remember the old saying, "Where there's a will, there's a way."

A goal can be as simple as waking up early to see the sunrise. To accomplish that, you need to plan and organize yourself, to set your alarm clock, select the best place to watch the day break, have a blanket ready in case it's cold, and choose the right shoes and outfit. As simple as this idea is, it requires preparation and planning. It needs thought to make it a pleasant event. Your goals need organizing, to be realistic and achievable.

A goal could be to buy a new car at the end of the year. You'll need to study the models you like and figure out how much you can afford. Monthly payments must be based on your budget, and you have to factor in where you're going to park it at work, how much you'll spend for gasoline, tires, servicing, and the like. How many people will use the car? The more questions you develop in the process of making a decision, the fewer mistakes you'll have in the end.

Everyone has a goal in life for different things. Jerry emphasized the need to plan ahead and to understand that goals are created in order to achieve higher sales. He motivated his sales force to obtain better commissions. Goals should be challenging but realistic; they should contribute to the profits of the company and the reserves needed for future growth. These goals need to be planned out and unambiguous, clear to everyone. They must be considered from the point of view of their actual output and the timeframe wherein you expect the desired results.

Jerry trained his sales staff by going over all types of goals. He'd make them write down their goals for each category. For example, in terms of educational goals, all associates immediately put down their children's education. For social goals, they'd write about parties and get-togethers celebrating birthdays of their kids, and personal time with their families. As for health, staffers wrote and talked about going to dentists and doctors, while family goals meant satisfying all of their loved ones' needs. Jerry would end with financial goals, tying the exercise to the sales goal. Many employees had not even gone to school, but that did not mean they weren't talented and thirsty to learn and accomplish, so for him it was essential to use examples to make a connection to them and help him get to their sales goals.

He'd use the example of a crib. Imagine that your wife is pregnant or you are pregnant. Don't you want to buy the best crib available? Its price represents how many sales are required in order to make the commission necessary to buy this best crib. I have to make a certain amount of sales per hour to earn the commission necessary to buy the crib tomorrow. I won't leave until I make it.

Once the goals were presented to the employees, Jerry always made sure there was a negotiable agreement on paper, with a plan for each associate that included deadlines and comparable performance goal numbers. This document was important to Jerry because it helped the salesperson understand they were signing a contract of performance, a promise of execution, and their participation in the overall goal. The plan had to include a time for an evaluation during the same week to make sure the month was going to end with positive numbers.

Jerry ensured the sales associate received motivational talks at all times. He'd tell his group leaders all the time that it was essential to enforce constant recognition, daily if possible. Special attention was given to the areas that were on track. In the areas that were weak, the staff talked it over to make sure they'd reach their monthly goal and that their performance was going in a positive direction. It was all about making it possible. The inspired employees all wanted to achieve their individual goals. The associate who was not achieving his or her aims would undergo a step-by-step review to find out what was preventing him or her from achieving the goals. It was essential for the employee to measure what he or she wanted and needed.

Jerry frequently heard the comment that he was training his people only for them to leave and move on to another company, to his own competitors. He'd always reply that employees need to be happy where they are. If they're not happy they'll leave—although this does not mean that he didn't want them to perform to their highest ability while they're with him. This never made Jerry stop his ongoing training, as he believes everyone has an unlimited potential and that, drop by drop, you can make an ocean.

All employees need to feel as if they're part of the company, to believe they own the company, and to consider the company a part of them. Offer associates a career, not just another run of the mill job. They yearn to have a sense of satisfaction in their place of work so their productivity will increase and be converted into the company's overall success. Employees are your biggest asset, the ones carrying your brand around to your customers. A very strong message has to be delivered to each one of the employees when they're hired that makes them feel engaged with your firm's philosophy and leaders of the organization.

Employees are a company's most important investment, and having them learn all the time should be a business' goal. Employee satisfaction will translate into creativity and innovations that will help the company grow and change, and are guarantors of on-the-job honesty. The more successfully employees are trained and communications processes are accomplished, the more a company will progress.

Once a new employee is hired, he or she needs to always be reminded how important they are for the company. The development of each employee is essential for the advancement of the entire company. The associate needs to feel he or she wants to work at the company, and not just because there are no other options for employment. Instead, they work at your company because it's fun and they enjoy showing up to work every day. They understand how important they are for the whole operation. They need to feel essential and empowered for them to be able to reflect the fiber and being of an enterprise, and for them to feel like they're part of a strong skeleton, and part of that whole body. Motivational conversations between employees and their leaders must contain words that have real meaning to all of its members. It has to get under their skins, be inspirational, and answer questions. Deliver a speech they'll remember and will be repeated and repeated among all of them, encouraging an *esprit de corps*. You are creating leaders who express the reasons for the business' existence.

Shaping your company into an industry leader requires associates with the maximum expression of passion for what they do. You must be able to unleash this zeal in all of the team's newcomers and maintain the same high level of enthusiasm throughout the years. One of the first points is to make sure the individuals you hire understand your company's mission. Jerry was serving an overlooked, under-served mass of families who did not have any options in the financial world. They were consumers unable to open a line of credit anywhere else. Every associate working for the company had to feel that ardor inside and become a facilitator to that particular customer. They knew they were selling them their first TV, mattress, or refrigerator, and this was the first step to the American dream many had traveled thousands of miles to attain. It was the first step in obtaining their first assets after all of the suffering in their troubled homelands, where they had little to eat, were living in very poor areas, and sometimes even enduring war. Now a change was being provided to them. This was an opportunity to have better things, to raise their kids in a developed country, live in greater comfort, and an opportunity to lift their lifestyle to a higher level. These employees were a part of it. They had suffered the same things their customers had undergone, felt what they felt, and they worked with the fervor of one offering a helping hand.

How you unleash your employees' passion so that they give it their all at work, how you motivate these individuals to give it their all every day, how you make them protect the company and the brand by being consistent to what is required of them, and how you make everyone behave the correct way is always a challenge to accomplish. It is particularly challenging with associates who won't perform. Identifying them in time to re-train them or let them go is the most difficult decision a company makes. This is part of doing business and the responsibility of good leaders. Keeping someone who is not performing or acting improperly will frustrate those doing the right thing. If the superiors allow it to continue unchecked, their leadership will be undermined and the resulting loss of respect will deteriorate his or her image.

The principles regarding how you're going to deal with associates should be a mutual agreement; it has to have the company's goals in mind, but must also have a meaning for the whole structure. It needs to express the values and reasons as to why you want to work with this team. The principles of mutual respect for each other, between associates and their leaders, is one of the priorities in this mutual agreement. The structure has to be built on trust at all times because it has to make everyone in the company feel like their leaders will always be impartial and fair. The associate has to feel that his work and dedication is respected by the entire structure of the company and that their working environment is a guarantee of equal opportunity and integrity for all.

Chapter Eleven

Word of Mouth

Branding yourself to become the initial source of credit for any person is a hard goal. It is an even harder mission to accomplish when you know something is missing in the information these people are bringing to your credit desk. This missing element does not allow them to qualify at any other store or regular finance house. Even though members of this group may not have social security numbers, it does not mean they're unwilling or unable to pay their debts. Jerry and Ron were recognized for being the number one location where thousands of people, many of them immigrants, were starting to buy with their first credit and building up their credit history in the United States, and this gave their company its biggest strength.

Raul had become Jerry's best friend. No longer drinking, he had saved money and was able to bring his wife to Los Angeles, where she started babysitting Daniel at Jerry's home. Raul and his wife were both putting money away in order to bring the rest of their family to L.A. Raul was Jerry's right hand man, always protecting the Azarkmans.

In downtown Los Angeles, a big furniture store called Grand Bazaar was sold to a Jewish entrepreneur who visited Jerry one day. With his first words, he pronounced that he planned to shut Jerry and Ron's business down by relocating Grand Bazaar right next door to their operation, which at that time had a Western Union office as its neighbor. Jerry took him to the back of the store and offered him coffee. In the ensuing conversation, the stranger told him he had money to buy the property adjacent to their retail outlet, where he intended to move the Grand Bazaar to. The businessman knew the Latino community was growing exponentially and he was planning to do lots of advertising to this target market for his new venue. Jerry told him L.A. was big enough for the two of them, that they could both survive, and even join forces. The newcomer would sell his furniture and Jerry his electronics and they could make it a joint venture, collaboration between the two of them. But the competitor refused and told him, "Don't say I didn't warn you. I will shut you down."

This was a crucial moment for the operation. Jerry knew that if they could become a better company, their customers would stick with them. But the reality of the situation was that Jerry's outlet looked like a flea in comparison to the new neighbor, who'd look like an elephant, as his store took up eighty percent of the entire block. Once the remodel finished, the rival businessman started stealing Jerry and Ron's staff, hiring their salespeople away.

Jerry realized that if he did not place more emphasis on his own associates, the results were going to prove disastrous. So he went to a seminar on customer relations and learned about the six steps for customer loyalty at NARDA (North American Retail Dealers Association). He selected the top leaders of the company at that time to learn about this concept; Elsa, William, and Claudio took the seminar and then trained the rest of the team. William was responsible for all of the salespeople and Claudio started out in the mailroom, putting stamps on the catalogs mailed out to customers, and now handled the company's credit.

Elsa was then taking care of the operation's accounting and the paperwork pertaining to credit. She came from El Salvador and had immigrated to America through her mom, who brought her to L.A. via Ronald Reagan's Immigration

Reform and Control Act of 1986, which granted amnesty to three million undocumented aliens. During Elsa's job interview with Ron, he asked her if she knew how to type and she said yes, so he gave her an electric typewriter to use, but she had never seen one before. Elsa told him she knew how to type, but on a regular manual typewriter, and Ron understood that he was dealing with an upfront and honest person. The next day, she was working with him in the back office. She would process all of the invoices and orders. One day, he assigned Elsa to do inventory in the jewelry department and he asked her to count the stock three times, and in the end, she came up with the same number each time. But, he'd shake his head and told her that it was impossible, the numbers were far from what his papers showed, and signifying there was a loss in merchandise. Elsa always remembers this situation because her best friend at that time was the jewelry saleslady (who she never saw her again after these discrepancies were discovered).

The six steps revealed in the seminar were crucial and simple, and can be summarized as:

1. Smile
2. Maintain eye contact with the customer
3. Greet the customer
4. Solve their problem for them
5. Go over the details of their purchase
6. Shake their hand before parting company

This might appear to be simple and common sense, but the sales associates needed to be reminded of this process all of the time to ensure it was completed and that they had created that bond with the shopper. These simple steps increase that connection with the customer, which the business needed now more than ever—especially since an elephant had moved next door.

Jerry immediately got involved with a buying group called AVB Buying Group (Associated Volume Buyers), which negotiates national prices for its members. This was going to bring about a big change in the way they bought their merchandise. By increasing volume, their buying power would get them better pricing than they'd previously had. This opened up other advantages that they did not even realize at first. For example, co-op funds, wherein the vendor would give the retailer back certain amounts of money in exchange for advertising their products. These funds helped the company to increase its advertising and bring more foot traffic into the store.

Once the training was finished, Jerry knew everyone was ready to deal with customers and prepared to achieve 100 percent customer satisfaction. The training and more competitive pricing would help them to compete better, but they were still scared that their business would be shut down by the tremendous power next door. The competition's display of products—enhanced by an interior decorator—looked much better, making everything look exceptionally beautiful.

Jerry then decided that if Grand Bazaar was going to add tons of advertising he needed to work with the media too. He wanted to piggyback onto and take advantage of Grand Bazaar's promotions. If the public was going to pay a visit to Grand Bazaar, they'd know the little store next to them also had merchandise and special deals; it was an opportunity for savvy shoppers to check them out, too, and compare prices and choices.

Raul heard what was going on and told Jerry all they needed to do was put boxes of merchandise in the parking lot so that people could see their activity. He was sure that with heaps of goods they'd attract the bargain hunters. Grand Bazaar was hiring many employees who'd already been trained by the Azarkmans' emporium. Their competition was big: it was far bigger, with more than 20,000 square feet, versus the Brother Azarkmans' more modest 8,000 square feet. But the interesting thing was that while most of the advertising was done by Grand Bazaar—which even created an event similar to a fair at the store site, with merry-go-rounds and a circus in front of the property—most shoppers went straight to La Curacao, because they thought the whole shindig was being thrown by the business they'd already become accustomed to patronizing. They told their friends, and through word of mouth the advertising was even stronger than the media. It was fascinating to see La Curacao full of people while Grand Bazaar lay empty.

La Curacao was the name that was given to the new store when the brothers moved from their 1625 to 1313 address on Olympic Boulevard. Patricia was the first one to suggest that Jerry should use this name. They'd asked customers for a familiar sounding name, and they always repeated "La Curacao." This Dutch company had started as an import operation shipping coffee from El Salvador to Europe, but the cargo boat would return to Central America empty. Some of the farm workers started to ask the importers if they could ship radios, then TVs, and little by little the Dutch firm started exporting electronics. Soon the ships would leave El Salvador full of coffee and on the way back its hold would be full of electronics. The firm's main office was on the island of Curacao, so it was a simple decision to name it La Curacao. The storeowners were Jewish, and when Jerry decided to use their company name, they went to El Salvador to seek permission to use it. As their Caribbean counterparts had no plans to open branches in the United States, they signed the papers authorizing the Azarkmans to use the name for their enterprise.

Nowadays La Curacao exists all over Central America with new owners, since the original Dutch company closed its operations. La Curacao in USA is a separate business from the one operating South of the Border. The name captures the attention of the countless Central American families now living in Los Angeles, especially the biggest group, which comes from El Salvador. In the City of the Angels, anyone who encountered La Curacao felt like they were in a familiar location—not only because of the name, but also because of the associates who, in the beginning, were mostly from Central America. In addition downtown L.A. could be called Little Central America because of the vast number of people who had migrated from there to this urban hub.

Grand Bazaar continued its advertising but remained empty, while next door, La Curacao was packed and sales went through the roof. Each weekend, La Curacao pulled merchandise out onto the parking lot, which meant someone had to stay overnight to watch it, and this would always be Raul. He'd park his car next to the boxes where he'd remain all night, guarding everything.

During one earthquake, Jerry was at home and the first one who called him was Raul, making sure he was all right. Raul inquired about Patricia and Erick. Jerry told him they were in Burbank visiting family and that he'd called, but as there was no reception he could not reach them. Jerry had no idea how they had faced the quake, but could not drive to Burbank as he was trapped at home, due to electrical poles that had fallen on the street where he lived. Raul told Jerry not to worry, and he drove up to Burbank, where he found that Patricia and Erick were safe and sound. Once the poles were removed from the streets, the anxious owner went straight to the store, opened it and everything was fine—thankfully, no damages at all.

Raul was a very important part of Jerry's success. He was a loyal associate who was always there for him. This was during Reagan's presidency, when amnesty for undocumented aliens was announced all over the United States. Jerry had paid an attorney to fix their residency paperwork. They had paid thousands of dollars to get their green cards, but years had passed and they still didn't have papers. The two Israeli citizens were in the same situation as many of their customers. When the amnesty was announced, they immediately went to ask their attorney about it, but he advised them to not go that route. It would slow down and even obstruct their residency process. Acting upon the advice of their counsel, they held themselves back and decided not to present their papers. But the news was everywhere. Every day was bringing them closer to the deadline. The pressure was so intense that as the amnesty deadline loomed, on the last day they decided to fill out the form. Once they closed the store, they completed the paperwork and gave the documents to Raul to drop off at the post office.

That night, while Raul was keeping an eye on the boxes inside of the parking lot, he boiled some water in an improvised little electric stove with exposed cables. Somehow, a circuit started, transmitting high voltage through the wires and then to the metal fence, electrocuting Raul. He died in the parking lot. The first employees who opened the store the next morning found his body and called the police.

Jerry was devastated. Raul was an honest, hardworking friend, who had been by Jerry's side for years now, and on many occasions had walked the streets with him, selling door-to-door. In addition to the tragic situation, the Azarkmans never knew whether or not Raul had mailed the amnesty forms. Months passed before they received their first communication from the INS stating that the process had started. In the end, they got their green cards—thanks to trusty Raul, who had dropped off the mail that evening before his unexpected, untimely, and much lamented departure. It's amazing how important loyal employees can be, protecting your business, helping you develop, and raising it to the sky. They, along with loyal customers, are the gifts that keep on giving, the true treasure that companies must cherish and nurture in order to sprout and succeed.

Bad karma apparently caught up with Grand Bazaar's owner, who was found dead one day in his home, after someone had shot him in front of his wife and kids. Although he was already in bankruptcy, his obstinate widow would not sell the business to the Azarkmans. The property went into foreclosure and the brothers had to find a third party to make an offer on their behalf; they bought it from the bank for $1.2 million. Their operation grew to 28,000 square feet now, offering both electronics and furniture. Sales were multiplying every day, new and referred customers were walking through the doors, seeking their credit lines, in search of their first TV, their first mattress, their first camera—their version of the American Dream.

Opening a business can be a very simple idea, but it has many aspects the would-be businessman needs to review before doing anything; you have to take many steps before you actually make the first one. Put your ideas together, create a plan of where, what, how, when, and how much you will need to start. You'll need to decide what kind of legal structure you must have, the type of protection you'll need from insurance companies, evaluate all of the taxes you'll be paying, select your business name, and do your due diligence to make sure the name is not being used by any other entity (trademark and copyright infringement can be costly propositions). When you have a name for your business, you'll have to register it with the county clerk and the state. If you chose to start, then get a federal trademark and a domain name for use in cyberspace. If you've already selected the location where you'll open your operation, you'll need to sign a lease. If that's the case, learn all of the legal implications of this real estate agreement. Then you'll need to have all of the licenses and permits, like employment identification numbers (EINs), so you can report seller's permits, local sales tax, business license, etc., to the IRS. Accounting and keeping the books are essential to making sure your business is profitable. It sounds exhausting because it is, but this is the real world of creating a business. It is not a simple thing and, if for any reason you skip a step, you'll be in trouble.

Inside of their operation, Jerry developed different ways to communicate among the associates and always trained their supervisors and group leaders to improve their level of service. This included being more professional and building trust between the customer and the salesperson. They would train their employees in their responsibilities as leaders in the organization, and show them their highest priority was to maintain a family-oriented, excellent, honest, sincere, positive, caring, and respectful relationship with all associates at all times. They wanted each and every one to feel that it was a must to adopt this positive lifestyle and make it the culture of the company.

There were many associates that had intimate relationships with other associates—something normal in any neighborhood, in any workplace. These were the pre-Anita Hill/Clarence Thomas hearings days, when sexual harassment regulations were not established, but La Curacao's vision was already very clear and advanced for its time because they wanted to protect the integrity of both parties and of the company. Associates who were in relationships could stop their romance at any time and one party could end up hurt, which could definitely affect the company. Some would leave the company so they would not have to see each other, or stay and start a new relationship, causing more fire and internal problems. It can be a very sticky situation when employees bring their private lives into the work space, so there have to be guidelines for them to follow in order to avoid harassment and even abusive situations.

Tito was born in a city named Cuscatancingo, which is very close to San Salvador, El Salvador's capital. His father was an auto parts salesman and his mother a dressmaker. He was their only child, and both parents were out working all the time. Tito was often home all by himself. At the age of nine, he was already taking care of all of the household duties, so when his parents came home exhausted after working hard all day, he'd already have cooked the family meal. Dedicated to his studies, Tito became his school's top student, which honored him with a scholarship to a private school. He walked a long distance from his home to his elementary school, but now, with the new middle school, the distance had doubled.

Bullying has always existed in schools all over the planet. This abusive treatment was the first thing Tito experienced at his new school, where all older pupils mixed with younger children. When the school year started, the new arrivals were the target for harassment by the older students. Tito would just observe and ignore them. He let them bother him until, one day, he had his hand on one side of the desk when one of the older kids smashed his hand against the desk with his foot. The calm, inoffensive, skinny Tito stood on his two feet and, with one hand, lifted his desk, threw it on top of the older pupil, and grabbed him by his hair; at that point, they had to be separated. Tito went home and told his father, who came with him to his school to talk to the principle. When he saw how much bigger and older the other student was, he couldn't believe that his son had won the fight.

He had to move elsewhere to finish middle school, and when Tito, who loved to sing, attended high school, he learned how to play the guitar. He'd often go sing with his two cousins at various places where they'd pass around a hat to make money. It was cash for him, money that he was learning to earn. His mom was sewing for a company that asked her to travel with it to France to help them at a wedding dress store, so off she went. Meanwhile, Tito and his father had to make it on their own. One day, Tito got sick and didn't show up at school. The next day, when Tito returned to class, the teacher asked him why he had been absent. When Tito explained that he'd been sick, she didn't believe him and called the principal, who was strict and practiced corporal punishment. Once the headmaster was called, everyone started shaking. His M.O. was to take the pupil and kick and hit him or her in front of the entire class.

Tito prepared himself. He was not going to let anybody touch him. He made it very clear to the principal that he should not dare to get close to him. Tito left and never went back to school from that day onwards. He was ready to take his life into his hands and move into his future, and he told his father that he wanted to study drawing through Modern School, a correspondence school where students studied by mail. His father agreed and bought him the course. Tito completed his drawing classes, earned his diploma, and went to work for a magazine company.

Operating any business requires a division of labor. Every employee has an important role to play, and the sum is greater than its parts. One of the most important tasks they had was making this point clear to their associates. It was important that everyone understand their role in the labor structure. Each worker needed to understand what his or her responsibilities were. Associates were trained to understand that each one needed to be productive, because everyone was accountable for reaching the department and company goals at all times. Each and every employee had to follow the rules, respect their duties, the company policy and philosophy. The associate was carrying the company's brand, message, and image, which the executives wanted to be recognized by the public.

La Curacao was now bigger than ever and full of merchandise. Customers were from many different countries. Mexicans formed the majority of the customer base; Salvadorans and Guatemalans were tied as the store's second best customers. Jerry, who loved history, read and learned about Mayan and Aztec cultures. He had traveled to Spain and could see the cultural differences amongst his customers. He started reading about how advanced both cultures had been. The Mayans had a written language based on hieroglyphics, created their own mathematics system using dots and bars, and invented the zero, while Europeans were still dealing with Roman numerals. They had a solar calendar with 365 days that included ten months with twenty days and five days in between. Mayans had developed and flourished in the southern part of Mexico, Guatemala, El Salvador, and Honduras.

The Aztecs were located more in the northern part of Mexico. They dominated the region beyond the Mayans and were much more organized in towns. They had their own education system. Those younger than fourteen years old were selected to go to two different schools. One school was called Telpchcalli, where students were trained in military strategy. Pupils went to the Calmecac School to learn astronomy, writing, statesmanship, and theology. They developed irrigation systems, drained swamps, and were even able to cultivate crops on manmade islands raised on lakes. Aztecs domesticated the wild turkey and knew how to cultivate maize, avocados, beans, squash, sweet potatoes, tomatoes, and chilies. The Aztecs were the dominant race, and they had cities everywhere, collected taxes, and developed the Aztec sun calendar.

The big temples and pyramids Mesoamericans constructed amazed the world. Jerry kept reading, visiting the region, and understanding the power of this race. He believed that all descendants of the Mayans and Aztecs—including the mestizos, (children of indigenous and white parents, with a mixed racial ancestry)—should be extremely proud of their past. But instead, they were not as confident as him. They were more shy and quiet, exhibiting completely different attitudes than what you could see in their own land. The power reflected in their art, temples, and pyramids was not present when you saw them at the store. Jerry started thinking that he had to bring these symbols to the stores and make his customers feel protected and proud of their past.

He visited the western part of Honduras at Copán, a powerful Mayan city located in the southern part of Mesoamerica, close to the border between Honduras and Guatemala. This was the biggest representation of the Mayan empire in the region. They settled in the Copán valley, which was a fertile area with a river. The city was developed by Mayans who came from Tikal, and their stories were found in ancient manuscripts. The city was founded by its first king, K'nich Yax K'uk' Mo, who called it the new Mayan Empire. According to the old stories, it is said that a coup was organized in Tikal and a warrior was sent to eliminate K'nich Yax K'uk' Mo.

There have been studies to trace the dynasty through bones found in the region and they discovered that the king's wife was from Copán and that K'nich Yx K'uk' Mo had been sent by the Tikal dynasty years before on a mission to conquer and establish this kingdom. All these theories only support this culture's high development in mathematics, engineering, and survival techniques. It still remains an archeological mystery as to why the Mayan Empire fell. Theories include the collapse of trade routes, epidemics, and droughts. But the final reason has never been definitively explained.

Jerry found out about Copán, the Corn God, who symbolizes life and death. He reworked the icon, using only the part that signifies life, and made it the emblem of the company. He knew that many other companies were abusing immigrants because they had no papers, which made it easier to take advantage of them. Jerry did not want the vulnerable newcomers to feel like strangers in a strange land; he wanted them to sense that they were welcome and treated with respect. He was giving these transplants the impression that they were equal members of America's gorgeous mosaic of cultures, and as good as any other person. At La Curacao, they could be sure they'd develop all of their confidence, without any fear. The image of the Corn God was a way of delivering a warm welcome to anyone from that region, an opportunity to send a friendly message proclaiming that inside these portals were people exactly like them.

La Curacao's associates needed to serve these descendants of the continent's biggest civilizations with the deference they deserved. What was most important for the staff was to assist, respect, care for, and be honest with them as customers; this was pounded into their consciousness during all training sessions. In addition, they needed to demonstrate esteem at all times and be on their best behavior. To be and to continue being part of the company's family, everyone had to contribute equally to its success. It was part of almost every single conversation between supervisors and associates. Anyone who was not performing as an individual opposed the company's philosophy, and definitely placed all of their co-workers at risk.

Meanwhile, Tito continued singing and working, developing magazines in El Salvador. Over time he moved to another firm. One day, the owner's sister had an accident in Panama and the entire family moved there to take care of her. Tito was out of a job, but his music connections helped him to start as a sales agent selling clothing, such as Levis, town to town during the worst time of the war between the guerillas and the army. Driving his car from a town where he had collected payment for a shipment, he tried depositing the money at a bank, but fearing a rebel invasion, the branch had closed early. Once back on the road, Tito was stopped by guerillas who were burning cars and killing people. Next in line, he didn't know what to do and was thinking about his only property on earth, and his boss' money. Once the guerilla confronted him, Tito said, "Why do you want to destroy my car? I'm not a government person and this car is all I have. You guys shouldn't hurt poor people like me."

The guerilla yelled at him, "So get out of here. I won't do anything, but hurry!" He looked like a very young guy. His face was covered by a bandana. Tito stepped on the accelerator and did not look back, thanking God all the way home.

During his singing phase, one of his fans became a close friend and invited him to travel to Miami, but Tito told him that he'd never been on a plane and that he didn't have a visa. His amigo asked Tito if he had a passport. As he didn't, the friend gave him a name and told him to get one through one of his contacts. Once Tito received his passport, he went to the U.S. Embassy. After waiting in line to be interviewed, his name was called and he was escorted to an office. Once the door opened, Tito saw his friend sitting behind a desk inside. His amigo was the U.S. Consul General for El Salvador! Needless to say, Tito got his visa, but as things developed, he never traveled to Miami. Time passed and he kept hearing about the opportunities in America, where the streets were paved with proverbial gold. Tito's band was bigger now and he had contracts to play all of the time, but most of the money he earned was spent on renting equipment. So he decided to go to the U.S., work hard there, buy all of the equipment his band needed, and then come back to live and perform in El Salvador.

It sounded simple. One of his friends told him that he had a cousin in L.A., who he asked to host Tito. The musician had married a woman in El Salvador and they already had a daughter. Saying goodbye to his little girl was the most difficult thing for him to do. Tito cried all the way to the airport, retaining the image of her standing on the sidewalk outside of their home in his head for years, along with her parting words, "*Adios, papito.*" Once he arrived in Los Angeles, his friend's cousin was indeed waiting for him at LAX,. At first, he shared the family's one room apartment with their two kids. Tito started working, earning $4.25 an hour unloading containers—hard work for little money. He had to send money to his wife and daughter, plus send part of his meager salary to his mom, since he had used her house as collateral in order to take out a loan to buy equipment for the band, which he then had to sell to pay for his ticket to America.

Tito went on to live in several different homes and work at all different kinds of jobs. His frequent singing won him friends who always helped him. One day, one of these friends showed him a catalog with many drawings of products. His friend told him that he worked for this company, and one of the owners was the one doing the drawings. Tito, a talented draftsman, immediately thought he could help, so he went to meet Jerry and started working for him as a freelance graphic artist, drawing the products for the catalog.

Tito's wife had kept the money he'd been sending to his mom and one day he received a phone call from some coyotes, informing him that they had taken his wife and that he had to pay $1,500 in order for them to release her. Tito put some savings together, sold his guitar, and got together most of the money. As she was the last border crosser to be delivered, they agreed to release her for that amount of money. She had left their child behind to stay with her grandmother, and Tito continued drawing La Curacao's catalog.

Meanwhile, the La Curacao's sales strategies were working, the associates were trained, and the avenues of advertising started expanding. TV and radio ads were extremely expensive; most advertisers could afford to show only a very small example of the whole operation. Jerry had created the catalog by drawing its products, but now he had Claudio and Tito helping him to produce it and he was mailing it out. It was very simple—Claudio had beautiful handwriting and Tito knew how to draw. It sounded easy enough but in reality, the catalog involved a lot of work. It was produced by drawing every single product by hand. Initially, they didn't use any photos. Claudio had great calligraphy. He'd write all of the messages, plus features and benefits of every item, by hand. Claudio also wrote the address of each customer and pasted stamps onto the envelopes.

Drawing all La Curacao's products took lots of time. One day, Jerry told Tito he was looking to hire salespeople, and asked him to refer any potential employees to him. Tito told him that he was a salesman, but Jerry could not believe it, so he told his employer how he had sold apparel for Levis, and other clothing companies. Jerry hired him as a sales associate and kept using him as a freelance artist for the catalog on the side.

Always one to keep up with the times, Jerry decided he wanted to use a computer to develop the catalog. He wanted to use Corel Corporation software. Corel is derived from the name Cowpland Research Laboratory, a computer software company specializing in graphic processes and programs. It became known for creating the graphics program CorelDRAW in 1989. When Jerry bought the computer and the program, Tito refused to use it. Jerry took the program home and promised Tito he was going to learn how to use it, and then teach him how to operate it. He did just that, showing Tito how to start the computer, then how to draw and add colors, step by step.

Jerry always explaining to their management team the responsibilities they had toward each associate, and emphasizing their wellbeing. This included creating accurate and understandable associate compensation programs, which would build confidence in the system for each one of the staffers. Members of the sales force often had questions as to how they were compensated. So the management team would sit with each salesperson and calculate sample commissions. They also created automatic reports enabling the associate to check how they were doing and to see if their sales had been posted. This became a simple way to build confidence in the system, thereby removing the element of uncertainty.

The main message would always be telling their associates that the only difference between their position and a management position was the respective tasks each had to perform. Other than these different types of duties, there was no superiority in any way. They were all associates. And when they heard these words from the owners, they felt like they were part of the family and had ownership of the company.

Jerry would often be on the floor, selling to the customers, and competing with the sales force. To ensure that everyone knew their sales goals were attainable, the Brothers Azarkman made sales, too, and were the biggest, best examples of hard work for their team. This was an additional opportunity for customers to build confidence in the company. They directly encountered the owners and could ask them any question, face to face. For some shoppers, it was a great chance to see Jerry, whom they knew from when he was knocking on their doors, selling them their first products. For the sales force, it encouraged their competitive spirit.

You could always talk to them. They were always available to chat with their staffers, too. The Brothers were the first ones to tell everyone that the company had an open door policy. Any associate had the right and was invited to visit any manager's office, regardless of his or her position within the company. Jerry would often repeat this mantra to everyone. The owners gave all of their associates the confidence and assurance that if one had a complaint or problem regarding his or her department or manager, the manager would not mistreat this worker or retaliate against him or her. Any associate must feel free to speak his or her mind at all times, without fear of retaliation.

Jerry would always tell his sales force in the training meetings that they needed to get to the customers heart. If they were able to connect on that level with the buyer, they'd become return customers. Customer loyalty was not only for the company, but for them as associates as well. Getting to the customer's heart had to start by delivering above expectations and showing the customer that the associate knew what he or she was talking about. Building that knowledge could only be done by studying the features and benefits of the products they were selling.

They continued stressing their training, working hard to prepare their management teams, making them understand that it was their responsibility to encourage and support all of their associates, and help staffers continue with their education, to the best of their ability. This included helping them with schooling, seminars, and company/outside training programs. Their education was seen as a gain for the company, as well as a benefit for the individual's personal and professional growth.

Jerry's fourth principle for converting his twenty dollars into a multimillion-dollar operation was his vendor connection. The sales representatives of the many companies who knocked on his door would find in Jerry a warm, open individual, who always had enthusiasm and energy and was tirelessly looking for deals for his customers. The relationship Jerry developed with the companies' representatives made them seek him out each time they had a special, a close out, a rebate, etc.

These representatives offered La Curacao products and services. They were always seen as partners. The manufacturers and dealers who represented these lines were paid according to the terms established by their agreement with La Curacao. There was always a friendly welcome for the vendors, who felt like that they were part of the operation. The representatives were asked for their opinions and suggestions regarding how to improve sales. They were invited to train the sales force, were part of the sales strategy, and involved in improving the knowledge of the sales force regarding the features and benefits of the products.

Creating this relationship with vendors made La Curacao's operation an important part of the vendors' agendas. When a product was recalled, the vendors were immediately asked to come to the outlet and explain why. When their companies discontinued an item, or there was a rebate or a price protection, La Curacao was the first to be notified. When an item was closed out, they were the first to find out. All of these benefits were transmitted directly to La Curacao's customers.

1981 to 1982 cutting and pasting pictures, manually building catalogs which created great response rate from the clients. These were the seeds of what latter will be the Marketing department.

Chapter Twelve

The Sky is the Limit

What a joy when all of your plans start to materialize! It is exciting when your vision becomes a reality, your business starts operating, you open your doors to the world, and you launch your online e-business. Jerry never stopped. He kept going, motivating his people, buying, working his campaigns, and creating all kinds of promotions. The customers kept coming. Meanwhile, they continued working at the office with the banks, inventories, and accounting.

Once your business is open and it's up and running, any new idea has the potential to bring you additional revenue. Some departments or categories give you a profit margin from the get-go. Some will take time to actually generate profit. And, the only reason some of the others exist is to create traffic; their immediate income may be little or nothing, but they attract customers and produce buzz. There will be departments or lines of products and services you'll have to build on for years until you'll see any results. Keeping a close eye on every single product you sell is your everyday duty. The company's profit is its good health, but if you don't watch it carefully, all of your hard work will have little or no pay off. Even worse, in this cyclical, competitive economy, there's always the possibility of losing everything you've struggled to accomplish.

La Curacao kept growing. The energy you felt when you visited the store invited you to return over and over again. Every weekend, there were events with music, food, raffles, clowns, and balloons for the kids. The sales were growing, and the associates were getting more benefits. Selecting the right products was key for increasing the volume of sales. Electronics formed the biggest department; customers came for their TVs, boom boxes, cameras, and the latest technology. It was essential for La Curacao to keep up with the times. Jerry was always involved in choosing products. He had an uncanny knack for understanding what the consumer wanted and was looking for. The firm's buying power and negotiating muscle was growing, but the Brothers Azarkman were still buying from distributors, not directly from the majority of brands they sold. Jerry was always trying to open accounts directly with the main offices of the electronic companies, and always seeking better pricing and credit lines.

Jerry learned very early on in life that creating a relationship with people always yielded much better results. He'd try to get to the heart of people, even with the most difficult personalities. He'd attempt to penetrate their inner world, to touch their soul, and let them lay a hand on his. Vendors were not any different. They were trying to sell their products, too, and for Jerry, it was a great opportunity to bring the newest products to the store. He'd treat his vendors like part of the family. They didn't need any appointments to see him. If he was eating when they showed up, he'd split his plate in two and share his meal with them. Even the most stuck up sales representative ended up at the kitchen table eating with Jerry. This made them feel welcome, like they belonged to the extended Azarkman clan.

Jerry always personally answered their calls and made them feel important. He was always ready to jump on their offers, but made it clear that there had to be a benefit for the salesperson, too. Any business negotiation had to work for both sides and be a win-win situation. Even though negotiating with Jerry meant additional value needed to be brought to the table, both parties always ended up happy, which was the purpose of doing business with each other. Vendors needed to feel that they were business partners; if La Curacao was successful, the vendor would be, too.

Jerry always listened to ideas and suggestions on how to set up products and how their features were different from comparable goods. Product features that were not important to his customers meant nothing; what made all the difference was the kind of benefit this feature would bring to their home. Customers were already expecting the staffers to train them and explain all of the features on the products. That made the biggest difference in their business.

Les Wallace, Ralph Chamberlain, and German Season had been selling to Jerry since the beginning of his door-to-door days. Les Wallace started out at a very young age, selling Christmas trees at a friend's lot in California, where he made a record by retailing more than 3,000 trees. But even then, Les thought sales was not for him and he started working at Sound Design, a consumer electronics company. One day, top management asked Les if he could oversee the administration of sales since he was the most knowledgeable employee, and he did. There was an opening in the sales team and he was offered this opportunity, which came with a great increase in salary, so he took it. Jerry called to find out how he could buy directly from the Sound Design manufacturer and the representative sent him to Les Wallace. This was when Jerry was still going door-to-door. Jerry started buying radios, telephone clocks, and clock radios from Sound Design, adding them to his catalog.

Les observed Jerry to see how he was growing his operation. Les was interested in how Jerry sold the product for a fair price and then stood behind the sale. Customers felt that he was someone they could go back to for more sales and to complain about defective products. In Les Wallace's eyes, Jerry was a soft-spoken man, and when they were negotiating he'd get straight to the point. Les believed Jerry didn't take advantage of his customers and gave them a unique opportunity, one many of them could not find anywhere else. The best thing about working with him as a vendor was that Jerry always paid on time.

While representing Sound Design, Les saw that the Yorx vendor was not representing the company properly, so he called this electronics company to offer his services. But once he phoned the company, Les couldn't make an appointment with La Curacao buying office. This compromised the security of his current job. Les decided to call Jerry to tell him that he had things to sell. Jerry told the vendor to come over right away, and introduced Les to each one of La Curacao's buyers, telling them that if Les Wallace called them with a deal, they should buy it. Les vividly remembers this as if it happened today, as Jerry proved once more that he was a *mentsch*, an individual with character and great moral fiber. He was a person who wouldn't forget where he started and who had helped him along the way. Les is still a vendor at La Curacao after thirty years. He currently represents Coby Electronics.

Ralph Chamberlain was the representative for Bulova watches. Ralph knew Jerry from his door-to-door days, too. When Jerry tried to open an account with him, Ralph said he needed an address to be able to sell Jerry watches. The first requirement for delivering the merchandise was to have a physical address; even though it was a prepaid order, they wanted to make sure the product had a responsible person to sign for the shipment. This is one of the reasons Jerry decided to open his first location at Laurel and Santa Monica. By doing this, he was able to open an account directly with Bulova, a leading watch manufacturer. This was one of the first brands Jerry was able to buy directly from, and at that point, this was his biggest accomplishment.

Bulova was created by Joseph Bulova in 1875 in New York. Like many others in the United States he was an immigrant, originally from Bohemia in what is now the Czech Republic. Bulova started his company at the age of 23 by opening a small jewelry shop in Manhattan, similar age Jerry started his business. His story is similar to that of many immigrants, tales of hard work that resemble Jerry's own saga. He started selling clocks, pocket watches and table watches in big quantities. Bulova found a helluva product, a niche market and he kept on ticking. He learned how to fix watches, make his own watches and developed new parts and tools. But he wanted to be different from the rest of his competition: While Bulova was not the only one selling or making watches, the quality he produced and the level of artistry he brought to each and every piece caught the attention of customers. They bought his product because Bulova timepieces had the highest accuracy, and the caliber of his products separated him from the rest of the competition. Thus, he added to his product value.

The stories of how companies are built have many points of coincidence; here you had an innovator who masters his business to make it different from his competition. Jerry identified a niche and provided them with unique credit, he sold them packages of product which no one could compare the price and both entrepreneurs made their companies different from the rest.

The Czech's watch-making operation was so successful he decided to open a manufacturing operation in the world's most famous country for watches: Switzerland. The city best known for watches was Geneva, located in a French speaking Swiss canton the Reformation.

Wristwatches were invented during the First World War, and people moved from the pocket watch to the wristwatch. Bulova stayed on top of the world of watches, introducing the first line of men's wristwatches. This brought many changes to the industry: not only was the watch now going to be worn on the wrist, and not in the breast or trouser pocket, but for the first time Joseph developed a standardization of parts never seen before.

An innovator, the Czech-born manufacturer was the first to create a line of wristwatches for women, too and the first to add a diamond to it. A stickler for function as well as form, Joseph Bulova believed in accuracy: the time had to be perfect in all of his watches, so he created an observatory tower in Manhattan to take readings, and hired a mathematician to log all of the data for accuracy, as all Bulova watches had to tell the same exact time. The clever entrepreneur likewise believed in advertising, and when Charles Lindbergh made his transatlantic solo flight from New York to Paris, Lucky Lindy won the Bulova watch prize and became the official spokesperson for the Lone Eagle, a line of men's watches. Joseph made 5,000 of these watches and sold them in three days. He created the world's first clock radio and first electric clock. Bulova was the first company to invest $1 million dollars in TV advertising during the Depression years, and supported retailers by offering payment plans made in installments over a period of time. He used clever advertising slogans: in 1941 ads depicting a clock superimposed over a map of the U.S.A. proclaimed "America runs on Bulova time"—reportedly the world's very first television commercial. And radio ads announced: "It's five o'clock Bulova watch time."

By providing Bulova watches, Jerry was able to offer his customers not only the latest watch models, but a prestigious, high quality brand that brought status to La Curacao. Minus any middleman, he was buying directly from Bulova through his relationship with Ralph Chamberlain, thereby making a higher profit margin. He now had all the benefits that buying without a middleman offered, such as manufacturer's warranties, the possibility of repairing the product for his customers, debuting the latest models, better pricing, and more profit. In addition, this bought more reliability, inventory consistency, and a stronger negotiating position to his company.

In addition to all of these benefits, Jerry was able to observe, firsthand, the power of a brand and the power of advertising. He saw how a name like Bulova opened doors for him and his salespeople, and how people trusted the brand. The quality of the product enhanced the perception of La Curacao's trustworthiness and its standing with customers, vendors, and sales associates. Jerry was selling quality items and this helped his own brand.

Jerry developed great connections with all of those who had helped him to start his business—his customers, his associates, and especially with other companies' sales representatives. He had already been doing business with the electronics import company, Century. Even though Jerry was buying directly from Century, there were other brands he had to buy so he could showcase variety and display the latest in technology. Customers were always asking for brands they knew from back home in their countries, like Fisher and Sanyo. When Jerry was buying from Midtown Electronics, he met German Season, a Sanyo representative. They had a short talk. German gave him a business card and Jerry went on to cultivate a close relationship with German.

Born and raised in Chicago, like many men of his age, German served in World War II, and when he returned home after the war, he and his family moved to California. In January 1971, he started working for Sanyo because he knew three other men who'd gone to Japan and went on to represent Sanyo in the United States. German was good at sales. He was a real people person and he loved talking with people and developing strong relationships with them.

Jerry dreamt of the time he would call German in order to deal directly with Sanyo. One day, he made up his mind and phoned him. German told Jerry that to open an account, he had to buy $3,500 worth of products in one order. At first Jerry was not ready to order this amount, but now he had a goal to accomplish. He knew that he had to sell to more families to be able to increase his buying power and accomplish the minimum order of $3,500. German hooked him up with one of his other accounts and Jerry was able to buy the small quantities he needed through them. He'd place the order through German and then pick it up with cash. It was always a smooth operation. They operated this way for around three months and the quantities increased little by little. The transactions were crystal clear; Jerry went to pick them up when he said he would, and paid in cash, just as he'd promised.

He knew that once his business grew, he was going to be able to buy direct. Jerry had moved to Burbank and his volume of sales had grown, so he called German again to tell him he could buy $3,500. He'd saved up the money and was ready to buy. Jerry knew that by buying direct, his price would improve and he'd expand the company. But, his place of business was still only a hole in the wall, so small only three people could fit in it.

German understood Jerry's determination, but the minimum purchase had gone up to $12,000, and opening an account required more than just the buying capacity for the first order. Jerry had to fill out a form, have credit lines from other companies, and needed a picture of the store. Jerry asked him if he could come and help him fill out the form, and German agreed to come and assist him. German not only filled out the form for him, he convinced Sanyo's main office to give Jerry the opportunity and provide him with credit. At that time, all Jerry had was a bank account, but not even a credit card of his own or, of course, for his business. Thirty days passed and he got a letter confirming that he now had a Sanyo account for a minimum order of $6,000. He actually got his first line of credit without a prepaid account.

Jerry had made a good impression on German Season, who was able to understand Jerry perfectly because he had dealt with several Israeli customers before. But in German's eyes, Jerry possessed huge potential. He always paid on time in cash, kept all of his promises, and when they moved to 1313 Olympic, he brought soap and toilet paper for the bathrooms, just as a contribution to better customer service. German trained the salespeople, always bringing them bagels and orange juice. From the very first moment they met, Jerry gave German the impression of being a very honest business man, and this word of mouth brought the brothers more and more business. German was able to get Jerry's payments extended from thirty days to ninety days, and he always paid on time. German remembers that when he went to major meetings, he'd get special deals then call Jerry to offer him the promo. Jerry would tell him, "German you do not need to call me. If you think it will be good for us, just ship it. You make the order for me."

That's how a trusting relationship developed between them. German would help them sell when big promotions came; while he did not speak any Spanish, he was still able to help on the floor at the store.

Although currently owned by Panasonic, Sanyo is a Japanese company that was created in 1950 by Toshio Lue. The firm's name means "three oceans," which the owner chose because he believed his company would one day be a worldwide enterprise selling its products across three oceans: The Pacific, Atlantic and Indian oceans. As an electronics company Sanyo, manufactured radios, speakers, video cameras, black and white then color TVs, refrigerators, tape recorders, IBM computers, digital cameras, vacuum cleaners, batteries, and more. Sanyo's philosophy was very clear: "We are committed to becoming an indispensable element in the lives of people all over the world."

All of Sanyo's operations and relations with customers were developed according to three points: "Excellent human resources, superior technology, and first class service." Its founder would always say, "We seek to be like the sun, which shines upon all alike, regardless of race, creed, religion or difference in wealth." Mr. Lue's words for his employees were: "Work with wholehearted sincerity." One of Sanyo's principles was to anticipate customer satisfaction, which was also one of Jerry's strong suits—he'd have immediate insight into what customers would like and want, which he had learned from them.

With direct access to Sanyo, Jerry now had quite an opportunity in his hands. He could buy the latest technology, select the models, pay on terms, and select his ideal product. Once it arrived at his location, payment wasn't due for thirty days or more. This inevitably changed the world for Jerry, who now had his third direct line of credit from manufacturers; if he regularly paid on time (which he, of course, planned to do), his line of credit would increase over the years and even help him start dealing with other vendors. Just by having a first relationship, everything would change. He understood selling electronics required him to stock the latest in technology, and now with Sanyo, he would have the newest goods; he was not at the mercy of whatever merchandise he was able to find in downtown L.A. or at Century.

In just a few words, German expressed why Jerry was so successful. He said, "He had a winning way of seeing everything. He is an honest and reliable human being, and there are not many people like him. He's a *mentsch*—Yiddish for a person with integrity. In his entire way of doing business, he had a big smile. Sales people love him because he treats everyone well and is upfront with you."

Jerry is a big believer in the need to push yourself to accomplish what you want and need to obtain. Push and push to accomplish more. If you push less, you'll get less. He makes an analogy based on what he learned by observing the handbag his father had bought his mom. When he was little, Jerry noticed his mom took her handbag everywhere. Her handbag weighed half a pound and was full, so his father went and bought her a bigger handbag. Now Muluk's handbag weighed two and half pounds and was also full, so Oscar bought her an even bigger handbag. Then she'd fill it up with five pounds worth of contents. To Jerry, life is similar to Muluk's handbag: The bigger the opportunity that's presented to you, it's your job to fill it up all the way to capacity. The more capacity you have, the more you need to push yourself to make more, know more, get more—the sky's the limit. Any space Muluk had left in her handbag, she'd fill up.

When Jerry opened his operation in Burbank, the person responsible for the place's real estate office was not an easy person to deal with. The leasing process was hard and many applicants were turned down. Jerry heard about how difficult it was to lease space at the Golden Mall, and he prepared for rejection. He used the charm that opened doors for him and promised to be a good tenant who promptly paid his rent every month. He used simple words, the right words, sincere and not arrogant or pretentious words. Jerry presented himself exactly as he was, and this opened doors for him. The realtor gave him the papers for the lease and he had a location. However, he forgot to ask for parking spaces. He later learned—from the other tenants—this was one of the most difficult negotiating points with the realtor. The next day, the leaser provided the parking information, giving Jerry four parking spaces in the back and one in the front. In his first visit he had already walked out of the office with a lease in his hands.

The new location had traffic during the week and he'd transport customers to the Golden Mall via van to see and buy merchandise. Jerry had food available there all the time and the operation mainly took place on weekdays. But on Sundays, the whole square was empty and he'd setup speakers and hold a party for Latinos in an Anglo neighborhood. Customers eager to buy his goods were transported from Downtown L.A. to wonderful downtown Burbank by the company's van. Inside of his place, Jerry worked with shoppers, showing them the line of products.

Jerry knew what his customers wanted to buy. By now, he'd walked the streets for several years. He had knocked on his customers' doors, sat in their living rooms, installed TVs in their bedrooms—he knew what their needs were. When a vendor approached him to sell any product, he perused it with a customer's eye, immediately knowing whether or not this product was for them. Selecting the right line of products is the biggest decision when starting a business; you can enjoy buying the goods but if your selection is not saleable, your business suffers. The worst ending for your story would be shutting down, closing your doors, losing money and very valuable time.

Jerry's challenges kept growing. He leased a bigger space in Burbank and had to pay rent for the business, his employees' commissions, and rent for his own apartment. He held these goals very clearly in his mind. He had to make enough money to pay both of his rent and meet his payroll in order for his business to continue. He'd repeat this in his mind all the time; he was constantly focused on his objectives. The situation remained the same when the operation moved to 1313 Olympic. They had a larger outlet and similar challenges, but also bigger loan payments, bigger commissions, and bigger supplier payments.

The strategy on the floor was designed by both of them. The brothers discussed presentation, and how they wanted the layout of the products to look and be developed. It was all based on how much money there was to invest in the display and to select the lineup. When they bought the Grand Bazaar, they had a lot of space to fill and their product selection included furniture. Some vendors offered discounts for the floor samples. Some even sold their merchandise on consignment. Something was crystal clear in Jerry's mind: it was impossible to compete in every product category. There were many stores in downtown L.A., competition was extensive, and many businessmen had already followed in their footsteps by targeting the Latino market. But Jerry was certain about one thing: "I want to be the king in one category." He sought to be the biggest and the best, bigger and better than anyone else in one particular department. By doing this, word of mouth would spread faster than advertising and being the go-to guy and location for that specific product was a way of creating customer loyalty. The idea made sense and they selected one particular product line—cameras.

The good relationship with their vendors gave the operation access to more product selection. These vendors always thought of Jerry when they had a great deal, knowing he had the capacity to buy closeout sales with killer prices in large quantities. Closeouts went out within hours and vendors that had closeouts needed immediate answers from the buyer, which was always possible with Jerry. He'd answer the phone and give them an answer right then and there. Jerry added all kinds of accessories to particular product categories; with this, he'd give the store the possibility of creating unique packages that no one else could have, providing customers with an easy way to obtain all they needed in one shot, and at good prices. Cameras sounded like the right line for Jerry to focus on because there is a large variety of photography-related products and accessories. By creating this department chock full of merchandise, they could be the camera kings of all Los Angeles' downtown area, one of the biggest markets in the entire United States. This was not an impossible dream, but a possibility. They could make it happen by selecting correct merchandise and accurately pricing it.

In addition, this department could attract customers away from their competitors. Now these shoppers would prefer to check out what was new and cutting edge at La Curacao. Jerry added a whole line of them to the department, opening up a door to new traffic for a store that not only sold cameras, but also exposed buyers to the rest of the product lineup. Customers now had a one-stop shop location for all of their electronics, as well as for watches, gold, and furniture.

The word camera comes from the Latin words "camera obscura" or dark chamber. People love the possibility of preserving special times with their cameras, being able to go back in life and check out their kids when they were little, or the last picture of their parents. Indeed, a longtime giant in the photography field coined an advertising phrase that has now become part of our everyday parlance: "The Kodak moment." For years cameras have been a very important part of people's lives, to the extent that today's cameras are found in all kinds of electronic devices, such as tablets and cell phones. Jerry had the vision of turning this section into *the* department La Curacao and making it the undisputed king. He had a longtime interest in this area since his early years when he grew up helping his mom with her sewing machine and saving money to buy his camera and the chemicals required for developing photographs. The photo department brought back childhood memories and family struggles; after all of these years, his own business was up and running. Now Jerry's early ambition to own a good camera and be able to take as many pictures as he dreamt of was coming true, but in the form of a sales opportunity.

He wanted a complete department that included still cameras and point and click models, because they were simple for anyone who wanted to use them. This particular camera did everything for the photographer, such as lighting and automatic flash—even though, at the time, cameras still exclusively used film. This provided an even bigger opportunity for repeat customers to return to the store to buy film supplies. Jerry added Single Lens Reflex cameras, professional cameras which allowed photographers to change lenses. He also added accessories that create better lighting and tripods for stable, better quality pictures, among other items. Jerry trained the sales force very thoroughly in this category, knowing they needed extensive knowledge in all of these matters…Jerry instructed salespeople that if a customer left the store after buying a SLR camera with only the lens mounted on it, the buyer would probably stay with that lens the rest of his or her life. Therefore, during an initial sale, an associate's main goal was to sell the customer much more on the same day. It was a great opportunity to add more profit and more value to the customer—and possibly the only chance the associate had to make multiple sales to this consumer.

The accessories were unlimited. La Curacao carried all types of lenses, including the telephoto, a long focus lens used for different distances. By having many kinds of brands for various distances, they created sales opportunities for the staff. Flashes built for external applications provided another selling opportunity for them, as did the wide variety of film, including Kodak, Fuji, and so on. The point was to convince customers that everything they needed to become the next Ansel Adams was in one package worth $1,200.

The art of selling to customers was not only in cameras but also in other areas, like adding headphones to portable cassette players, adding components to their TVs, microphones to stereos, and many other accessories that made the sale more profitable and higher than the original price. This gave customers unique differences in their purchases that, in the end, added value to them. In other words: Accessorize! Accessorize! Accessorize!

Inside the store, the customer always found coffee and cookies. Salespeople were trained to refer to customers as cousin or brother-in-law. This made the shopper laugh, broke the ice, and opened the conversation up with the salesperson. Many of these customers became company associates. They knew the neighborhood, had family and friends there, and this generated even more customers. Jerry joked around with his customers, and he'd change their names, creating something like a nickname. He made up a name for one lady who he'd call Hola Mola whenever he saw her. Up until this day, everyone in her family calls her Mola, and although she moved from Los Angeles, whenever she visits family back in L.A., she always calls Jerry to say hi.

They often sat down to plan the products layouts. Renovating the store was essential to keeping it fresh and looking like there was something new available. It also had to do with the money they had to invest in the look of the store. The brothers opened a furniture department because they had to fill up more space in their store. But the main purpose was to fulfill customers' needs, as the Azarkmans provided credit for them to buy their first mattress, refrigerator, and TV. They were able to develop a furniture product with Century, a furniture manufacturer at South Central, L.A. (a different company from the original consumer electronics outlet). The product they developed was called Bolo, which was made of foam, covered with a strong fabric, and functioned both as a sofa and bed. Before futons were introduced to the marketplace, Bolo became a sensation. It was a very convenient item to have at home for any guests sleeping over. In countless cases, it became the first bed for many immigrants. The killer price lured tons of customers to come and buy the bed, as well as see the rest of the products La Curacao offered, and take advantage of their credit.

The strategy created on the floor was very simple—arrange the product line up by both category and price. All products were always set up in a step up program that started with a lead item then arranging the rest by price. This helped the salesperson take the customer through the different prices and benefits of the product, presenting the opportunity for selling better products. The product display was self-explanatory but the items' advantages and features of the product had to be explained by the sales associate, and credit was his or her biggest sales tool. The credit plans were adjusted to the individual customer's needs. If they wanted to make a fixed monthly payment, they'd determine how many months of credit they needed. There were no interest charges at the beginning of La Curacao's operation.

Since the company's first steps, it was very clear that a system was needed to handle the sales and the inventory. The tests kept increasing—the more sales the store made, the more challenges there were to know the inventory levels, what was in the warehouse, and what was on display. The credit lines, the accounting, and everything were all done manually, which was very time consuming. So the brothers started developing the idea of a computerized operations system.

Since their space was limited before the expansion to 1313, they used the attic of their Burbank storefront as a warehouse. The sheer volume and weight made it dangerous—they were afraid that one day the entire attic would collapse and cause a major accident at the store. So, when they moved to 1313, they decided to open a warehouse a few miles away. The problem was keeping an accurate inventory. Since sales constantly reduced the stock, it was nearly impossible to keep up inventory. In addition to sales, all of the customer information regarding credit and payment was handled by hand, rendering the probability of mistakes very high. Physically counting merchandise at the warehouse, and recording each sale, was the only accurate tracking method. But this was exhausting. In addition to sales, credit accounting was also still done by hand. There was no modern method to support the operation.

Ron Pinglas and Eric Baruch were hired to create a computerized system to enable the company to handle inventory, input customer information for credit risk management, process customer payments, and update accounts. The complexity of the system was challenging. They called the software the AR.

At his small operation in Burbank, Jerry had already created the firm's first credit card and his original system was entirely manual. It was the first steps of what later became a strong financial department. For the majority of customers, this credit card was the first credit they'd ever received—most were not eligible for credit in their homelands, either. Ron found an embossing machine previously owned by another company and used it to create his cards. Then the cards were hand delivered to customers. In reality, most applicants were approved; the company became famous for providing newcomers with their first line of credit in America.

When customers applied for credit, their application had a number of questions and it was a very fast process. Almost everyone got approved. At the beginning, the process for approval was not sophisticated. The idea of customers agreeing to pay a down payment was the strongest tool for protecting the company from losses. It was all a learning experience that required understanding the different countries' identification cards and developing a database of information to enable the merchant to find relatives if, for any reason, a customer did not pay his or her debt. In reality, the overwhelming majority did indeed pay for their purchases via their La Curacao credit card.

The key was gathering as much customer information as possible; a higher line of credit was approved if that person had been recommended by an existing customer in good standing. In terms of credit criteria, this was an important factor that reduced risk for the merchant. The application sought additional information, such as country of origin, province, or department. Incidentally, in addition to obtaining recommendations, this data helped La Curacao to open new accounts. The more references or contacts this person had, the better his or her rating became because La Curacao had more options for looking for that person if they didn't pay their bills. But the main reason for obtaining references was the opportunity to call and verify the identity of the new applicant, as well as asking the references if they, too, wanted to open a new credit account.

The amount of new accounts being opened was growing and growing. All of the information provided an opportunity to study that particular customer's purchasing behavior. They asked detailed questions to understand what had brought that customer to the store. This also allowed them to know which departments had more traffic and more demand. They also asked the customer how they had learned about La Curacao, which was important for determining the most effective media advertising. This helped them figure out which form of communications provided the most bang for their advertising buck?

Converting twenty dollars to $200 million. Not even by gambling is one able to get so much with such little investment! The biggest investment Jerry made was his convincing words, and his dedication. His fifth principle was creating an excellent floor layout and floor strategy. He'd already identified his niche market, customers, associates, and vendors. Now La Curacao had to stand out and be different from the rest of the competition. The rivals for his niche had customers, associates, and of course vendors and suppliers of the same products. But, Jerry developed a floor strategy. The store had a particular ambiance and a particular setup. The way the products were laid out was inviting. Vendors admired the creativity of the store, such as developing a wall of televisions, which that took days to setup. The cost of making a TV wall was outrageous, so they created their own by painting the wall and shelves black, then covering it with black carpet. Setting the TV sets on the wall made the place look huge, and the display gave the store a high tech look for everyone to admire.

Rodney Glen King was born in Sacramento, California in April, 1965, the second child of five siblings. His father, Ronald King, worked in construction and maintenance, and the family eventually moved to South Pasadena. Rodney started to work when he was in the fourth grade, cleaning commercial buildings with his father from 5:00 p.m. to 2:00 a.m. His concentration in class was "really wacked," as he later said in an interview. Like any other kid, Rodney attended school, but he had learning disabilities and studying was too difficult for him, so he was left back a year in high school. He decided to drop out in his senior year when he was nineteen. He married Crystal Waters who also had two children, so Rodney now had to provide for four kids, but he had trouble making ends meet. In July 1987, his wife filled a complaint with police contending that Rodney had beaten her up while she was sleeping and dragged her outside the house where he beat her again. He was placed on probation and ordered to attend counseling, but never showed up. Rodney's struggles continued; he'd hang out with his friends and drink alcohol every day.

At 6'3", Rodney was always considered a tall guy. His family found him to be gentle and kind, they nicknamed him the "gentle giant," while his friends called him Glen. His mother, Odessa King, raised him to be a Jehovah's Witness. She had converted due to her husband's drinking. Some say that both husband and wife were members of the Jehovah Witness faith for a long time.

Chapter Thirteen

The Riots

I t's incredible how little things in life can snowball into big things, going on to cause unexpected consequences. On the evening of March 2nd, 1991, parolee Rodney King was drinking while watching a basketball game at a friend's house. Shortly after midnight, King was speeding with two passengers, Bryant Allen and Freddie Helms, on Interstate 210, heading westbound. California Highway Patrol Officers Tim and Melanie Singer, a husband and wife team, spotted the vehicle on the Foothill Freeway and turned their patrol lights on. The Hyundai King was driving didn't immediately come to a halt, and the high-speed chase heard 'round the world was on.

In November 1989, Rodney was arrested on charges of assault with a deadly weapon, second-degree robbery, and intent to commit great bodily injury. He had gone to a convenience store and, brandishing a tire iron at the clerk, Rodney ordered him to empty the cash register. The clerk grabbed the tire iron and Rodney fell backwards on top of a pie rack. He swung the tire iron and left with $200. He subsequently pleaded guilty and was convicted of attempted robbery, though all of the other charges were dropped. Rodney was sentenced to two years behind bars and served one year at the California Correctional Center in Susanville, until he made parole and went home. Finding a job had been difficult in the past, but now, with the stigma of parole, finding gainful employment became even more difficult. Nevertheless, he got a part time job at Dodger Stadium.

The CHP officers followed him in hot pursuit, and the freeway chase reached speeds of up to 117 miles per hour. King drove off of the 210 and sped through residential neighborhoods, reaching eighty mph. By this time, he was being followed by several LAPD police cars and helicopters. After an eight-mile chase on city streets, King's car was cornered and he finally stopped the vehicle. King—who was on probation—had refused to stop because he knew he'd be charged with driving under the influence.

What happened next would trigger the largest urban rebellion in the U.S. during the 20th century. George Holliday, a plumber from Argentina who had been woken up by the police sirens, walked out onto the balcony of his Lake View Terrace apartment with a video camera. He proceeded to shoot a nine-minute video that shook the world. Holliday's riveting video is arguably among the most watched footage ever shot in human history, ranking up there with the Zapruder Film, the 8mm Kodachrome home movie bystander Abraham Zapruder shot with a Bell & Howell camera at Dallas in 1963 that captured the assassination of President Kennedy.

Meanwhile, blissfully unaware of what was to transpire, Jerry and Ron had begun operating their business every day of the week. The brothers vividly remember the day they decided to open La Curacao on Saturdays and Sundays, because it was a major decision, since most of their business had been conducted Mondays through Fridays. This decision greatly increased their sales, which almost doubled in volume. Weekends became so busy that the employees' schedules had to be planned very closely, in order to have enough people to take care of the customers. They had to hire new associates frequently to cover the different schedules.

Byron arrived to the states at the age of twenty three; his mom had left him in Guatemala to care for her sister Carmen who was ill and battling cancer in Los

Angeles. Carmen had a little boy Juan Carlos who would visit La Curacao with his mom all the time and Jerry would tell him "Get good grades and I will give you a gift". Juan Carlos was twelve when his mom past away. Byron's mom decides to stay in the states and bring him there. Once in Los Angeles Byron who was studying to become an architect decided to look for a job and Juan Carlos took him to meet Jerry. Once in the store the only opening they had was to wear the mascot's custom, don Paco, he was so skinny that wearing pillows to fill the spaces was the only option.

Byron's grandfather, his mom, and Juan Carlos were living in an apartment building next to La Curacao, it's was the easiest place for him to find a job. When he was not wearing the custom, he would be responsible for the decoration with balloons, and welcoming everyone to the store. But he didn't stop there he wanted to get promoted and after pushing and pushing he was promoted to the maintenance department.

Mike Falkenstein had a BA in Business Administration at Loyola Marymount, and started his career in cameras. One of his accounts was La Curacao, where he started as a vendor. One day he asked Jerry to hire him, and the owner said, "I cannot afford your salary." But Mike was so convinced of the company's potential that he encouraged Jerry to make a deal with him. Mike told Jerry to let him select the merchandise for the camera department and to pay him a percentage of the department's increased sales. It sounded reasonable to Jerry, who thought his investment would be the cost of the product for the inventory and he knew he had terms with his supplier, this would give La Curacao enough time to get their profit and pay Mike's his percentage.

The camera department became the strongest department in terms of growth and sales. Its stock included Sony Handycam camcorders—the type of video camera George Holliday used to record the Rodney King video. Those scenes would set off a tumultuous chain of events, ensnaring Los Angeles, as well as La Curacao. In any case, Mike proved his point; after demonstrating strong returns and results, he was hired to run the store and became La Curacao's first store manager. Standing 6'2", Mike was tall; with a complexion as white as snow and hair so blond it looked white. He became part of the team and, because his background in sales was strong, he was the perfect fit for the booming retail outfit.

Elizabeth Aldana was not the original name of the employee who was first known to everyone as Liliam Musgrove. Liliam had emigrated from Guatemala to Illinois and had started her college career when she met and married her boyfriend. However, things did not work out and she decided to move out. She got a divorce and her options where to keep her last name or go back to her birth name. From both of her names, she picked the second one. Instead of Liliam Elizabeth, she selected Elizabeth. The change was huge because people generally expected her to go back to using Liliam, thus, she became Elizabeth Aldana.

The college graduate moved from Springfield, Illinois to Los Angeles, where her sister was already living, and came with the dream of earning her law degree. She started by researching which law schools she wanted to attend. Her first choice was Loyola Maryland University, located on Olympic Blvd. in downtown L.A.

Elizabeth had moved to Los Angeles to become a lawyer. When she drove to get information from Loyola Marymount University, located a few blocks from La Curacao, she decided to park at the store's lot in order to avoid paying a parking fee at the college. When she parked, a security guard approached Elizabeth, who said she was going shopping at La Curacao, and the guard believed her. Upon entering the store, a woman asked her if she was there for a job interview and the aspiring attorney immediately said yes. She was given an application to fill out and went on to be interviewed by Mike Falkenstein.

He asked her several questions, which she confidently answered, and he told her "You're hired. We have openings in two departments—cosmetics and electronics." Elizabeth responded, "Do I look like I would enjoy cosmetics?" She wasn't wearing any makeup or heels, just jeans and a T-shirt. "You're right, you look more like you're right for electronics," Mike agreed. He then asked her what she knew about electronics. Elizabeth explained to him, in detail, how she'd connected her stereo to her TV set. That was all Mike needed to hear, and she started working in sales with Jerry.

Elizabeth remembers the competitive nature everyone had on the floor. If she was not fast enough, another salesperson would steal her customer. But, they were making so much money that she didn't worry about it. She soon became one of the top salespeople. She was fast, soft spoken, and could help three customers at the same time. She learned all about the features and benefits of the products, so she was able to easily explain them to the customers and move shoppers from one product to another. And the more she sold, the better her commission became. She knew the formula for her commission and that the bigger the margin on the product, the bigger her check was. The smarter you were on the floor level in identifying the products with bigger margins, the higher the income the associate received.

Since the inventory was increasing all the time, La Curacao rented storage space nearby. The inexpensive inventory was stored and secured only by a lock. So the management decided to open a warehouse in the vicinity. They called this space Oak, because it was on Oak Avenue. The 5,000 square foot space contained their entire stock of furniture, appliances, TVs, etc., that were not in the store. Two associates were assigned to oversee the operation of the new warehouse and, before the AR program was created, the duo spent much of the day counting and updating the inventory for the store sales, an extremely time-consuming procedure.

The operations side of the business was Ron's number one issue, who took it on as his baby. He wanted to make a computerized system that would handle all of the company's operations and, with the help of Ron Pinkas and Eric Baruch, the AR started. AR stands for Accounts Receivable, because the process was initiated in the accounting department. All of the different departments were included: accounting, sales, credit, purchasing, and inventory.

Eric came from Israel, where he had been Ron Pinkas' friend and had graduated from Ben-Gurion University of the Negev with a BS in Computer Sciences and a MS in Physics. He had already worked in Ludan Engineering as an MIS Director then embarked on the adventure of moving to the United States, looking for his own American dream.

When he moved to California, Ron Pinkas told Eric that if he needed to purchase anything, he should go to La Curacao. When he went there, he met the Azarkmans. Ron helped Eric buy a mattress and TV. Eric became a close friend of the Azarkmans and, as a programmer, heard all about their need for a computer operations system. Soon, he was working with them.

At first, the AR system Eric Baruch started was very limited and had everything exposed. There were no security passwords —virtually any computer savvy person who worked there, or any hackers, could go in and check everything and anything in the system. All of this private information—including the credit applications— was out in the open for anyone to see. The credit lines were determined by a conversation with the customer and, based upon the words and ways this person conducted himself, the line of credit was applied.

When Rodney King stopped his Hyundai, five Los Angeles Police Department officers arrived on the scene: Sargent Stacey Koon, the supervising officer; rookie Timothy Wind; Laurence Powell; Theodore Briseno; and Rolando Solano. CHPs Officer Tim Singer ordered Rodney and his two friends to get out of the car and lie face down on the ground. The two passengers complied and were taken into custody without incident. Rodney stayed in the car. After a few minutes he came out, acting differently from the other two. He patted the ground, waved to the helicopter, and grabbed his buttocks. Believing that King might have a gun, Officer Melanie Singer pulled out her pistol.

She ordered Rodney to get onto the ground, which he did, and approached him with her gun drawn. Sergeant Koon ordered Singer to holster her weapon, as officers were not allowed to approach suspects holding guns in their hands because it was possible someone a perp might pull the weapon from his or her hand. Sergeant Koon ordered the officers to subdue King using the swarm method, a technique wherein several officers grab a suspect with empty hands. However, at this point Rodney resisted; he stood up and pushed Officers Powell and Briseno. Koon then ordered all of the officers to fall back.

In the eyes of the officers, Rodney King was acting as if he was under the influence of drugs, like PCP (or phencyclidine). Also known as "angel dust," PCP is considered to be a recreational, dissociative drug. It was formerly used as an anesthetic agent; as a recreational drug, PCP might be ingested, smoked, or snorted. In any case, subsequently, when they tested Rodney later, his exams came back from the lab the toxicology results were negative, conclusively proving that he was not under the influence of PCP.

Be that as it may, King was a strong, tall, powerfully built individual who was not following Koon's instruction, so the sergeant fired a Taser. When a Taser is used, victims usually loose total control of their muscles, due to neuromuscular incapacitation. This high tech stun gun was created in 1969 by NASA researcher Jack Cover, who named it after his childhood hero Tom Swift: Taser means "Thomas A. Swift's electrical rifle." Koon tased King twice, but he was still not subdued (a faulty battery was later held responsible for this failure). In the officer's subsequent statement, Rodney after the first time he was tased, Rodney fell to the floor, screamed for five seconds, but got up again, facing Koon.

In the video shot by George Holliday, King can be seen standing with Taser wires coming from his body, and he is hit in his head with a baton, which is contrary to LAPD's rules of engagement. Officer Powell hit King with the baton several times, and in the video Officer Briseno is seen moving towards Powell to try to stop him. Powell stops. In subsequent declarations it was claimed that Sgt. Koon had ordered him to stop. Rodney again tried to get up and is positioned on his knees. Powell and Wind pummeled King with their billy clubs while he's on the ground. By this time Koon ordered the men to give the suspect "power strokes," but Rodney still tried to stand up. Koon then ordered the officers to "hit his joints, hit his wrists, elbows, knees and ankles." After 56 baton blow and six kicks, five or six officers handcuffed King and put cord cuffs on his arms and legs, then dragged him off to the roadside to wait for an ambulance.

The next day Holliday contacted the police, letting them know that he had a video of what happened the night before in Lake View Terrace, at Foothill Boulevard and Osborne Street, but they fatefully dismissed him. Holliday then went to KTLA and the local TV station broadcast Holliday's grainy video in its entirety on the air, for all of L.A.—and eventually the world—to see. This incendiary videotape was repeatedly aired by countless TV stations and channels all around the globe, becoming one of the most sensational events ever broadcasted.

On May 16, 1991, Los Angeles Superior Court Judge Bernard Kamins, a former public defender, set July 17, 1991 as the trial date for LAPD officers Koon, Powell, Briseno, and Wind, whom L.A. district attorney had charged with excessive use of force. As supervising officer, Sgt. Koon, who had Tased but not hit Rodney with batons, was charged with "willfully permitting and failing to take action to stop the unlawful assault." Kamins denied a defense motion for a change of venue outside of L.A. County, and the defendants' attorneys appealed. However, on July 23, 1991, the California Court of Appeals unanimously granted the change of venue motion, and also removed Judge Kamins from the case on the grounds that he was biased. The King beating case was reassigned to Judge Stanley Weisberg, who transferred the trial outside of Los Angeles County to predominantly white, suburban Simi Valley—where many police officers reside—in neighboring Ventura County.

The state court trial started on Feb. 3, 1992 at the East Ventura County Courthouse in Simi Valley. On March 2, 1992—a year to the day when Rodney's partying set in motion this fateful chain reaction—the jury was selected consisting of six male and six female residents of Ventura County. There were 10 whites, one Latino and one Asian juror. Not a single member of the jury was Black, although the prosecutor, Terry White, is an African American.

The verdict in the Rodney King case was highly anticipated. The court proceedings were followed by everyone. Of course, the violent video had gone viral. Day after day, televised airings of Holliday's infamous video of the LAPD officers pummeling the motorist pushed viewers to be part of what had gone down; everyone wanted to know what the results of the police brutality trial would be. Holliday's footage was presented as a key piece of evidence during the trial; it was broken down, shot by shot, and repeatedly screened in the courtroom.

On April 29, 1992, the jury reached a verdict. Within a matter of seconds the news media swarmed the Simi Valley courthouse, as everybody wanted to know the outcome of the case. Would the LAPD officers be found guilty? If so, would they go to jail? The whole world was watching as the jury's verdict was announced at 3:15 p.m. The jurors acquitted three of the policemen, but were unable to agree on one of the charges against Powell.

Tom Bradley, a former LAPD officer who had become Los Angeles' first Black mayor, said: "The jury's verdict will not blind us to what we saw on that videotape. The men who beat Rodney King do not deserve to wear the uniform of the LAPD." President George H.W. Bush stated, "Viewed from outside the trial, it was hard to understand how the verdict could possibly square with the video. Those civil rights leaders with whom I met were stunned. And so was I, and so was Barbara, and so were my kids."

As seeing is believing, these politicians were not the only ones who weren't "blinded" by the jury's verdict and "stunned" by the trial's outcome. So was the proverbial man in the street, as all hell broke loose in Los Angeles.

Elizabeth came in to work at 9:45 a.m. on Thursday, April 30. The day before, she'd seen as many as 300 African Americans on TV protesting at the East Ventura County Courthouse in Simi Valley after the verdict was announced—the city, as a whole, felt it was wrong. The news reported that at around 5:00 p.m., April 29, two dozen officers had confronted a growing group of outraged people gathered at Florence and Normandie, in South Central Los Angeles.

The mob was bigger than the police unit, and the policemen ended up retreating. At 6:00 p.m. the crowd at Florence and Normandie turned violent and began looting shops and attacking vehicles driving by and people. At 6:45 p.m. Caucasian truck driver Reginald Oliver Denny, who was hauling 27 tons of sand, stopped for a red light at the intersection of Normandie and Florence, where he was pulled out of his truck by a mob and severely beaten up, as cameramen in news helicopters hovered overhead shooting the entire event. Denny was lying unconscious when he was rescued by an African American civilian named Bobby Green, who had been watching TV when he saw what was happening, ran to the scene, pulled Denny up from the ground, put him inside of the truck, then drove the 18 wheeler and victim to the hospital.

Denny was far from being the only casualty that evening. Fidel Lopez—a construction worker and immigrant from El Salvador—passed the same intersection, where he was also pulled out of his truck and robbed of around $2000. Damian Williams, one of the so-called "L.A. Four" who had already assaulted Denny, smashed Fidel's forehead open with a car stereo and tried to slice his ear off. Lopez lost consciousness as the crowd sprayed black paint on his chest, torso and genitals until Rev. Bennie Newton, who had a ministry for troubled youth in the area, placed himself between Lopez and the crowd, shouting: "Kill him and you have to kill me, too." The minister then took Lopez to the hospital.

Once inside of La Curacao, Elizabeth saw that the TVs had been turned on and everyone was glued to the sets, watching what was happening outside in the streets. The store's metal window covers had not been removed and the door was not open to the public. Ron was working with warehouse employees to put as many TV sets as he could into a truck parked outside the building. Eric Baruch was trying to copy all of the AR files onto a disk in order to have a backup. All of these measures were just precautions, they said. Meanwhile, Jerry was putting all of the jewelry into his car, along with a new shipment of video cameras—the very piece of equipment which, as fate would have it, Holliday had used to record the beating that had set the wheels into motion for all of the dramatic events leading up to this moment.

Some employees were on the roof watching what was going on in South Central. The rioters were still far from them, but the looters had started to move closer toward downtown. Inside of La Curacao, they watched on television as the nearby store owners armed themselves to protect their property and area, as they had learned LAPD had abandoned the whole area. The storekeepers and residents were on their own. The police weren't as bold now that they were the ones who were outnumbered, unlike when they had outnumbered and outgunned Rodney King. You could see the shopkeepers on the roofs of their stores with rifles guarding their property.

In happier days, Jerry had decided that children needed special entertainment and he selected a penguin character to serve as La Curacao's mascot. He chose penguins because of how they lived, staying together as a community, taking care of their young ones. Although many companies select aggressive animals to represent them, Jerry saw in this inoffensive, friendly, and warm animal an analogy for his associates. A penguin family became the store mascot. The family was composed of the father, Don Paco; the mother, Dona Cata; and three children, Memin, Lulu, and Paquito. It was a great tool for bringing families to the store, where kids loved to shake hands or high five Don Paco, who was portrayed in a penguin costume by Bayron.

Before Bayron's aunt had become extremely ill. She came to talk to Jerry one day, asking if he could watch for her young son when she was gone. She had cancer and knew that she could lose her battle with the disease any day. She passed away and the 12-year-old child was left under the supervision of the child's aunt, her sister and grandfather, who was eighty-five years old. Jerry started to check up on him, getting him out of trouble all the time and even giving a job to his cousin.

On the day of the riots, Byron and Juan Carlos were watching what was going on from the balcony of their building. Byron ran to tell Jerry that the looters were close by and that they should leave. Mayor Bradley had announced a dusk to dawn curfew, the National Guard had been called, and about 2,000 Guardsmen were deployed. But they did not arrive until the next day because they did not have proper equipment, training, or available ammunition. Despite all of the money the government spent on the Pentagon, America was militarily unprepared to respond to a domestic uprising. Comedian Bill Cosby went on NBC-TV, asking people to stop what they were doing, joking that they should just stay home and watch *The Cosby Show* instead.

La Curacao's employees were sitting around watching the unfolding riots on the store's TVs when Ron Azarkman came in yelling, "Go home everyone, go home!" On her way out, Elizabeth was asked if she could transport some boxes in the back of her truck, and she replied, "What am I going to do with them? I don't have anywhere to put them. I live in an apartment building with open parking. There is no security or anything like that. I'm afraid the boxes will be stolen." She got in her truck and left, driving all the way home. As soon as Elizabeth put the key in the lock to open her apartment, she heard her phone ringing and rushed to answer it. On the other end of the line, her sister was crying hysterically, yelling, "Where were you? I was calling and calling!" Elizabeth answered that she was fine and asked, "What's going on?" Her sister said, "Put on the TV. La Curacao is burning!"

As Jerry was driving home later that night and, at one stoplight, he saw a man with a clarinet playing for the cars that approached his vehicle; the musician's hand was outstretched for money. Jerry put his hand into his pocket and pulled everything out, about seven dollars, and said to himself, "I don't know what is going to happen now. All I know is I'm starting again." And Jerry, who had started the business from scratch, with just hard work and sheer determination, already knew how he would rebuild his dream.

Safely back at home, he watched TV until very late that night. He saw all of the destruction wrought on so many businesses, properties, people, and his own store. When he drove to work, the freeway was empty, devoid of the traffic usually found on L.A.'s clogged streets.

Everyone had watched what was happening at La Curacao. First, looters broke down the doors and then the store went up in flames. It was like that old 1960s slogan: "Burn, baby burn!" As Elizabeth had left the downtown area around 10:30 a.m. and it took her no more than forty-five minutes to reach North Hollywood in the San Fernando Valley, one could tell how quickly it had all transpired. The next day she drove back to what she believed was the store. Several employees were crying and crying. There was nothing left, only one wall.

On the floor, nothing could be recognized in the debris, everything was in ashes. Even the truck where they had loaded all of the TVs had burned to a crisp, with all of the merchandise inside.

Jerry found many employees at what had been La Curacao, including Edna from accounting, who was weeping. He hugged her and proclaimed, "Don't worry. We will start all over. We know who our customers are, we know where they live, what they want to buy. We are going to start again. Don't worry, we will start again."

Byron's building had burned to ashes leaving them all sleeping in the street. Many other employees showed up that day and were across the street in a Greek coffee shop that had survived the rioting, where the brothers told all of them: "This is not the end. La Curacao did not burn down, because La Curacao is *us*."

Two days after the store had burned; Edna was at home when she received a call from colleagues asking her if she had documentation, and as she did, Edna was told to go to the state unemployment office to apply to collect unemployment insurance. When she got there, Edna found several other La Curacao associates also in the process of filling out the government forms.

The following days were extremely crucial for La Curacao and its survival. First, the store set up a table on the sidewalk across the street from where their emporium had stood. The building's manager had offered them an empty space where they setup a sign emblazoned "La Curacao." Jerry went to all of the Spanish language TV stations and said on the air, "If you took merchandise from La Curacao, we forgive you. Just come and we will put it under your account or call us and we will pick it up." This message was very strong, and it inspired confidence, making everyone believe La Curacao was alive and kicking, still open for business. After four days of riots, the store was already operating in a small office across the street and people were coming to pay their bills. "Customers were noble people," Elizabeth would say. They saw the disaster on TV and wanted La Curacao to get back on its feet, so they came to make good on the lines of credit that the store had extended to them.

After the third day of the L.A. Riot, Rodney King held a press conference. Quite eloquently, and without a trace of vengefulness, Rodney spoke words a Shakespeare might envy, simply saying, "People, I just want to say, you know, can we all get along? Can we get along? Can we stop making it, making it horrible for the older people and the kids? It's just not right. It's not right. It's not, it's not going to change anything. We'll, we'll get our justice…They won the battle, but they haven't won the war…Please, we can get along here. We all can get along. I mean, we're all stuck here for a while. Let's try to work it out…"

That same day, California's then governor, Pete Wilson, requested the intervention of the National Guard and 4,000 troops were dispatched to ravaged L.A. In addition, 1,700 federal law enforcement officers from different agencies across the state came to protect federal facilities and help the beleaguered local police force.

Vendors had called Jerry and Ron to tell them that they could ship them merchandise in order to start all over again. A day before the riots, it just so happened that La Curacao had signed a contract with Panasonic. The sales team set up a few TVs, video cameras, and jewelry. They called Elizabeth and a few of their top employees, for a total of six, plus Eric Baruch, Jerry, and Ron. They all came with the mindset to start selling. Eric the computer whiz had recovered most of the information saved on the backup disks he had made, and printed a file listing customers' available credit and sales history to understand who owed how much and what could be sold to them.

In a week, they went back to 1605 Olympic Boulevard to rent a space and they were given room on the first floor, which was connected to the parking structure's first floor. They closed part of the parking area and set up furniture. Without any help, they got the merchandise and set it up every day before they started selling. During this period of recovery, one had to improvise, creating a step-by-step program with a strategy of what the objective is—mainly to sell higher margin and volume sales. And, of course, to survive while one rebuilt.

The Mother's Day Catalog had been mailed on April 30, the day when the store burnt down. Vendors had already sent the merchandise for this promotion, so when the riots broke out, La Curacao had been preparing for the Mother's Day promotion. Within one week of the riots, La Curacao was—rather miraculously—already operating and ready for business. They worked really hard on the finances, seeking extended terms from vendors and higher credit lines, while discussions with the insurance companies started. The team all worked so hard to sell that they reached their sales goal for the month of May.

Meanwhile Bayron's family were homeless waiting for FEMA (Federal Emergency Management Agency) to help them with the situation and it took them

April 30, 1992 La Curacao burners down in the Los Angeles riots.

over thirty days to get help. During this time La Curacao employees will collect money and clothing to help them.

Everybody at that time knew each other from their neighborhoods in their home countries; many were relatives and friends of relatives. One customer who always wanted to buy directly from Jerry would come and wait until he was available to serve her. One day, when she came and asked for him, Elizabeth told her that Jerry did not come to the sales floor too often anymore that he mainly worked in the office. The client replied, "These people, when they make money, who do they think they are? I've known Jerry since he was a boy, running with no shoes in El Salvador." She probably thought that the Israeli transplant was the son of an immigrant from El Salvador, which explained why he spoke in broken Spanish.

Sales at La Curacao were incredible. Another customer, Juliana Ramirez, purchased a Sharp projector for $9,000, telling Elizabeth she planned to take it to Guajaca (also known as Oaxaca), Mexico to setup a movie theater. Juliana also bought a surround sound system with all the accessories she needed to make it work. The sale was partially cash and part on credit. "Those were simple days," Elizabeth said. "The credit department was not as sophisticated as nowadays. All they needed to do was show the customer to the credit supervisor to answer a few questions and the decision was made right there."

The name of the Azarkmans' corporation is Adir International, which has several meanings for the brothers: A for Azarkman; D for Doron; I for Jerry's name in Hebrew (there are two ways to spell this name: Yoran or Ioran); and R for Ron. Adir is the Hebrew word for giant and the Brothers Azarkman wanted to have a giant operation. After the riots and the store was incinerated, they had to redouble their efforts and energy every single day to motivate everyone.

La Curacao's insurance did not cover manmade fires or riots, and this was exactly what had happened, as the looters had started the fire. The brothers looked over their insurance policy and there was one clause that covered them for loss of income. Their stipulation applied to this circumstance and their broker helped them through the detailed process of applying for compensation.

The store's media partners helped them by reminding the public that La Curacao, which had gone up in flames just a few days before, was already up and operating at a new location. The Azarkmans learned a big lesson from this experience—they shouldn't put all of their proverbial eggs into one basket. Instead of owning only one outlet, they had to build stores at multiple locations in order to be able to survive horrific situations such as this one in the future.

Jerry started working with the architects to rebuild their operation at 1313 Olympic Boulevard and the art designs were readied. The concept was to create a Mayan-Aztec style building that would be seen from far away. The City of Los Angeles, which had failed to protect the original building during the uprising, requested that it authorize the design, asserting that La Curacao would have to build a different place for the 110 Freeway off-ramp. This would cost an outrageous amount of money, especially coming at the same time that the building at 1605 West Olympic Boulevard was in bankruptcy. At this time, several buildings in downtown Los Angeles were suffering from the financial fallout of the S&L Crisis.

The savings and loan crisis of the '80s and '90s was due to the collapse of financial associations that provided customers with savings accounts and loans for mortgages, cars, etc. During this period, 747 out of 3,234 loans failed. In 1986, a reform of the tax code was made; causing the value of investments to come down; many listed this as an income tax reduction. This stopped the era's real estate boom and the prices of property came down. People with loans for properties that were not worth the price of the loan were defaulting on them; many sought Chapter 13, filing for bankruptcy.

They decided that the investment they needed to make in order to build up their old location was bigger than just buying the entire building. The bank that had the property was very flexible with them and the Azarkmans made their move, buying the property. They knew they had to go through lots of remodeling to be able to get the store to where they wanted it to be.

Following a Department of Justice investigation, a federal grand jury indicted Koon, Wind, Powell, and Briseno, charging them with violating King's civil rights on August 4, 1992. The officers' trial began February 25, 1993, and on April 16, Powell and Koon were convicted, while Wind and Briseno were found not guilty. There was no civil unrest after the verdicts were announced. Judge Davies sentenced Powell and Koon to serve two and a half years in a federal correctional facility, but civil rights groups grouse that the judge's sentence was too light. Later that month, the DOJ announced that it would appeal Davies' sentences, but after lots of legal wrangling that ended and the sentences stuck. Although a jury initially denied Rodney King's $15 million civil suit against the LAPD officers, on April 19, 1994, a jury in an L.A. Court awarded King—who'd also filed a civil suit against the city—$3.8 million in damages.

But if the Rodney King who turned millionaire knew back in 1991 what his case would lead to, would he do it all over again? We don't know for sure, but what we do definitely know is that this was a calamity for the 53 families who lost loved ones and for the 2,383 individuals who were injured. Another 7,000-plus people were arrested. Approximately 7,000 fires were set, 1,100 buildings and retail stores looted and burned down during the riots that wreaked havoc on up to 3,100 businesses—including La Curacao. Property damages and material losses caused by the L.A. Riot were estimated to be $1 billion-plus.

The sixth step of how Jerry converted his twenty dollars into $200 million was by making products accessible to customers through credit. The niche market Jerry found was not composed of middle class people; the majority of his customers were newcomers just starting their lives in the U.S. Many had minimum wage jobs, and most remitted money to relatives back in their home countries. All had limited discretionary income beyond paying for their own expenses, in addition to sending money back home. This was a clientele that wanted to own what they saw at the store, but for most, it seemed impossible. But providing them with credit changed their world in an instant, from not having anything or very little, to now having access to a line of credit to buy TVs, computers, furniture, and many other products. Jerry helped turn these have-nots into haves.

This opportunity was important not only to the customers, but for La Curacao, to the point of that they opened more than a million accounts in Southern California. Who were these million-plus customers? People like you and me, with the same dreams and fears, with families and children, just like any other human beings, seeking an opportunity in this society.

Jerry first gave credit to his customers when he was selling door to door. As these first customers brought more and more new consumers, the small store led to a bigger location, and even after being scorched by the riots, growth remained the number one objective. That bitter experience left the Brothers Azarkman with nothing else in mind other than the need to have more than one store where they could continue operating, even after—God forbid—another chaotic situation wherein they lost a store. This led them to open a second store. Selecting the new place was very important because it had to mimic the same profile customer they currently had.

They selected Panorama City, a district located in the northern part of the San Fernando Valley. It was one of the first planned communities built by Henry J. Kaiser, who dedicated his life to the construction business, building roads first, then ships for World War II. Kaiser was known for constructing cargo ships within forty-five days. They were called Liberty Ships. He became a real estate magnate who built complete communities in Hawaii and went on to organize the Kaiser Permanente healthcare program for his employees. Panorama City was different from many other parts of the San Fernando Valley, where growth came as a result of the development of jobs in the downtown area. Panorama had its own work centers, such as General Motors and Anheuser-Busch. Once GM shut down, its facility was converted into a retail area.

The Azarkmans used all of their creative ideas to construct 1605 Olympic and the new Panorama store, leading to the opening of their first store in a mall. The whole design was made with Aztec and Mayan figures, with a children's area, so parents could safely leave their kids while shopping. La Curacao was the first retailer that targeted Hispanics in the whole U.S., and it was very successful. The day of the grand opening, they invited Don Francisco, a Chilean TV personality and host whose programs appear on the Spanish-speaking Univision television network, to cut the ribbon. Don Francisco was so well known by everyone in the Latino world that the area's freeways were blocked and the entire mall was so packed that the ceremony was cancelled by the city because too many people were in attendance.

Launching their second store in 1995 led to the Azarkmans to aspire to open four more outlets and to become a chain of stores in Southern California, with facilities in other states as well. Their growth became exponential and gave the chain buying power that increased every day.

During his childhood, Jerry's family fled Islamist extremists in Iran and moved to Israel. He left the Holy Land to avoid war, and came to the U.S.A.—only to be confronted by America's biggest urban insurrection of the 20th century. But with more hard work and steely determination, a Phoenix arose out of the ashes.

Chapter Fourteen

Nothing Can Stop Us

S electing who will work with you is a very important part of developing your company. What if you select people who are more intelligent than you are, sharper, more aggressive, ready to take over? It sounds scary but the best way to grow is to select people who will push the bar higher. Demanding more from these special personalities can be a real ride. Some will understand their role, some won't. The ones who get it will immediately start producing and changing things, looking for opportunities, developing those opportunities, and improving areas. The ones who don't get it cause problems for the leaders, because it will demand lots of time to train and educate them.

Jerry surrounded himself with people who were smart, and who had the same thirst for growth and ambition burning inside of them. Their sales goals increased every year. The brothers had the feeling that if they had been able to make the sales goal for May after their store was burned down, the sky was their limit. They knew it in their bones because, after the store was torched during the riots, they had no place to conduct business out of for days. From there, they opened a little outlet in the building across from their old store, then the operation was moved to the basement of another building, all in the same month—and they still miraculously managed to reach their sales goal. This made them think that everything and anything was possible.

Before Ron brought in the first desk for the company's undertakings, everything was done standing up: there were no desks. This simple act of introducing one desk internally changed how the firm did business. It started shaping a department that would become, in the future, one of the company's backbones. The sales force had their mission to accomplish: selling. The venture had its goals: open the store every day, have it organized, cleaned, cashiers ready, and all merchandise already placed in the inventory. In the public's eyes, this was what it took to run a store. But, behind the scenes, there were many other areas that made the entire process successful.

In the beginning, the credit department was the enterprise's biggest investment. Since the founding of La Curacao, the company carried the paper, this meaning they provided the credit on their own means and was potentially liable for incurring any unpaid debt. This means sales were done on credit. Once the customer applied for credit and a certain amount was allocated to them, the store backed this person up with merchandise and a sort of capital outlay. This client got his or her first credit in America and now the store would have to pay the vendor for the product and wait until the customer finished paying it off before they got back what, in essence, was a loan. They had to wait to make a profit. The entire process was managed internally by accurately calculating the appropriate monthly payment and establishing the correct line of credit, according to the customer's ability to repay. Recording the history of these processes, and being able to see all of this information instantly on a screen with all of the data computerized, was a big achievement. The customer's confidence and trust, wherein all of their charges were crystal clear, was another challenge that became possible with time.

Building your customer's trust from the moment he or she takes his first step inside of a store is the biggest accomplishment of any operation. Just looking at the way the merchandise is set up could trigger a customer's like or dislike. Every single step a customer takes inside and outside of your business will affect the process of building trust in that brand. There are many ways customers can encounter a business, such as through a phone call. If the person who answers a call is not friendly enough, or the answers don't meet that customer's standards and expectations, the business will not only start losing clients, but they might generate bad word of mouth that can gather momentum and build to such a big extent that it will boomerang on the business, harming its efforts to achieve growth and stability. Especially in this age of social media, any disgruntled shopper can start a website critical of a place of business and all of their followers will read about.

In its initial stages, the credit department started with lots of trial and error. Customers were asked simple questions and credit lines were established depending on their answers. Then, modules were developed with computerized systems to more scientifically qualify each applicant. The FICO rating system for determining a person's creditworthiness did not work for this particular niche segment of the population; at the time, there was no other company in the United States handling what La Curacao's credit department was doing.

Marvin lived in El Salvador. His mom had immigrated years before and promised her son she'd come back for him. But as time passed, he just couldn't wait any more. So, when many of his neighbors and friends said they were going to the States, he was first in line. They were all the same age, mostly college students. They traveled by bus and they felt as if they were on a school field trip. Reality hit them in the face like a splash of cold water once they got to Tijuana and met their coyotes.

Once they started crossing the border, the marathon began. Marvin was not an athlete. He played ball in the neighborhood but this was more of "run for your life." After they were on the other side, they sensed the border patrol on their backs and started running. The three split, running as fast as they could. The undocumented workers felt the helicopters above them and started hiding in tunnels around the route the coyotes had given to them before crossing. The Salvadorans kept going and going until they reached a road where coyotes had parked cars on the road and were waiting for them. The newcomers arrived in Los Angeles in the back of a pickup.

After a few years in the U.S., Marvin's mother had obtained her green card through her employer and she finally received it in the mail. Marvin had still been in El Salvador when she had submitted the papers so her son could join her in America. She had explained this to Marvin in letters and phone calls to him back in El Salvador. But he couldn't wait, so he'd decided to take the big risk of illegally coming across the border. Marvin's mom couldn't believe what he had done, but now the family was united.

Like many before and after him, Marvin started working in construction until a friend told him about La Curacao, where he decided to apply for a job. He went to the store with the familiar sounding name—back in his country, there were several stores with that same name. Claudio Miron conducted the job interview with Marvin. Marvin had been studying business administration at the University of El Salvador before he made the fateful decision to go to El Norte.

The store was looking for someone to take delinquent customers to court. The job was simple enough—gather the internal paperwork that proved the purchase and history of payment defaults. At the court, he'd fill out all the paperwork required to bring the case before a judge in small claims court. This person would need a vehicle, because once the claim was filed, he'd have to go to the customer's house to serve the court papers.

Claudio asked Marvin if he had a car and driver's license, and he said no. So, Claudio explained that, unfortunately, La Curacao would not be able to hire him. Not wanting to lose the opportunity, Marvin asked, "What would happen if I took the test and got my license?" Claudio responded, "Then we're talking. I won't have a problem hiring you." Marvin went to the DMV, passed the written exam and then the driving portion of the test. He returned to the store with his driver's license, showed it to Claudio, and was hired.

To process the papers at the court, Marvin would take the bus, which was easier as he didn't have to look for parking spaces near the courthouse. He learned how to file all of the legal papers, which was easy. The hard part was when he had to go to the homes of the people being sued, as he still had no car.

Marvin would get all of the papers from the small claims court, then go home and wait for his brother to come home from work, as he had a car and knew the city better than the newcomer did. His brother drove with him to serve the court papers to the customers at their homes. It took Marvin several months to finally save up to buy a tiny car with no back window and a really bad paint job—but he didn't care, as he was able to move around freely.

The school Jerry's son Daniel was attending asked his parents to have their son undergo several exams to determine what was preventing him from paying more attention in class. The administration wanted to find out why he was always talking and disrupting class; the teachers believed Daniel could possibly be suffering from Attention Deficit Hyperactivity Disorder. The Mayo Clinic defines ADHD as a combination of problems, including difficulty in sustaining attention, overactive and impulsive behavior. Children diagnosed with ADHD may struggle with low self-esteem, troubled relationships, and poor performance at school. This chronic condition affects millions of children and often persists into adulthood.

If Daniel was found to have ADHD, he most likely would have to take medication and have his behavior constantly checked, with possible adult intervention to help him understand what he was going through. The doctor explained to Jerry that the treatment would not cure Daniel but would help him deal with the symptoms and that early detection was the key. When the symptoms were being explained to him, he realized that they started manifesting when children were two to three years old.

As the symptoms were elucidated one by one to Jerry, he understood what all this meant and started thinking not only about Daniel's behavior, but his own. The indicators include frequently failing to pay close attention to details and making careless mistakes. Jerry thought to himself, "This happens to me." He often lost focus when doing a task, could not seem to listen, even when spoken to directly. Sometimes it was difficult for him to follow through on instructions. He remembered that he sometimes did not complete homework or tasks. Jerry realized he had problems organizing chores or activities, and he thought he was lazy because he'd avoid jobs that required mental effort. He felt it was normal to often lose things he needed, like books or tools, because he thought these were things everyone does. All of his colleagues knew Jerry was easily distracted when he was in meetings and could be forgetful.

Jerry's said to his doctor, "What you're saying describes me." The doctor explained to him that ADD occurred more frequently in boys, although it could occur in girls, too. In addition to all of these symptoms, Attention Deficit Disorder has an additional branch that includes hyperactive and impulsive behaviors, but when the doctor described these more hyper symptoms to Jerry, he did not recognize them as being applicable to Daniel or himself.

The doctor described additional related behaviors and symptoms, asking, "Do you see any of these symptoms in Daniel? Have any of these symptoms been happening in more than the last six months? Are they occurring in more than one place—for example at home and at school?" And of course Jerry knew the answers. He told the doctor it was happening at both places and that it had been happening to him and Daniel for a long period of time."

When Marvin started at the company, there were no more than twenty associates. The most exciting time for him was Christmas, because Jerry took the staff out to eat at the Tony Roma's located at Universal Studios City Walk. It was a big deal for him because it was unexpected and, more importantly, it made Marvin feel like both brothers were thanking him, and the other associates, for all of their hard work. At the same table, they had operations people, salespeople, and credit people—they were a small company that could fit at a single table for dinner.

The people applying for credit were asked were very simple questions, including: where they lived, what their home phone number was, where they worked, and what their work phone number was. The same person who asked the questions would go to a backroom and use the phone to confirm the information. This was a very simple verification process—nothing sophisticated, especially compared to what exists today. The caller just asked the person who answered the phone if they knew this person. It was as simple as that.

If, for any reason, he or she was unable to verify the information, the staffer would start asking the applicant additional questions based on his or her observations. For example, if a lady applying for credit said she made tamales for a living, the questions were about tamales. The interviewer would ask about how the tamales were made, how they were different, what time they'd wake up to prepare the ingredients, how long it would take, how many they'd sell, and the like. If the customer sounded knowledgeable and/or showed passion regarding the work he or she claimed to do, the application was then given to Jerry or Ron to decide whether or not to approve the sought after credit.

Sometimes, one of the brothers would personally come to have another conversation with the same customer and ask more questions. This simple process determined the customer's down payment for each product and their line of credit.

In this way, the credit department started seeing recognizable patterns of people with the same activities, coming from similar neighborhoods in their countries, and began developing a simple behavior score.

It sounded like a simple enough process, but it carried a lot of pressure. If, for example, employment could not be verified, the entire process became based on perception because the store could be dealing with an imposter who'd never make the monthly payments and simply abscond with the merchandise. For this reason, they had to create as many precautionary steps as possible to defend the company from possible theft.

The credit department grew from being a small crew of four people to a much bigger operation. The increase in new accounts and in sales naturally brought changes to this area. The credit department was split in two, with a new division created to do collections. Claudio stayed with credit while Natalio was hired for collections. Both sections were critical for the company's expansion—the more new accounts that were opened, the more systems were required to control the risk of giving credit lines to people without any credit history. The methods were developed and modified constantly.

Marvin vividly remembers how hard it was for him, and understands now the risks he went through. A few months after he arrived in the United States, he got his green card, and then found a career working in collections for a major company. Claudio was promoted to store manager when Mike Falkenstein was promoted to become the first Vice President. It was Ron's vision to bring second level leaders to the company so vendors understood the potential and growth of the company.

Iche was an Argentine Jew who spoke some Spanish; his parents had moved from Israel to Argentina, where he was born. When he was six years old, they moved back to Israel. When Iche came for a job interview, the first thing Jerry asked him was to cut his hair. He looked like a biker, wearing a ponytail, leather pants, and leather jacket. Iche was hired to run the credit department, where he went on to make significant changes in its processes and applications. He even created a department of approvers so the brothers didn't always have to authorize the credit awarded to applicants. This change came naturally because the volume of credit was increasing every day. They could not be there all the time.

The credit department's success was due to the smart dedicated people developing the system, not only in regards to programming but in identifying the characters to evaluate and creating modules to determine internal behavioral scores. This credit department became an example for all financial institutions in the United States. Many top banks have asked for meetings with the department to better understand the way La Curacao manages its credit portfolio. Having credit with La Curacao provided stability for many customers; with this proof of credit, they could buy a car, rent an apartment, or any number of things that require credit. In the community, it became the card every newcomer needed in order to start gaining a position in society.

Jerry could not believe what he was hearing from the doctor. He began blaming himself—was Daniel's condition his fault? Did he do something that affected his son? Or was it his mom's fault? He started asking more and more questions. The doctor explained that the actual causes were still unknown and being studied. Some research conducted at several universities indicated ADD is related to DNA or inherited traits, rather than being a choice or behavior. Other studies suggest environmental factors can contribute to it. While the exact causes remain unidentified, recent anatomical reports on the brain's structure have found that the area that controls mental activity is less active.

Some ADD studies have indicated the disorder may be caused by exposure to environmental toxins or lead, as well as by women smoking during pregnancy. Jerry was sure this was not the cause of Daniel's condition—even though they'd lived in old buildings, it had just been for short periods of time. In any case, the doctor explained that Daniel's condition could cause other complications, including struggling in the classroom, a tendency to experience more accidents and injuries, trouble interacting with peers and adults, and an increased risk of alcohol and drug abuse. After all of the explanations, they knew Daniel would undergo an evaluation and, if he tested positive on six or more of the symptoms established by the American Psychiatric Association's Diagnostic and Statistical Manual regarding ADHD, they would have to deal with it as a family.

In thirty years, La Curacao became what it is today because of the dynamic leadership of Jerry, Ron, and a great team. The sensibility each area of operation needs to possess in order to take care of business makes a big difference and sets the Azarkmans' enterprise apart from their competitors.

How do you put together a winning team to take over everything pertaining to your business and to control all of the departments, from sales to credit to collections? This is one of the most difficult aspects for growing a business. A top management officer in a sister company of La Curacao once said, "This is the first company I have worked at where the associates are the ones that make the decisions." Empowering associates is a big step towards expanding. Being able to train employees to make the right decision when management isn't around to guide them is essential for the wellbeing and development of any company.

The seventh and final element for transforming twenty dollars into $200 million was empowering each and every associate to feel like they could make a difference. In trying to figure out how to make ends meet, Jerry was not alone— many others had the same needs and thirst to succeed. These people met at La Curacao and made this company produce millions of dollars with Jerry, his brother, and other executives.

Empowerment sounds like such a big word, but the essence of this word is for any person—no matter how simple and humble they might be—to draw from their own self the strength to think big. It involves the motivation to develop that internal force to act—not just react—to life, the job, or relationships. It's up to you to make things happen. Empowerment transfers that internal fiber everyone has, giving it an opportunity to be expressed so that it can be externally manifested. "Si se puede" means yes you can! You can do it! You can manage your circumstances. An employee might think he or she is not part of the decision-making process, but, if your employees feel empowered, these are the moments when your associates will turn from good to great to extraordinary.

Associates are trained to do their job and the company gives them sufficient tools to be able to perform their jobs. With this, the power has already been given to them to accomplish their goals. What then is empowerment? Empowerment is letting all of their potential out, unleashing all of their inner strength after receiving all of the knowledge required to execute the work. It's the capacity to analyze options and make the right decisions, to look for the information required to finish a task. It is being positive about change, seeking skills to create a better job environment, and being able to sort out the difference between good and bad. This is the new way to see the workplace—empowerment is the new management skill. In Thomas A. Potterfield's book, *The Business of Employee Empowerment, Democracy and Ideology in the Workplace*, empowerment is identified as one of the most important and popular management concepts of our time. This is definitely a strong tool for motivating your associates.

Jerry implemented this process throughout the entire company to make sure there was a constant ladder of opportunity for associates who possess the thirst to move up to higher positions. The course of action started with training associates, evaluating their accomplishments, and measuring the success of the team, as well as of the overall company. Empowering each associate and department should be the goal of every company in order to achieve success.

They bought the property at 1313 Olympic Boulevard, which included their first LA Curacao location. Then their operation expanded by buying the Grand Bazaar building, although the city owned the land. After the L.A. riots, the city took over the property at 1313 and compensated the Azarkmans for it. The municipal government designated the location for educational purposes and a school was built in the community. This was badly needed because of population growth. Meanwhile, the company kept growing in sales and expanding its locations. While the challenges increased every day, Jerry always felt his military training gave him the ability to never show weakness, to not give up, and to patiently wait for the best opportunity. The entrepreneur also knew the information he gained about La Curacao's niche market from his associates, as those hired by the store were representative of the people he was targeting. Jerry knew this was the company's biggest asset.

How to select associates was a big question for the company. What were the right questions to ask them? Jerry always looked for ordinary things to ask the person being interviewed for a job opening. At his office, Jerry always had a bunch of magazines and books and he'd ask an interviewee to pass him a blue book. The reaction to this simple question would provide him with a zillion observations. For example, did the job candidate stand up immediately to look for it, or did the prospective employee give him a questioning look? Once next to the table, some candidates gave him a look of insecurity, of not knowing what he wanted. Others would take the initiative, directly going to look in between the magazines and getting the first blue magazine or book encountered. All of these movements were observed and analyzed in order to make sure the right person was hired.

There is a saying that goes, "It's not the people who have to do things who actually do them, it's those who really want to do them." This is part of the good attitude needed for creating a special team. The crew that raises the bar all the time tries to take advantage of their opportunities and deliver above expectations results. That kind of team needs to be guided by leaders who know when to push and when to let go. Motivation and recognition are the strongest tools leaders have to get their teams to succeed.

After his test was administered, Daniel was diagnosed with ADD. It was recommended that he start using medication and prepare special accommodations at his school. These were not options, but rather requirements. He was going to need all of his family and their community's support. However, Jerry did not agree with giving him prescription drugs. He knew he had the same symptoms and believed that if he had gone his whole life without pharmaceuticals, he and the family would help Daniel to understand how to live with his condition and handle himself. Jerry was sure they could work it out together—this would be the best way to help Daniel.

He read about ADD and learned that now Daniel would need extra attention and lots of affection. He understood that Daniel needed to be told all the time how much he was loved. Jerry was the first to understand what he was going through.

Indeed, Jerry understood himself better through his son's condition. Now he understood he was the one pushing himself, even when something inside was telling him he could not accomplish a task. He now understood perfectly that this condition had made him stronger, had made him push himself to overcome his own negativities. Jerry was going to create a lifestyle necessary for protecting Daniel and give him the attention and affection he needed. He knew he could not focus on the negative part because this would frustrate Daniel; he had to motivate his son, increase his self-esteem and discipline. He knew he had to be patient and understanding. He had big expectations for his child, but also doubts as to how Daniel would approach school and other challenges. Jerry had to accept Daniel as he was and reduce as much of the stress placed on him as possible.

Reality unexpectedly showed up when his son Daniel was diagnosed with Attention Deficit Disorder. Jerry was so scared when he heard the doctor's diagnosis—how could he turn this thing around, what did he need to do next, and how could he help his son? All these questions popped up in his mind and he felt powerless and incompetent. Jerry had surpassed every obstacle life had thrown in his path with sheer will power. He had never given up; he'd worked hard, even in moments when he felt like there was no light at the end of the tunnel. But now reality was catching up to him, and this was unknown territory. He didn't know what to do.

One of Jerry's first steps was to find out if any of his other children had ADD. Erick was given the same exams and tested negative—he had none of the condition's symptoms. Once Ilanit became of age, she too took the test, underwent the same process and also came out negative. More good news.

Daniel grew as an A+ student at school, and did well in all of his extra activities, with the same challenges any other child or teenager faced—but he always had the undying support of his family to fall back on. There has not been any difficulty that Daniel has not overcome. One silver lining from this ordeal has been that Jerry learned how to overcome some of his own symptoms, too. To this day, after a meeting finishes, Jerry sometimes asks his close associates, "Did you pay attention?" Of course they did, but this really means that, at the end of the meeting, he could not remember the entire conversation, just pieces from here and there. Jerry's collaborators become his right hand in these moments. Minutes from meetings provide a written record and are his strongest tool for focusing and keeping track of his desires. A few phrases here and there help him to communicate the things he really wants to get across. At his next meeting, he comes prepared with a summary of the previous powwow. He goes from one meeting to another, trying really hard to keep focused. However, some days are more difficult for him than others in order to be able to operate at full speed, especially when he has not slept enough.

Jerry discovered that sometimes the topic is the biggest challenge for him. When the subject is important to him, if he wants to make a change or improve something, he is fully alert and participates with his ideas, suggestions, and examples. He was very young when he discovered that he lost interest easily in class because of the language barrier in Israel, when he knew little Hebrew. He also stopped paying attention because he was put in a class where he did not belong or because he just didn't like the topic. But time passed, with his attention deficit increasing and isolating him from the rest of his schoolmates. He did not understand himself and started noticing he was daydreaming more frequently. Jerry forced himself to pay attention, but his grades were not as good as they could be, until that fateful teacher turned him around with motivation and self-esteem, and he climbed to the top of his class.

The company's growth was tied to the Information Technology Department; developing any idea across the firm required support from the IT bureau. Its team of professionals came from different parts of the world: Eric Baruch from Israel, Eryck S. from Poland, Mauricio from Mexico, as well as other rocket scientists from India, the Philippines, Bolivia, Mexico, and Argentina. These whiz guys and programmers developed software from scratch to take care of any crazy idea the company comes up with.

The single strongest support this team gave the stores was providing them with a working system for cash sales when there were steep discounts, one of the biggest traffic and sales events of the year. The high volume of sales brought an amazing quantity of traffic that was so big that the lines of people would make the fire marshal shut down the stores. It was planned for several dates during the year, taking into consideration the expectation that the associates would have to do it offline, since the system usually could not support such a high volume of transactions. This frustrated the operation, because it slowed down the process of taking care of the customer. Top management had to hear on the Monday morning, after the weekend sale, that the retail group complained that many sales were missed because there was no system. The transaction operating system went through many phases at the point of purchase. It automatically needed to update the information on several company platforms, requiring reports and statistics that made the transaction very slow. It was one thing to make it slow, but quite another story when the system would crash.

On the other side of the company was IT's version of the situation—it did not have enough systems to support the high volume of transactions at the same time during cash sales, which were crashing the system. All of these growing challenges were faced every single day until they were able to upgrade to more powerful systems—even including a backup system. Thus if the regular, everyday system crashed, there would be a local backup system per store that would continue to support the sales and no one would notice the difference.

This high traffic was generated by the promotions Jerry and the marketing team developed, and sometimes they turned out to cause trouble with the authorities. The big turnout at a store in L.A. made the City require La Curacao to acquire parking lots all around the flagship store to accommodate the sales and overflow of cars. They also had to provide for the associates' cars, too. The store was remodeled, and more space was taken for displays. The bigger the store, the more additional associates were needed to serve the customers. In addition to more support staff, all of them were hired to provide better customer service.

The credit department was growing each day too, so there was a big demand for space for parking. The Azarkmans bought the building behind 1605 9th Street, which is known today as James Wood Street. This tall building had a big sign on top of it that read "TEAMSTERS," and they were the owners.

The Teamsters are the largest union in the United States and Canada, an important part of organized labor for more than a century. The organization was founded by drivers in 1903, and its membership grew to include freight drivers and warehouse workers. Today, the Teamsters consist of blue collar and professional workers organized in unions in both the private and public sectors, with more than one million members.

The organization used part of the 9th Street building for years, as they owned it. On the first floor, there was a large room where meetings were held. The union decided to sell the building so it could move to another property at a different location. The building was very old, and many of its features were failing. For example, the elevators would get stuck and stop operating and the water pipes had problems. The investment the labor union needed to make it operate properly was not worth it. The only value it had was in the land beneath the building.

After the Azarkmans bought the dilapidated structure, they first considered keeping it running and renting out the unoccupied areas. But, very soon they concluded this was not possible. The inspectors contracted to assess the property for the selling process made several observations about the quality of the property, and tested the levels of asbestos, which were at such high levels that the cost to remove it was enormous. The building was worthless—it was only the land they were really buying, in addition to the cost of building's demolition.

Asbestos was banned for health and safety reasons from construction products in many developed countries of the world; in the United States it's still used in cement asbestos pipes. In the '80s a white asbestos powder was added to materials used on surfaces covering ceilings. In a 1998 study called "Mechanisms in the Pathogenesis of Asbestosis and Silicosis" published in the American Journal of Respiratory and Critical Care Medicine, author Churg A. Mossman of the University of Vermont, College of Medicine reported that asbestos has been related to health issues for years and is recognized as one of the causes of lung cancer.

The costs of removing all of the asbestos from the Teamsters' building at 9th Street was so high that it was less expensive to simply demolish the entire edifice. The building was still partially rented, and the long process of relocating every single tenant took years and many evictions. But the space was needed for additional parking in order to comply with city regulations. In the beginning, they thought they could continue renting offices during the week, and during the weekends, use the building's parking lot for the overflow of cars. The idea was ingenious, as it would take care of the high volume of customers and associates for the retail operation—but the reality proved to be different.

Meanwhile, the building at 1605 and 1625 Olympic Boulevard was developed as La Curacao Business Center. Several floors were leased to tenants in all kinds of businesses, from attorneys to schools. Ray, the building manager, always emphasized that it had incredible potential, with views from the different floors of the world famous Hollywood sign, downtown L.A., and Santa Monica beach.

Demolishing the Teamsters' building was a nightmare. First, the building's management looked for Hollywood movie companies to sell a video of the demolition to as a way to pay for it. It took years before all of the tenants had left the building and the location looked like a ghost town. One day, a few homeless people entered the building and pulled out copper pipes, which the building was full of. What they did not know was that the water system was still running; water started flooding the building and spilling out onto the street. The police came and, when the thieves were caught, they claimed they worked for the building's owners and were actually doing a job for them.

Finally, a Hollywood company decided to buy the film of the demolition. Once the permits were processed, to the surprise of everyone, the city announced that the closed building next to them had been a gas station previously, and that made the explosion for a demolition impossible. What a fiasco! It was a great idea that did not pan out.

The building had to be torn down piece by piece, floor by floor, until the last rock, pipe, and wire had been taken out. A full, empty lot was unveiled and another parking lot was developed there to please the City of Los Angeles and the neighbors, as it reduced the competition for finding a parking space. All of this added parking allowed La Curacao to run as many promotions and bring in as many people—and vehicles—as necessary. As they used to say on Star Trek, "space, the final frontier."

Part IV

Now What?

Can you repeat your success? Can success transfer to other areas of your life, other businesses? When you hit once, can you continue hitting and getting the same results?

Chapter Fifteen

Where Do You Want to Be?

Y ou see people walking next to you at a bus stop, a mall, school, at the work place, and you ask yourself: are any of these individuals going to change their lives and become millionaires? The odds of winning the lottery are close to impossible. Getting money through inheritance is slime. Becoming a millionaire from working is even less likely.

What it takes to turn your life around is not only hard work but smart work. Jerry discovered a niche, and he worked hard to give this group of people valuable and excellent service. His business grew to higher volumes, and he hired associates to support him and his customers. Vendors became his partners and he got credit lines, great deals, and the right merchandise. Next came opening new stores to serve this niche in different regions. Jerry and Ron developed at the store level:

strategic product displays with a clear traffic flood and common sense. Plan-o-grams were designed to create a logical product flow, with different step-ups to naturally walk the consumer to better products. All these strategies were done to bring an extraordinary shopping experience to customers and to provide them with a great selection, variety, and quality of products. Credit became a tool to make any product available to this niche. They empowered their associates to be able to execute and perform accordingly, and they were able to grow towards opening more stores.

All this took them years of effort, years of the 4 Ds: Discipline, Desire, Determination, and Drive. That is what business is about—never taking a step back not even to propel you. Take a good look at your business and see the path it's traveling down. Watch it closely to improve your next step. Use every mistake as an opportunity to grow and not judge yourself. Instead, nurture your business and make a difference. Maturing as a business owner requires thinking, watching, and analyzing what you are doing and making it better the next time. Never stop improving yourself, learning new ideas, observing what others are doing, and making it better. Raise the bar constantly, pushes you to the next step, and climb that business ladder.

Jerry saw every challenge as an opportunity. The table was set for them, and he had two choices: take it or leave it. Jerry took it in the early days of walking the streets of Los Angeles; once he made his first sale, he kept coming again and again, with more products and more offers with better deals. He was always adding special value that his customers could not find anywhere else, and giving them all of it on his own credit with four month payments with no interest, and a special gift at the time of delivery.

The surprise gift after the purchase brought a smile 99% of time. It was unexpected, and it left a good impression and made the customer more likely to buy again. The free warranty on the product gave additional value to the purchase. Any product bought from him had always a value no matter how long ago they had bought it, if their product was damaged or it didn't work. Jerry used a formula and gave them some kind of credit towards the next purchase.

Jerry never forgot the people that gave him a hand, which helped him start his business and made it grow, especially his vendors. Every year, the company prepares a vendor event where they are honored and recognized. Recognition is one of the most important factors in people's life; it's a psychological element that makes people compete for greatness. Vendors are acknowledged for their efforts, their support, and the growth of the business year to year, most of the time due to their dedication to the account. The event brings together all of the Sales Executives and the top management of their companies. It's a moment of sharing, giving them a token of appreciation. One award in this event is given to those vendors that gave Jerry his first push and support when he needed it the most. It is given to the vendors that gave him support to continue selling in the early days of the operation by providing him with lines of credit and product; some vendor products are still part of the lineup today.

How do common people do extraordinary things? How do you motivate yourself to continue your efforts to change your life and the lives of others? How do you mold the future today to make those unexpected moves that will convert your steps into models of success? The most important answer to these questions is inside you—never, never, never give up. Never say *this is it*. Always try to make a change and lift the bar to unlimited and unreachable goals. Never stop pushing. Never stop short.

Every year, in the month of March, everyone expects changes in the company. This has become, for years, the month where people are moved around. Some get promoted, and some are moved to different departments. This time of the year, everyone is, in a way, expecting the company to become better, to acknowledge the quality and the importance of its associates. These changes are done all over the company, not only at the sales level, or operations teams. These movements bring an expectation that is positive, because people understand that somebody is watching and, by watching, improvement is on its way. Everyone gets evaluated, and these evaluations are done to every single associate of the company. It's like in the Jewish traditions of Passover when conservative Jews clean the house from top to bottom.

The Passover is a commemorative holiday and festival of the Jewish community, celebrating their Exodus, when the Israelis were liberated from slavery in Egypt. It's celebrated on the 15th day of Nisan in the Jewish calendar. This is the first month of the ecclesiastical year of the eighth in the leap year. It's the month when spring starts and happens during March or April, measured in the past when the barley was ripe. In the Bible, the story says that God send the 10 plagues to Egypt to liberate the children of Israel. The worst of the plagues was the last one where the slaughter of the first-born child happens. Jews were instructed to mark the doors of their homes with the blood of a spring lamb for the spirit of the Lord to pass by. The traditions are not to eat leavened bread, so they eat Matzo instead. The Torah says that the use of *chametz* is forbidden, which is one of the five grains use as a leavening agent. Homes are scrubbed to make sure there is no left over *chametz* anywhere.

At Sylvia Arteaga's table, there was not much to eat. Her mom had left her in the hands of her grandmother and grandfather. She was only four years old, but she already understood that her mother, who had her at the age of fifteen, now had a new husband and her grandparents didn't want her to be raised by a step father. She was born in Mexico City and her grandfather was extremely strict. Sylvia was in sixth grade when the family decided that she was not going back to school. Her aunt had run away with her boyfriend and now her grandfather was so mad that he said he was not going to spend more money on their education. Instead, he wanted them to see how hard life was in the construction business, and took them to work with him. Once he calmed down, they stayed home. Sylvia was always looking for something to do; she would find little jobs here and there, but she had to make sure to be home before her grandfather came home from work to avoid any problems.

One day, she and her aunt decided to come to the United States for a better life. She was eighteen and they both took a train for four days from Mexico City to Tijuana. They knew a coyote would be waiting to pass them to the other side for $350, but they did not know the person—it was all by references. She was not scared. She felt invincible. They tried two times. The last time, they dressed her like a chola. She remembers that they layered her hair with gel. Once at the border, the border patrol asked her name, but she knew nothing of English and she could not answer, so they sent her back. The third time, they asked her if she dared to go in the engine of a car. She was short and skinny and so she said yes. The only challenge she had was with her hair; her hair was very long, and she felt like it was going through the car slits. The coyote had told her that, when she could not take it anymore, she should slam on the sides of the car and they would stop. The line to cross the border was long, and she was holding out ok, but she began to get scared that the engine would pull her hair, and she would be swallowed by it, so she started making all the noise she could, but they kept going. Once the car stopped, she felt relief. They had passed San Clemente, the last border patrol check point.

Her sister was not with her. She was passing through the hills and had been returned several times already. When Sylvia arrived at her family's apartment in Los Angeles, and her sister was not there, she immediately said she was going back. They had made the decision to make it together, and she was not going to let her sister be by herself. The coyote told her, "give me two days, I will bring her to you," and in two days, the aunt and sister was there with her.

A relative of the family had a job at an agency for his sister, but she had decided to go back to Mexico. He offered it to Sylvia, and she started going to different job interviews. One of them was La Curacao. Ron asked her several questions and she was able to answer them all. She was hired and told to come back on Monday. On Monday, she had an emergency and called to say she was not going to be able to show up and that she needed a couple of days, Ron told her that it was no problem. The days passed, and she called Ron to let him know that she had another job offer and that she was going to try that one first. If it didn't work, she'd go back to La Curacao.

Today, Jerry still believes that the communities that opened those doors to him in the beginning, and that continue to shop at their stores, are the real heroes of this story. This community with many faces, many different skin colors, those who came running away from poverty, political persecution, civil wars, or devastating natural disasters. Giving back to these people has been the brother's top priority. The creation of La Curacao Children's Foundation was extremely important to the brothers. This organization serves the communities around each of the stores; it has brought basic necessities, such as beds, to thousands of families. All of the local and neighborhood organizations: churches, schools, children services, and any registered organization in the community; families are referred to La Curacao Foundation for help. The store personal is trained to visit these homes and answer a questionnaire to approve the donations.

The decision is made at the store level, and the next day, La Curacao is in the neighborhood, in the home of the intended family delivering bedrooms, dining tables, sofas sets, refrigerators, and any product that the store has and that the family needs, for free. Even in the worst days of the recession, La Curacao never cut this budget. The promise to help those in need has been always part of the business model. This is done totally for free, and as a contribution to society and to children, and is a way of giving back to that specific neighborhood that has supported the business.

The company is very appreciative of their community and giving back is the biggest and most important element for Jerry. The social promise of La Curacao is a portion from every sale goes back to the community. The foundation is like a department and it is the whole company's mission to be there and help. They believe that there are not enough ways to give back to the community. The Azarkmans' have donated thousands of dollars to local charities and have provided a lot of support in times of disaster—particularly the Northridge Earthquake and Hurricane Mitch.

In 1998, Hurricane Mitch qualified at that time as the deadliest hurricane in history for the North Atlantic, and especially for Central America. It started on October 22, and it was qualified by Saffir-Simpson's Hurricane Scale as a category 5 hurricane. Hurricanes actually weaken with time, but when this one hit Honduras and continued its path through the rest of Central America it was brutal. Even though by that time the hurricane hit, it had grown even weaker, the disaster was outrageous. It took the hurricane from October 29 to November 3rd to pass through Honduras, Guatemala, and Nicaragua, bringing high quantities of rain. A record 11,000 people died and more than 11,000 were missing. In addition, more than 2.7 million were left homeless and there was over 8.5 billion dollars' worth of damage to the infrastructure.

When the news brought the story of the disaster, the community got organized at La Curacao. They created a place to donate. The parking lot of the Los Angeles store was converted into a collection center for food cans, clothing, blankets, medicine, water, and money. A nonprofit organization collected all the cash resources. Volunteers from the community and La Curacao associates received the donations and organized them by category. They were boxed and shrink wrapped in pallets, and all these pallets were taken to the warehouse. The warehouse started to fill out: more than one hundred freight containers were collected in a matter of twenty-four hours and they were all ready to be shipped to the disaster areas. La Curacao contacted the Red Cross and many other organizations and were told that they only accept money donations. Now what?

What were they going to do with all the donations the community had brought? They could not throw them away. No one wanted to take them into the eye of the hurricane. An important decision had to be made. The affected communities needed help and La Curacao could not lose the communities' confidence, in addition to all of their effort to prepare the donations. They made the decision to get an airplane; leased it and all the donations were taken to the different countries. And guess what? These were the first donations to arrive in Central America. At each country, local La Curacao partners were waiting and the donations got to those who needed them within two days.

This is once more a token of the promise and appreciation these two brothers have, and will continue to have, for the community that has taken the company to unimaginable levels. In the beginning, the Central American community opened their homes to Jerry, and as the company grew, the Mexican community opens their doors, too.

Sylvia did not like the job and came back to La Curacao, and started immediately. There were less than ten associates, and she was the first Mexican hired. It was hard for her to understand the way they spoke. Even though it was Spanish, each country used the words differently—bad words from one country might be normal vocabulary for the other. Juanito was a supervisor in the group and he told everyone—without Sylvia knowing—that she was his niece because he was trying to protect her. He trained her, saying that there was always something to do, and if there were no customers, she had to find something to do. She would see other associates talking, but she would clean the glasses and make herself useful.

She would sell jewelry, and she would prepare the inventory models. She would observe how Jerry would sell an item and she would mimic him. She would even use the same words as him. An earring is *aro* in Spanish and Jerry would call it *jaritos*. Sylvia would call them the same as a joke, breaking the ice with the customer. She felt like she was among family because of the way that Jerry treated everyone with respect and made it easy for them to learn how to sell and treat their customers.

She started noticing that electronics sell faster, and she followed Jerry to learn how he sold to a customer. She noticed that he would bring a cassette with music and set it up in the system and show the customer how it worked. With the next customer that came in, she offered him a boom box, and pulled out a cassette and gave it to the customer for him to set up while she was learning. She worked hard to get the sale, and treated the customers like family. They would come back and wait until she was available. She was working a $7,000 sale and it took several weeks.

Each time the customer wanted to change an item, she would say the invoice was already done, and the customer would say, "so I will talk to Jerry then." She knew that if the customer went to Jerry, she would lose her sale. Jerry was a sales person on the floor the same as she was. This customer worked for a liquor warehouse and, each time he returned to the store, she would joke about him sending them a bottle of wine.

Finally the delivery was done and a bottle of wine was sent by the customer, the driver drank it and lay down on a park; he was intoxicated, and for his bad fortune a police helicopter lost control and landed on top of him, and the driver lost his life there. What are the odds of something like this happening?

Sylvia was making $3.35 an hour, plus commission, and she had two jobs. She worked at La Curacao during the day and at a restaurant at night. She would make $150 in tips a week, while at La Curacao it would be a monthly commission check. She wanted more money and she knew the electronics department was where the money was made. She tried to sell there and one of the salesmen told her that Jerry didn't want her selling here. She kept pushing and learning. She knew she had to learn how to calculate percentage and tax for each invoice, in addition to the monthly payments with the interest. She practiced and practiced until she got it and began selling everything around the store. The Mexicans would come to her and wait for her as much as they had to. One day, her supervisor asked her if he should give out tickets since she had a big line. She answered him, "Please do."

She had to survive in an environment of different people. She had a customer that used only bad words and had a furious attitude. She helped her once and, to calm her down, offered her a cup of coffee. She asks her how much sugar she wanted and the lady said four spoon full. Sylvia realized the sugar container was empty, and a coworker volunteered to bring her more. Sylvia finished preparing it, and gave it to Rosa, her angry customer. Rosa took a sip and threw it all at once, yelling, "Are you trying to poison me?" It was salt instead of sugar. After that, they became friends.

All these people have the same dreams and fears, with families and children just like yours, looking for opportunities in this society, with a great desire to work and support their families, here in the States and back in their countries of origin. When Jerry was walking the streets, people would ask him if he could deliver these same products to their home countries. They wanted to be able to export a gift to their relatives back in their towns. When Jerry was planning to use La Curacao as a name, which already existed, they visited El Salvador and met with the owner of La Curacao in Central America. They had no intention of coming to United States and they were authorized to use the name. Jerry proposed selling products in the United States for the La Curacao of Central America, to be delivered to families in El Salvador, Guatemala, Honduras, and Nicaragua.

The operation started with El Salvador, and it was a huge success. The product was already in the country to be delivered. The customer was able to select the product from a catalog of pictures, and in some cases, the actual sample was brought to the stores for customers to be able to verify the actual product that was going to be delivered. The operation was difficult because the customer in the United States wanted products to be delivered back in their countries, not in cities. They wanted to deliver products to remote locations where, in some cases, there were no roads or rooms, even in the small homes, for big items they bought. Sometimes, there was no electricity. There were many challenges for the company, but they always delivered, even if it had to by boat.

The department grew to the rest of Central America, and became a very successful operation. When the company grew to the Mexican community, it was necessary to have a partner to deliver there. Agreements where made with Mundo y Hogar, a chain of small stores all over Mexico. Once the operation grew to bigger levels, this company was replaced with Viena and after growing even more, it moved to FAMSA. The Export Department of La Curacao was growing to such a high level that soon it made sense to open their own warehouses and have their own products ship directly to their own locations in each country. This was the next step and those warehouses are fully operating today. Many products are exported from United States to Mexico and Central America, in addition to the products bought locally. All this happened before the Hurricane Mitch. The community knew that there was a connection back in their country with La Curacao, so when the company decided to help, people felt comfortable to come and donate. They trusted their donations would arrive, and they did.

When Mike Falkestain was hired, Sylvia was assigned to be his assistant, and he asked her what changes she would suggest. She told him that everyone came late, including herself, and that this could be an opportunity to set everything straight.

She told him to talk to everyone and to give them a warning so that everyone would be disciplined for it. The following Saturday, she showed up at 10:10 AM, and a few minutes later, in front of everyone, Mike showed up with a white paper with something written on it and gave it to her. He said that this was a warning for coming in late. She was so furious. She told him that he had no right to do that, to humiliate her in front of everyone. He had to bring her to the office and even notify everyone about it ahead of time. At 1:00 PM, she left work and she did not show up to work the following days. Jerry called her to ask what had happened. He knew that she worked with her heart; he had seen her changing light bulbs even when she was pregnant. She was a valuable associate and it didn't make sense to lose her. He knew her very well. He remembered that she delivered her baby came into work the next day—she was an extremely loyal and dedicated associate. He was not going to lose her. She came back. He convinced her by saying that he would not allow that warning to go into effect for now.

Jerry saw her as an authentic Mexican Ambassador for the company. She had set up her own goal of $80,000 in sales in a month, and she had asked Jerry if he would give her a microwave if she reached that goal. Jerry knew that the amount was unreachable and said sure. She went and asked Ron the same question for a 13" TV. He also said yes. The amount was overwhelming. Sylvia remembers that she did not even go to the restroom so that she would not lose one sale. She was sitting at a dining room set when she saw Mike and Ron walking towards her with a white envelope. She thought that they were going to fire her. Ron gave her an envelope with a $1,000 commission. She was the best salesperson. No one could come close to her numbers.

Once Sylvia reached this goal, it made Jerry realize that it was reachable. By making a strategy of identifying the product with higher margins, the salesperson could reach higher goals. Goals were set up for each salesperson, and the floor strategy was explained to everyone. Sylvia was the example that proved the goal was reachable. Jerry developed a spiff program to give additional incentive to the sales person when they sold specific items on the floor.

One additional reason for La Curacao's success is the combination of the two brothers who were so different that they came from two different business worlds. Jerry, who we know well through this book, developed through the years as the marketing guru of the business, and Ron became the finance guru.

They both complemented each other in the business, but what makes Ron different than Jerry? Ron transmits authority, strong will, and a great capacity to organize and order what nobody can foresee. One of Ron's biggest gifts is the ability to organize and structure a business. He dedicated a lot of his time to understanding banking regulations to obtain the loans necessary to grow. He learned accounting, balancing the funds, payroll, and budgets in addition to the warehouse, Human Resources, and IT Group. This gave the company the strength to grow and to deliver and created the necessary structure to support the operation.

Jerry, on the other hand, developed his abilities in the marketing parts of the company, the purchasing department, and the sales force. Jerry is always ahead of the game with advertising campaigns and sale strategies on the floor. His eye for product gives him the advantage to see in it what most won't see. Because he is a great motivational speaker for the sales force, he is a strong leader.

Companies need leaders—leaders that will transmit leadership, and authority too. This respect will develop with time and with example. Both Jerry and Ron have, through the years, brought security to their associates. Because of this, associates are able to project to the customers the message that La Curacao is here for the long run.

At 1313 Olympic Boulevard, there was a procedure for closing the store. The associates in the jewelry area had to pull all the gold and set it up on a box that was kept overnight in a safety box. Sylvia and three more associates pulled all the gold and set it up in the box. It was ten minutes before closing; four men came in separately and requested the help of the three associates. They had already left the box for the supervisor to put in the safety box. They helped the men, but they did not buy anything. Instead, the jewelry box had disappeared. The associates knew it had been the plan to distract them and to steal from them. Sylvia noticed that each time something bad happened to the Azarkmans, many good things happened to them immediately. She would always say that they were blessed by God. The sales that month were the best of all, and they had the *cambalache* promotion where you would come with an old product that was given a price. The number given to that product could be used towards a new item. Sylvia received $20,000 in commissions that month.

Amelia, as Sylvia remembers her name before she could get her legal status, felt that she had to push herself and try even harder because she had no education;

every new manager had their style and their way to demand from them all. She had already become the electronics supervisor, and she was pushing to become a manager. She was like a sponge for learning anything La Curacao had offered her. She was a role model for many sales people, and she delivered anything that was asked of her. Jerry would tell her not to take the customer's credit card. What she did was, if she was busy with a customer and another would approach her, she would say, "Do you have an account with us?" That person would say yes. She would ask for the card and keep it with her until she was able to come back and help them. She became the first woman to have the position of Store Manager.

Human Resources was always happy with Sylvia. Every sales associate that worked close to Sylvia became supervisors and group leaders. She was given the nickname of The Incubator. Great opportunities to grow in the company followed her because of her knowledge and experience. She knew how to follow all the directions that Jerry gave in his training. One of the examples that has never left her mind was when Jerry was training them about achieving goals, and he asked them if they had to pass a broken bridge, where there were lots of crocodiles and a million dollars on the other side, if they would risk their lives. Most of them said they wouldn't. He then asked if they would cross that same bridge and the crocodiles if their son or daughter were there. Sylvia remembers that she said yes she would. Jerry then said, "That is your sales goal. Achieve it for your kids."

She would work long hours, and when the month came to an end, she would work even longer to make sure all of the contracts were accounted for. Sylvia would remind her children that she worked as hard as she could to bring milk to their table and so that they didn't have to experience what she had to do. Jerry was an inspiration for her, a motivator, and a humanitarian. She would never leave the brothers; she promised them forever because they opened the door to a world of possibilities, and they became her new family at work.

The plan of profit sharing is a very important part of growing a business; there are many bonus plans that work parallel to the salary structure that motivate people to work harder and smarter. The bonus plan works separately than the commission plan for the sales force. The sales associates have their clear commission plans and a bonus when they move above the expected numbers. For this, there is additional compensation. Ron developed a plan where, instead of flat commission for the sales associates, it's rooted in performance-based salary: if the person does not reach his required performance, this person would be moved to another area where he/she can develop better, and perform even better.

The bonus plans for associates that are not salespeople and that are not paid by commission is a tool to demand more. There will be compensation down the road if they deliver extra. The bonus plan is different than profit sharing because it happens before there is even profit. In some cases, when the economy has been at its lowest due to the recession, some of the bonuses were still paid because they were not linked to sales goals but to performance. These key bonuses were keeping the business going but the economy was hurting so badly that, at the end, all bonuses were cut to nothing.

Even though Jerry's ADD has been an issue for him all his life, he handles his thoughts when he is in a middle of a conversation by always trying to create new ideas. He might be in another place in his mind while the rest are in a meeting, but he is thinking about how to build what is coming. A word might have taken him somewhere else, but his mind is not blank—he is creating new programs, connecting two areas that make sense, tying the conversation to a previous meeting, and great things come out.

Jerry, in his vision, can never see an obstacle as something negative. He always sees it as an opportunity. He would say, "The bad economy is a new condition, a new opportunity to take advantage of the need for credit. Instead of buying Sony, people will buy JVC. They won't spend $5,000 now; they will spend $1,000 instead." This new economy brought a different tier of customers—some bought, others didn't. The pressure boiled and they needed to add traffic builders to the line of products to get higher numbers.

This gave them the opportunity to directly import products and put them under market price to bring the traffic into the stores. It brought a chance for new customers to make an impulse buy. The floor strategy was to make this new customer not only stay with this product with low prices or traffic builder and no margin, but also to expose the stores and show other products that will, in the end, bring more sales. In all the advertising and marketing campaigns, a store won't be able to expose all the products that are available. Once the customer has the opportunity to come and see them, they definitely find many other products that he/she did not know the store carried. Re-invent your company, the way the products are displayed, and the selection of products; changing all the time increases incentive and brings enthusiasm to the floor. These are some of the changes every company has to go through every year to keep advancing.

An influential character in Jerry's life has been Don Francisco, a TV legend in the Hispanic market. His stage name is Don Francisco but his birth name is Mario Luis Kreutzberger, and his show has been ongoing for over fifty years. Don Francisco came to the inauguration of the second store in Panorama, and the amount of people that showed up was so many that freeways where collapse and the streets were blocked for miles with cars. The mall where the event was taking place was packed shoulder-to-shoulder and even inside the store, to the point that the event was shut down by the fire marshal. Since then, Don Francisco has kept in contact with the brothers and has been a great influence in their lives.

In their conversations with Don Francisco, there is no negative comment that he doesn't turn around and make positive, making everything around him happy. Don Francisco is easy going and an instant friend. He has been part of the Azarkman's family prayers in Passover. Jerry sees him as a father figure, as a teacher.

Jerry remembers, through his conversations with Don Francisco, that when he was doing the training for Rena Ware, there was a guy who would walk with a limp. Around his neck, he wore many gold chains and he would walk with the catalog of products always in his hands. In his car, he had a booster chair to drive. He was always smiling and never said anything negative. He would neglect his disability, and when Jerry saw him as the top salesperson of the group, he said to himself "I can be anything I want to be. If this guy can, I can too." Jerry's mantra is "nothing can stand against my will".

Jerry remembered that Joe Roach, one of his vendors, had taught him everything about the business of small appliances. He would repeat his last name and make the analogy of a cockroach to break the ice, "I'm going to build you a department in thirty days. If you do not sell the product, I will take it all out, but I'm going to teach you how to sell it." The first thing is, you do not need a lot of merchandise. One toaster in the front and two of the same in the back of the sample—then when you sell the two, he would come and refill it. You do not need a big inventory, he would insist. He would say, "All you need is to call me and tell me what to bring, and I will bring it for you every day, if necessary." Joe did not work for money; he was a proof of success, and he would always acknowledge that success depended on the loyalty you create with your customers.

What stands against my will? Jerry would say, "I have to fight with myself not to be disconnected from what is going around me." He had to battle for his work, to make those sales, negotiate the best prices with his vendors, to build the company one step at a time, and build the associates one by one. Jerry would say, "You have to work so hard, to the level that you can sell ice to the Eskimos. Whatever it takes—cut wood, get your hands on it, do it too, build your work, keep working, even against yourself to make it happen." Take any goal you have, anything you want in life, dedicate yourself to making it happen, sacrifice your extra time for this, make your idea appealing for your potential customers, and always have a gift to thank them. You will have to extend your furthest muscle all the way out to make it a reality.

Your dedication to your business will always have side effects; you will be sacrificing time from other things, like family. Jerry would have loved to dedicate more time to his kids, share more of their lives, pick them up from school, be there for their school presentations. If he could go back in time and change something, he would have twelve kids instead of three. His family is the most important thing in his life.

Analyzing his life, Jerry would say that the customer is the judge of any business; they are the ones that will determine the success of your business. If you don't pay attention to your customer's complaints, you will be losing more customers than the amount of new ones coming in. You can increase the amounts of new customers but this could get to a point that they would not compensate the ones not coming back. The word of mouth of any experience is very important for your business, and a bad experience is even more important to listen and learn what needs to be changed or improved.

When Jerry goes back to see whom he would give thanks to in his life, he will never forget the struggles his family suffered, and how strong his mom Muluk was—how she had to bring food to the table and take care of her family. She taught him that life is not easy and that there is no limit to how hard you have to work. She taught him that, with every drop of water, you can eventually create an ocean. With every penny she accumulated for the family, it was for them to have a better life.

He is also thankful for the teacher that believed in him and that gave him the confidence to step up. Education in an individual's early years is so important in developing their self-esteem and creating a thirst for learning. Changing teachers brought light to young Jerry and turned his life around.

His father was another stepping stone for his development and another person he appreciates for his encouraging words. His dad taught him that the sky was the limit, but that the most important part was for him to be happy. Having money doesn't bring you happiness; you need to find your own happiness. Your happiness can start when you accomplish any of your goals, when you are with others, or when you give to others. Each one needs to find their internal happiness and their own joy.

Another moment of thankfulness for Jerry was being accepted to his military academy and all his military training after school because this gave him the strength to self-motivate and to be more disciplined. It taught him how to live on his own at a very early age. It gave him the opportunity to get a job to change people. In his job at City Hall, all he had to do was hang around at a park and get in a gang of young kids that had become a pest for the neighborhood. They were kids from twelve to sixteen years old; three of their friends were already in jail. One of the trials these kids did to him was to make him smoke marijuana. They insisted he smoke, so he took a drag and began choking and coughing. They laughed so much at him that, in the end, he was accepted. They asked him if he could help get their friends out of jail.

Jerry, at this point, had to demonstrate to them that he had power and that he had connections to be able to have leadership inside the group. He went back to the City Hall and the psychologist assigned to help him deal with these kids made it work out. Jerry was the hero for the kids now because he helped their friend out of jail.

They were planning a robbery, Jerry could not tell the police, he had to convince them not to do it. They had to wait for the guy to come out of the bank were they knew he was cashing money. Jerry was outside with them and he decided to use one of his biggest tools: math. He told them that with this job they would get $500 each the most, and if they would be caught they would go to prison for at least 6 years—was it worth it to take all this time of their liberty for so little money? He was able to convince them. He started taking them to classes of how to make jewelry, driving classes, until little by little each one began finding jobs and leaving the group until it disappeared. He was a few years later on his motorcycle in Tel

Aviv and something went wrong, he was trying to fix it when a taxi pull back to him and it was one of the kids he had work with him in the past at the park. He contacted several of them, and they had taxis too, they had a reunion right there in the middle of the street and helped Jerry with his motorcycle.

Another reason for Jerry to be grateful is his two wives that gave him his kids, who he adores and can't wait to spend more time with. He wants to be part of every step in their lives; he wants to be their friend, share his ideas, his experiences, his knowledge in business, and his warm heart with them.

Jerry will always be indebted with the Latino Community that opened their doors to a stranger, with all their rich culture of music, food, colors, respect for their elders, and their humbleness. He has learned so many things from them, and the most important one is that he didn't have to speak Spanish to be able to communicate with them.

He will always owe a favor to the vendors that gave him a hand and opened his eyes to the world of retail—from his first purchase of Pong at Midtown Electronics to everyone that came knocking at La Curacao.

Don Francisco will always be in his heart for giving him the peace that you have to have with any of the struggles that your mind is punching of. Don Francisco's daily preaching philosophy of always looking for the positive in any negativity and enjoying life no matter what.

Life is not easy we all know this and specially the life in the retail world. The fun may be taken away when in business there will be internal factors that will limit the flawlessness of the shopping experience. If a customer had a bad experience they will tell their family, their friends and these negative comments can be heard among hundreds of people that still have not put one step in your business. Your store or service is done in a particular location, from where are you going to get new customers? You need to listen to your customers: they are the source of information for the future of your company. Adjusting your operation to fulfill your customer's needs is one part of being successful in business, but to stay in business you will have to work on the shopping experience of your consumer, and make it so smooth that once the transaction is completed, they would love to come back and experience it again.

Creating loyalty from your customers is essential to continue doing business. In today's business world, people are looking for more value for their dollar and if your business is not providing that extra touch there are others that will. Rewarding your customer for his/her shopping is essential to create that connection and creating loyalty. Jerry develop the "Puntos" Program where the customer gets points for their purchases, for paying on time their monthly payment, for bringing new customers, and for connecting with the different services offer by the company. The more a customer buys, the more points and better gifts they can redeem. The loyalty programs assured the customer's continuity and make them coming back to keep adding to their points.

If Jerry is asked what his biggest internal challenge is, his answer is always that he demands more from himself than he would request from others. This gets him in trouble sometimes because some people do not forgive his comments. When his observations put him in the shoes of the customer, his critical observations are always with the intention of making the company improve, elevate itself to better customer service and better deals.

Jerry believes that even the impossible can be possible, like hitting in billiards with one shot one ball and the possibility of all balls going inside at once. How many times you will play and not even one will go in. The probability of this to happen of hitting once and getting them all in is very small, but it doesn't mean it can't be done. That is how he sees the universe he believes that there can be more than one big bang in the theory of the universe. The possibility of having several big bangs for him takes it to infinity of the universe. When you ask Jerry if he believes in reincarnation, he will give you his Theory of Multiplanets he thinks that somewhere else, there has to be someone like him and you, doing the same things you are doing now.

If he had to leave this life in any moment, and he could come back to talk to someone, it would be his kids. He would tell them that they have to finish what he started and make an emphasis of his life philosophy to have fun but not in a way that will go against their health. He would emphasize always giving back to people and to have a soft heart to always help others. He knows that business will never stop in this family because business is in their veins.

Jerry always recommends having gifts for customers; gifts can change any situation from negative to positive. Jerry will tell you that he has a solution for the conflicts in Gaza. He says that one side fires a missile and the other side responds with ten. One side gives hate, the other reproduces more hate. What if, instead of all this terribleness, you start releasing balloons with gifts inside and toys for the kids. Instead of hate, we give toys. Instead of bullets, we give toys. Once you do it 100 times, 1000 times, 10,000 times, the message finally will start penetrating.

What is the future? Asking Jerry about this, he answers, "I have done only ten percent of what I want to do." He has many plans for his family, and for the business world. He would love to create businesses and sell them to make people develop. The whole industry is going to change, he believes. Companies are changing and prices are changing. People with similar buying habits are creating buying groups and he believes that these groups are going to buy one kind of car, their kind of groceries, their type of electronics, etc. and they will have their own stores in the future.

People are constantly changing their habits, learning new ways to do to things. If customers are not feeling that you are renovating your operation, remodeling, bringing new lines of product, not adapting to what is new in the market, you will lose customers and they will go to more exciting retailers. Refreshing your operation with innovative ways to do business will keep your traffic coming to see what is new. Many of the original customers at La Curacao moved to other cities and states or some just felt that the company that gave them the first credit no longer represented them. It was a store for new comers, for the ones that could not get credit anywhere, and now they were on the fast track for acculturation. How do you keep being appealing for your old customers, even though you renovate and keep with the trends of the market? The answer is complex and not so easy to answer, but it's important to put yourself in your customer's shoes. You will see what it is that they are looking for. Are you a customer of your own store? Have you gone to the processes that each customer goes through? Go through the process and determine if you can be more efficient. Find out what is affecting your customer's shopping experience. The customer's satisfaction is the focus of your answer.

Customers are savvier now days. They can research prices on their phone where ever they are—they are the watchdogs of the retail industry. This will make retailers more cautious in pricing and creating new strategies to approach pricing. Access to buying becomes easier and easier for the consumer each day. If retailers want a better shopping experience, the paying process will have to change dramatically too.

The retailer's environment is changing due to technology and social media. The cost of keeping up with the latest systems affects the bottom line of companies and affects the price of products for consumers. If a balance is not produced, retailers will continue to disappear. Jerry has a call to build a new concept of retail with the same niche but with the highest technology, fair pricing, and extensive customer service that allows the retailer to be profitable. Jerry will build a store of this kind from zero but now with more than $20.

What do you think the future will bring? For Jerry, everything is summarized in one phrase—always remember; *where there is a will, there is a way.*

About the Authors

Ruth Garcia-Corrales

Ruth was attending Tenth Street Elementary School in Los Angeles, taking her first steps towards learning English, when the six-year-old's grandmother fell into a diabetic coma and changed the whole family's destiny. After 10 long, tense days, the grandmother awoke and her first words were: "I want to die in Costa Rica." Furthermore, the old woman did not want to travel by plane, so the whole family started a 30 day odyssey by car from L.A. to Costa Rica.

Back in the family's homeland, Ruth graduated from Lincoln High School and went to the University of Costa Rica, graduating as an engineer; grandma lived more than 20 years with them in Costa Rica. During high school, Ruth was part of all the clubs and programs the school offered, including the Lincoln Log yearbook and the basketball team. She organized the Junior Senior banquet, Halloween Ball, Coronation Dance and "El Troyanito" for the school newspaper, to name just a few of Ruth's activities.

Ruth has been writing since she was 12 years old, when the first diary was given to her by her Mom. She has collected all of these diaries from her teen age years, her first kiss, her peers, stories of her travels. Her reading hobby made her Mom and

Dad buy her the entire collection of books available at the time, and she passed her entire school vacations reading.

Ruth was appointed Consul General of Costa Rica for the entire U.S. West Coast. She organized support committees for cultural, sports and civics events, Rose Parade floats and the like, putting together more than 100 volunteers. Ruth even co-founded the Central American Federation of Nations, composed of all of the Consul Generals of Central America; by joining and working together on issues that affected their communities CAFN helped them became stronger.

During her Consulate years Ruth met Jerry Azarkman, co-owner of Curacao, who became one of the support businesses for community events. After her tenure in office as Consul General came to a close, she went to say *"adios"* to Jerry who went on to ask Ruth to become part of the company. She became the Advertising and Marketing Manager and help developed the chain of megastores that offers 85,000 products, as well as services such as local and long distance phone calling, Internet in Spanish, money transfers and exports to Mexico and Central American products.

Ruth was part of the company for more than 17 years, during its major growth period and as an expert in targeting markets she created many successful promotional campaigns. In addition to being the spokesperson for Curacao's TV segments, she was the creative head of messages and concepts for all of the company's campaigns.

Ruth is the founder of several programs as: Fundraise for a Cause a program for organizations for crowd funding, she created "Learn to Read-Read to Learn" a tutoring program for second graders, the Creative Hub where kids learn art projects and oversaw the company Foundation.

Ruth is a member of NAPW, the National Association of Professional Women, with over 850,000 members across the country, and is currently the President of its Los Angeles Chapter, she oversees 16 States for the organization and member of the board for Women's National Book Association. She was recently honored with ImpreMedia's Distinguished Woman (*Mujer Distinguida*) award and Civic Service Leadership Award by League of Women Voters of Los Angeles.

Jerry Azarkman

Jerry was born in Iran to Jewish parents who immigrated to Israel when he was little. He spoke Persian and was soon shocked to discover a new language, Hebrew. He struggled in school until a new teacher gave him the motivation to learn, to stay focused and confront the challenge of his internal battle with Attention Deficit Disorder. Jerry went on to become the top student of a class of 40.

Jerry went to high school at a military academy in Israel—he remembers that only 68 pupils were accepted out of 3,000 applicants. He would wait for the mailman every day until he received the long awaited acceptance letter. He was in the Yom Kippur War and saw, firsthand, destruction and the loss of life, including the death of one of his best friends. This experience made Jerry change his philosophy of life and how he viewed weapons and warfare.

He decided to move to the United States and start a business; he had no money, so with $20 in his pocket he started walking door-to-door in downtown Los Angeles, selling Pong, the first electronic game. In a largely Hispanic neighborhood where he didn't speak English or Spanish, Jerry took his first steps towards what is today a multimillion dollar operation. He made his customers work for him by bringing neighbors to him so Jerry could offer them his products and collect monthly payments from them.

He discovered an underserved, neglected niche of immigrants with many needs, and opened their first lines of credit and sold them the products they had dreamt of one day owning. Mostly immigrants from El Salvador and Mexico became his first customers and first employees.

Many of Jerry's ideas have changed the way most think of doing business, as he is an innovator in customer service, marketing and credit. The way Jerry sees the relationship with the customer is exceeding his consumer's expectations. Jerry would say, "Never offer more than what you can deliver; this is a simple way of losing your customers."

Jerry trains and motivates his associates, helps them find goals in their lives and the reasons why they have to try harder. His story brings them hope that after all of their hard work there will be compensation and the more you work the bigger that satisfaction will be.

Jerry has three kids, Daniel, Erick and Ilanid. Daniel is a graduate from Berkeley in Linguistics who graduated from Culinary Arts in order to become a writer.

Erick graduated from UC Santa Cruz in Computer Science and is developing new platforms for the company founded by his father. As of this writing Ilanid attends high school.

Jerry was awarded by Earnest & Young Entrepreneur of the Year for Greater Los Angeles in 2014. He works every day in the business, having back-to-back meetings in areas of marketing and finance for his new adventure Star World.

Left to right Paty, Erick, Ilanit, Daniel, Jerry and sitting down Muluk and Bob Banayan Stepfather picture taken in 2014.

Jerry Azarkman winner of the Los Angeles Entrepreneur Award for Ernest & Young 2014.

We want to thank each and every one who one way or another helped us put this Memoir together.

The authors

Morgan James
Speakers Group

www.TheMorganJamesSpeakersGroup.com

We connect Morgan James published authors with live and online events and audiences whom will benefit from their expertise.

 Morgan James makes all of our titles available
through the Library for All Charity Organization.

www.LibraryForAll.org

Printed in the USA
CPSIA information can be obtained
at www.ICGtesting.com
JSHW082229140824
68134JS00017B/797